The Arab Minority
in Israel's Economy

Social Inequality Series

Marta Tienda and David B. Grusky, Series Editors

The Arab Minority in Israel's Economy:
Patterns of Ethnic Inequality,
Noah Lewin-Epstein and Moshe Semyonov

Getting Started: Transition to Adulthood
in Great Britain, Alan C. Kerckhoff

Equality and Achievement in Education,
James S. Coleman

Ethnicity and the New Family Economy: Living
Arrangements and Intergenerational Financial Flows,
edited by Frances K. Goldscheider and Calvin Goldscheider

FORTHCOMING

Persistent Inequality: Changing Educational Attainment
in Thirteen Countries, edited by Yossi Shavit
and Hans-Peter Blossfeld

Careers and Creativity: Social Forces in the Arts,
Harrison C. White

Social Stratification: Class, Race, and Gender
in Sociological Perspective, edited by David B. Grusky

Inequality and Aging,
John Henretta and Angelo O'Rand

Children, Schools, and Inequality,
Doris R. Entwisle and Karl Len Alexander

Between Two Worlds: Southeast Asian Refugee Youth
in America, Ruben G. Rumbaut and Kenji Ima

The Arab Minority in Israel's Economy

Patterns of Ethnic Inequality

Noah Lewin-Epstein and Moshe Semyonov

Westview Press

BOULDER • SAN FRANCISCO • OXFORD

Social Inequality Series

Copyright © 1993 by Westview Press, Inc.

Published in 1993 in the United States of America by Westview Press, Inc., 5500 Central Avenue, Boulder, Colorado 80301-2877, and in the United Kingdom by Westview Press, 36 Lonsdale Road, Summertown, Oxford OX2 7EW

Library of Congress Cataloging-in-Publication Data
Lewin-Epstein, Noah.
  The Arab minority in Israel's economy : patterns of ethnic inequality / Noah Lewin-Epstein and Moshe Semyonov.
    p. cm.
  Includes bibliographical references and index.
  ISBN 0-8133-1525-5
  1. Palestinian Arabs—Israel—Economic conditions. 2. Palestinian Arabs—Employment—Israel. 3. Palestinian Arabs—Government policy—Israel. 4. Israel—Ethnic relations. I. Semyonov, Moshe.
II. Title.
HC415.25.L48 1993
330.95694'054'0899274—dc20   92-47403
                                                                CIP

Printed and bound in the United States of America

 The paper used in this publication meets the requirements of the American National Standard for Permanence of Paper for Printed Library Materials Z39.48-1984.

10   9   8   7   6   5   4   3   2   1

To the memory of our fathers,
Jacob Lewin-Epstein and
Gabriel Semyonov

Contents

List of Tables and Figures   xi
Preface   xv

1 Approaches to the Study of Arabs in Israel   1

Ethnic Stratification in the Economic Arena, 7
Notes, 12

2 The Arabs: Profile of a Disadvantaged Minority   14

Population Characteristics, 14
Sub-Groups in the Arab Population, 18
Legal and Political Status, 20
Socioeconomic Inequality, 22
Ecological Segregation, 28
Inequality in Resource Allocation, 30
Kinship and Economy, 33
Concluding Remarks, 35
Notes, 35
Appendix 2.A, 37

3 The Arab Economy in Israel   40

Historical Background, 40
The Arab and Jewish Communities—
    Economic Characteristics, 40
From Separation to Subordination, 45
The Changing Economic Base of the Arab Sector, 47
The Changing Occupational Structure, 51
Spatial Mismatch, 54
Educational and Occupational Mismatch, 56
Concluding Remarks, 58
Notes, 59
Appendix 3.A, 61

4 Community Segregation and Socioeconomic Inequalities   62

Community Effects on Earnings, 64
Evaluating the Contribution of
    Community Attributes, 67
Inequality Inside and Outside the Arab
    Labor Market, 68
Socioeconomic Attainment Across Labor Markets, 72
Decomposing Mean Differentials, 74
Discrimination Against Arabs in the Labor Market, 77
Concluding Remarks, 82
Notes, 82
Appendix 4.A, 84
Appendix 4.B, 86

5 Arab Women in the Israeli Labor Force   87

Changing Employment Among Arab Women, 88
Community Determinants of Arab Female Employment, 91
Occupational Differentiation, 94
Gender Differences Inside and Outside
    the Arab Labor Market, 99
Socioeconomic Attainment Inside and Outside
    the Arab Labor Market, 101
Comparing Workers Inside and Outside the Arab
    Labor Market, 102
Comparing Men and Women, 103
Comparing Jews and Arabs, 105
Concluding Remarks, 107
Notes, 109
Appendix 5.A, 112

6 Who Benefits from Economic Discrimination?   114

Conceptual Considerations, 114
Consequences of Discrimination for the
    Superordinate Group, 115
Examining the Outcomes for Jewish Workers, 118
Testing Competition and Job Segregation, 125
Concluding Remarks, 131
Notes, 132
Appendix 6.A, 133
Appendix 6.B, 134

7   Jews in Arab Labor Markets   136

Notes, 146
Appendix 7.A, 147

8   An Israeli Dilemma   148

Bibliography   157
About the Book and Authors   164
Index   165

Tables and Figures

Tables

2.1   Distribution of the Israeli population by continent of birth
        and religion   15
2.2   Total fertility rates for Arab and Jewish women, by religion
        and continent of birth   16
2.3   Infant deaths among Jews and Arabs by sex   17
2.4   Mean characteristics of the economically active labor force
        population of Moslems, Christians, and Druze in Israel, 1988   19
2.5   Years of schooling of Arabs and Jews, 1961–1990   23
2.6   Arab and Jewish employed persons by economic branch
        and by occupation, 1960–1990   25
2.7   Mean characteristics of the Arab and Jewish labor force
        aged 25–64 in 1974   26
2.8   Percent of population in regions by ethnicity, 1974 and 1990   29
2.9   The percent distribution of Arabs and Jews by size of locality,
        1961, 1972, 1983, and 1990   31
2.10 Local authority budget components in 1975/1976 and 1985/1986   32
2.A   Localities according to categories   38

3.1   Industrial structure of labor markets in the Arab and
        Jewish sectors, 1972 and 1983   49
3.2   Percent of employers and self-employed in the Arab labor
        market in 1972 and 1983 by age group   52
3.3   Occupational structure of labor markets in the Arab and
        Jewish sectors, 1972 and 1983   53
3.4   Occupational distribution of the population and of jobs in the
        Arab sector, 1972 and 1983   54
3.5   Educational mismatch among Arab males in the Arab and
        Jewish labor market, by age cohort, 1972 and 1983   57

4.1   Unstandardized regression coefficients predicting income of
        Jews and Arabs   65
4.2   Characteristics: means and category percentages of Jews and
        Arab population groups of Israeli labor force population,
        age 25–64, 1983   71

4.3 Regression equations predicting occupational status and
      income for Jewish and Arab population groups of the
      Israeli labor force   73
4.4 Components of occupational status differentials between pairs
      of groups, Israeli labor force   75
4.5 Components of income differentials between pairs of groups,
      Israeli labor force population   77
4.A Decomposition of income differences between Jews and Arabs
      for the total population and for men   85

5.1 Persons in the civilian labor force and labor force participation
      rates for Arab and Jewish women in Israel   89
5.2 Employment ratios of Arab and Jewish women in 1983 for
      specific marital and education status   90
5.3 Employment ratios of Moslem, Christian, Druze, and Jewish
      women for specific marital and education status categories   91
5.4 Means, standard deviations, and ranges for characteristics of
      communities in which Arabs reside   92
5.5 Distribution of the Arab labor force in Arab and mixed
      communities across major occupational categories,
      by gender, 1983   95
5.6 Unstandardized regression coefficients for models predicting
      gender-linked occupational differentiation among Arab
      women and men in 1983   97
5.7 Means and category percentages of workers inside and outside
      the Arab labor market, by gender   100
5.8 Components of occupational status and earnings differentials
      between Arab labor market and non-Arab labor market workers
      for men and women   103
5.9 Components of occupational status and earnings differentials
      between women and men employed inside and outside the
      Arab labor market   104
5.10 Component of occupational status and earnings differentials
      between Arabs and Jews   106
5.A Regression equations predicting occupational status and monthly
      earnings for ethnic labor market and non-ethnic labor market
      workers by gender   113

6.1 Regression results predicting two measures of economic well-being
      of Jewish workers in 33 Israeli communities, 1983   121
6.2 Regression results predicting two measures of economic well-being
      of Jewish workers in 33 Israeli communities, 1983   122
6.3 Regression results predicting share of income received by Jewish
      workers at the top 5 percent and the bottom 20 percent of the
      income distribution   124

6.4   Standardized and unstandardized estimates of two-wave
          regression models predicting income and percent Arab
          across 323 occupations   127
6.5   Estimates of two-wave regression models predicting income
          and percent Arab in 231 occupational categories in the
          periphery   129
6.6   Estimates of two-wave regression models predicting income
          and percent Arab in 267 occupational categories in the
          core sector   130
6.A   Means, standard deviations, and correlations among variables
          included in the analysis   133

7.1   Male employees—human capital variables and income means,
          economic branch and occupational distribution, persons
          aged 25–64   140
7.2   Female employees—human capital variables and income means,
          economic branch and occupational distribution, persons
          aged 25–64   142
7.3   Actual versus expected occupational status and earnings of
          Jewish commuters to Arab markets   145

Figures

6.B   Two-wave, two-variable model representing competition
          and segregation   134

Preface

In a socially and economically integrated society the Arab citizens of Israel would long have been marked for special treatment—the object of concerted compensatory policies—to redress their disadvantaged situation. Israel, however, is an ethnically divided society, in which the Arab population is a subordinate minority. Lagging behind in educational achievement, standard of living, and public services, the Arab sector has encountered for the most part a lack of concern on the part of Israel's (mostly Jewish) public and its leadership. By examining patterns of competition and inequality between Jews and Arabs we intend to both contribute to sociological knowledge and to draw out policy implications.

Israeli Arabs are citizens of the state. As citizens they enjoy formal political equality, but since its establishment over forty years ago Israel has not developed a genuine universalistic civil ideology that would equally embrace all its citizens, regardless of their ethnic affiliation. For many years the Arab citizens of Israel have been all but "invisible" on Israel's public agenda. One cannot escape the conclusion that the primary disposition of the governments of Israel has been to keep the Arabs in a segregated marginal position within the Jewish state. The "invisibility" of the Arab citizens of Israel was also manifest in mainstream social science discourse until quite recently.

The research reported in this book joins a modest, but growing, body of literature that aims to redress the paucity of scholarly work concerning what we consider to be the principal cleavage in Israeli society. In the following text we intend to explore the extent of disadvantage faced by Arabs, particularly in the realms of work and resource allocation, and to examine its sources and institutionalized patterns. As such, we intend the contribution of this book to be twofold: first, to provide a theoretical perspective on multi-ethnic societies based on the concept of group competition, and second, to highlight a crucial aspect of inequality in Israel and enhance our understanding of Israeli society. We hope that our endeavor will stimulate further interest in Jewish-Arab relations in Israel and serve as a catalyst for changes that will make Israel a more humanistic and universalistic society.

It is important to clarify at the outset that the research reported here concerns the Arab *citizens of Israel*—those residing within the 1948 state borders. It does not include the residents of territories occupied by Israel since 1967 who are not citizens of Israel, and whose legal and political status is fundamentally different. The predicament of the latter undoubtedly deserves extensive investigation, and indeed our book *Hewers of Wood and Drawers of Water*, published in 1987, specifically addressed this issue. While recent events have clearly out-paced the bearings of past research, an updated examination of the topic is beyond the scope of the present monograph.

The decision to focus on the Arab citizens of Israel, rather than on Palestinians in general, reflects our conviction that the central issues facing Israeli Arabs and those residing in the occupied territories, although related, are fundamentally different, and they should not be confounded. In the forty-five years that Israeli Arabs have lived as a minority in the State of Israel they have emerged as a distinct segment of the Palestinian people. Although fully sympathetic to the plight of their brethren in the occupied territories, their interests are diverse, and their position as part of Israeli society plainly sets them apart. In no time has this been more evident than during the recent years of the *Intifada*. The aim of residents of the West Bank and Gaza is clearly to form a separate state. For Israeli Arabs, by way of contrast, the terms of participation in Israeli society are the central issue of concern.

This book is not intended to address all issues surrounding the condition of Arabs in Israeli society. In particular we do not deal with the matter of the realization on the part of Arabs not only of full citizenship but also full membership of the nation. We recognize that the problem of symbolic identification and Arabs' collective aspirations cannot be fully resolved without a fundamental metamorphosis of the State of Israel. We surmise, however, that addressing the issues of inequality and subordination in a systematic and pointed manner in itself may facilitate a "re-accommodation" of the Jewish majority and the Arab minority in Israel.

Throughout the book we use survey and census data, and we frequently employ statistical methods of analysis in order to provide precise details of the topics under discussion. Our data sources are varied although the overwhelming majority of statistical information comes from the Central Bureau of Statistics. We are fully aware of the difficulty in addressing broad issues of a fundamental nature, or of attempting to substantiate theoretical arguments, using statistical information depicting a particular period. This is a perennial problem facing researchers, which is accentuated when the data are measured at different points in time.

We devoted considerable efforts to bringing our data up-to-date. In some instances information was available for certain points in time but unavailable for others. Naturally, we made use of the best data available to us. Some of our analyses required particular information and very large sample sizes present only in population censuses, the last of which was carried out in 1983. The reader should take note that, apart from the historical background, our discussion of the data and their implications is given in the *present* tense, even though some of the data analyzed were collected several years back. We chose to use the present tense in order to emphasize the urgency of the issues under study and to convey the point that the patterns revealed are descriptive of the position of the Arab minority in Israel. It reflects our belief that although specific figures may have shifted, the underlying patterns have remained substantially unaltered.

Our research was carried out over a period of several years and was supported by generous grants from the Israel Foundation Trustees (grant #14) and from the David Horowitz Institute for the Study of Developing Countries. Several superb graduate students helped out in data preparation, analysis, looking up references, and not least, in providing an attentive ear and commenting on our ideas. We extend our appreciation to Tammy Lerenthal, Anat Oren, and Rebecca Raijman. We benefitted from helpful suggestions made by Yitchak Haberfeld and Yehouda Shenhav on preliminary drafts, and we are especially grateful to Yinon Cohen, who took the time to read the entire manuscript and provided numerous illuminating comments. We take this opportunity to thank Yasmin Alkalai for her masterful handling of the large and complex data sets, and Sylvia Weinberg for her expert word-processing skills and for her never-ending patience. Deborah Golden contributed numerous suggestions while doing an outstanding job in editing the manuscript.

*   *   *

Some of the findings presented in this book have been reported in *American Sociological Review* 53 (1988):256–266, 55 (1990):107–114; *European Sociological Review* 8 (1992):39–51; and *Social Forces* 68 (1989):379–396, 70 (1992):1101–1119.

Noah Lewin-Epstein
Moshe Semyonov

1

Approaches to the Study of Arabs in Israel

Jewish-Arab relations in Israel have been molded under extremely turbulent circumstances—war, population migration, territorial disputes, nation-building, and economic competition—all taking place within one century. Over the years, mutual antagonism has not dissipated and conflict is ever present.

There have been several scholarly attempts to explore and analyze the situation of Arabs in Israel from different vantage points. No single approach appears to have untangled the complex relationship in which the two groups are engaged. The cumulative result of research in this area, however, has underscored the profundity of the problem and revealed the multi-dimensionality of Jewish-Arab relations in Israel.

Sociological studies of Jewish-Arab relations in Israel have been carried out along the lines of three major paradigms: the cultural perspective, the pluralism perspective, and the class (economic) perspective. The cultural approach stems from structural-functionalism which views common cultural patterns as essential for social integration. From this point of view, ethnicity, as a focal point for divergent cultures, is considered disruptive to social integration. Following this logic, cultural and social assimilation are required of subordinate groups in order for the successful realization of nation-building to take place. Over two decades ago Eisenstadt (1967) addressed the issue of the "non-Jewish minority groups in Israel" by focusing on processes of economic development and modernization. According to the analytical framework he proposed, the growing contact of the Arab minority with Jews was expected to bring about cultural change and usher in the values of modernity. Economic progress, according to this view, would serve as an integrative force which would diminish the potential for ethnic conflict. Eisenstadt noted, however, that these outcomes were hindered by the unique historical and political circumstances in which Jewish-Arab relations were shaped, namely, the broader context of the Israeli-Arab and Israeli-Palestinian conflict.

More recently an alternative cultural approach was proposed by Ben-Rafael (1982) who applied a general model pertaining to dominant and subordinate cultures to Jewish-Arab relations.[1] The underlying argument of Ben-Rafael's approach is that ethnic encounters between Jews and Arabs, rather than inducing assimilation, in actual fact, reinforce the boundaries of mutual exclusivity. The central concept here is "negative convergence" which, it is argued, characterizes the continuous interaction between Jews and Arabs. The cultural approach proposed by Ben-Rafael addresses ethnic stratification in Israel largely in terms of cultural dominance and subordination, where cultural dominance is derived from a modern scientific-technological orientation. According to this perspective, in order for conflict to dissipate, a sense of "Israeliness"—cultural contents and symbols drawn from shared experience and based on a modern orientation—must emerge and stand independent of "Arabness" and "Jewishness." The Jewish-Arab ethnic cleavage which, according to this view, is essentially cultural, is reinforced by the ongoing conflict between Israel and the Arab countries and the Palestinian people. By defining Israeli Arabs as a religio-linguistic minority, the dominant Israeli culture in fact reinforces the ethnic cleavage and limits the ability to develop "Israeliness" as a unified cultural construct (Ben-Rafael 1982).

Indeed, policies of social and economic exclusion, which are the focus of the present study, as well as other forms of separation, have frustrated the prospect of the emergence of such a shared construct. Smooha (1985) has pointed out that Israel's Jewish-dominated world-view sees Arabs as a cultural, religious, or linguistic minority rather than a national minority. In so doing, the Jewish majority sets the stage and conditions for political and economic subordination of the Arabs. From the vantage point of the cultural approach it is also emphasized that Israeli Arabs are part of the larger Arab world surrounding Israel. Hence they hold in common the primordial roots of Arab culture, values, and identity. This in turn leads to their further alienation from Jewish identity. Thus, the dominance of "Jewishness" in Israel on the one hand, and the continuing sense of "Arabness" among Israeli Arabs, on the other, set a course for negative convergence rather than assimilation. Indeed, the two groups appear to be committed to cultural and social segregation.

A second manner of conceptualizing ethnic relations in Israel is a pluralistic approach advanced and developed over the years by Smooha (1976, 1978, 1980). The version of pluralism proposed by Smooha may be conceived of as a controlled-conflict approach. Pluralism refers to the objective existence of distinguishable groups based on language, religion, national identity and separate cultural heritage, coupled with ecological and social segregation (residences, schools, friendship networks, and political parties). A basic premise of the pluralism approach is that the source of conflict is exogenous to the relations between ethnic communities. Rather than stemming from the differences between the groups (which determine the pluralistic nature of the social system), conflict originates in competition over scarce resources. This conflict over resources, however, may be exacerbated or attenuated by factors such as the level of inequality and the presence of mechanisms of inclusion or exclusion. While other paradigms have identified either the cultural or the economic sphere as central to the understanding of ethnic relations, pluralism emphasizes the predominance of the polity as the arena in which ethnic groups struggle for control and where structures of cooperation may form. Indeed, according to Smooha, pluralism connotes coexistence and the potential for reducing inequality and conflict. Smooha's approach is essentially prescriptive rather than descriptive—it does not describe present Israeli society but provides a model of pluralism which, if adhered to by Israeli society, might in the long run avert conflict and stabilize Jewish-Arab relations.

In line with the emphasis on the political arena, some social scientists (mostly political scientists) have applied the notion of "control" to analyze Jewish-Arab relations in Israel. Control, as a theoretical concept, has long been used to conceptualize superordinate-subordinate relations in ethnically divided societies. Typically these approaches have not gone beyond listing "control" as one of several possible mechanisms available to the dominant group. Esman (1973) for instance, referred to control as one means of managing communal conflict in multi-ethnic societies. His framework included, in addition, "induced assimilation", "syncratic integration", and "balanced pluralism" (akin to the approach put forward by Smooha). In his approach, the state is set apart from the ethnic groups comprising the society and is given a mediating or managing role. Consequently, the framework proposed by Esman largely ignores the use of the state apparatus by dominant ethnic groups, and the role of the state in creating and maintaining ethnic inequality.

In analyzing the Israeli case, Lustick (1980) takes the control framework one step forward in an attempt to outline the components of control and to examine the ways in which they are woven into the routine of ethnic relations. The "control" perspective adopted by Lustick focuses specifically on the political dominance of the Jews over the Arab minority in Israel. Lustick argues that " . . . thanks to a sophisticated system of control it has been possible for the Israeli regime and the Jewish majority which it represents to manipulate the Arab minority, to prevent it from organizing on an independent basis, and to extract from it resources required for the development of the Jewish sector" (pp. 25–26).

Lustick identifies three main components of control over the Arab population in Israel: segmentation, dependence, and co-optation. Segmentation, which comprises ecological as well as social and cultural dimensions, refers to the exclusion of Arabs from the political, economic, social and cultural core of Israeli society. Dependence refers to the enforced reliance of Arabs on the Jewish majority for important resources, an aspect particularly evident as it applies to economic resources (as will be elaborated in a later section). By co-optation Lustick refers to " . . . the use of side payments to Arab elites or potential elites for purposes of surveillance and resource extraction" (p. 77). This definition, however, is unnecessarily narrow, and co-optation may be viewed more broadly as the counterpart of dependence. Dependence establishes the conditions under which co-optation can take place at low cost to the superordinate group while it appears beneficial to both groups (more on this subject later).

The control framework proposed by Lustick makes it possible to study economic activity of Arabs in Israel as a dimension of Jewish-Arab relations. Nonetheless, it is essentially a political model in which economic activity is marginal and secondary to the political dimension. Without, at this point, debating the issue of the predominance of the different dimensions and institutions in the Jewish-Arab conflict, suffice it to note that a more specific and more concise framework is needed for a comprehensive and analytical treatment of the participation of the Arab minority in the Israeli labor market.

A third perspective applied to Jewish-Arab relations in Israel focuses on economic relations and derives primarily from Marxist and dependency paradigms. In a series of research projects, Rosenfeld (1964, 1978) studied the confluence of class and nationality in the case of Israeli Arabs. According to Rosenfeld, the central factors responsible for the class situation of Arabs in Israel are the Zionist ideology of the Jewish nation, and the state control of the economy. The restrictions and expropriations imposed by the Jewish state on the Arab minority, on the one hand, and the large demand for wage labor, on the other, brought about specific class relations whereby Arabs " . . . live in one place and work in many others, live among Arabs, work among Jews and are employed almost entirely by Jews" (Rosenfeld, 1978:393). The thesis advanced by Rosenfeld and his colleagues underscores Arab dependency as the major explanatory factor for the economic position of Arabs in Israel.

The most comprehensive and radical application of the dependency approach to the situation of Arabs in Israel has been made by Zuriek (1979). Zuriek evoked the theoretical framework of internal colonialism to characterize Jewish-Arab (Palestinian) relations. The internal colonialism model is essentially a class-relations analysis in which ethnicity and nationality are assumed to be aligned with the class cleavage. According to the internal colonialism model developed by Hechter (1975), national development has less to do with spontaneous social structural or economic processes, and more with the exercise of control over government policies concerning the allocation of resources. Referring to geographical territories in which several ethnic groups reside, Hechter contends that the obstacles to national development of the peripheral group relate not to a failure of peripheral integration with the core, but to *malintegration* established on terms increasingly regarded as unjust and illegitimate. Hence, the internal colonialism model would appear to account for the persistence of backwardness in the midst of industrial society and the apparent volatility of political integration. "[B]y linking economic and occupational differences between groups to their cultural differences, this model has an additional advantage in that it suggests an explanation for the resiliency of peripheral culture" (Hechter 1975:34).

Zuriek's analysis of Israeli society begins by defining Israel and the Jewish majority as a colonial regime. The focus of the discussion is on the distinction between capitalist and non-capitalist economies within the state. Zuriek proceeds to expose the features and position of Arab society in Israel and compares them to those of ethnic groups in other nations to which the model of internal colonialism has also been applied. The central features noted are the imposition of a capitalist economy on a traditional agrarian system, economic transformation, ecological separation which permits clear identification of core and periphery, and the establishment of an ideological system to justify superordinate-subordinate relations. This approach, then, views the economy as the central arena of Jewish-Arab relations and economic processes associated with capitalism as the driving force of ethnic conflict. However, the "broad brush" used by Zureik, rather than illuminating the unique features of Arab subordination in Israel, simply appears to equate ethnic subordination and economic inequality with colonialism. From this point of view, the model offered by Zureik is uni-dimensional and deterministic. Once colonialism is established it takes on static characteristics.

In a recent book, Raja Khalidi (1988a) offered yet another economic framework for studying the position of Arabs in Israeli society. He identified four aspects of the economic status of Arabs in Israel which set the Arab population apart from the rest of Israeli society: (1) state policies and popular attitudes which underlie the differential treatment of Arabs in Israel, (2) spatial separation of the Arab population from Jews whereby Arabs are concentrated in specific geographic regions, mostly distant from the center, (3) unique cultural and social structural features which still clearly distinguish the Arab population despite the many years of contact with the Jewish society, and (4) economic, political and social differentiation along ethnic lines.

Taking the above characteristics into account, and approaching the issue from an economic perspective, Khalidi proposed "regional economic analysis" as a tool for examining and understanding the status of the Arab minority in Israel:

> In the broadest definition, our conception of the Arab region in Israel . . . can be construed as a homogeneous region in light of common features (economic, social, and geographic): a functional region in terms of the importance of its relation to the national economy and polarized patterns of differentials in many regional-national characteristics; and a programming region in terms of the systematized context of Arab-state relations in Israel and the existence of specific state policies toward Arabs (1988b:26).

From an economic perspective, Gottheil (1973) has characterized the Arab region as having undergone transformation from a subsistence agricultural economy with an embryonic industrial and commercial structure, to a consuming entity with its productive capacity resting primarily on reproduction of exportable labor power.

While recognizing that the Arab sector is separated from mainstream Israeli economy, some social geographers (Arnon and Raviv 1980; Bar Gal and Sofer 1976) have proposed that the contact with the industrialized and modern Jewish sector has initiated rapid changes in the traditional, less developed Arab society. According to this view, continuing integration into Israeli society is seen to benefit rather than to harm Arabs, and to result in their improved economic conditions. By way of contrast, Gottheil, Zureik, Khalidi, among many others, have underscored the potential for the development of a dual economy whereby the Arab region is "integrated" as an external factor in Israel's national economy. One clear feature of this structure of relations is the "near-exodus of Arab labor (especially of young people) to available industrial and construction employment in the (Jewish) towns" (Zarhi and Achiezra 1966:5).

The above discussion of previous research on the status of Arabs in Israeli society has illustrated the multitude of perspectives put forward in an endeavor to understand the issue. More importantly, this body of literature has underscored the complexity of Jewish-Arab relations in Israel and has revealed several noteworthy findings. Arabs, on the whole, are disadvantaged relative to Jews in every dimension of inequality, be it economic, social, or political. Their standard of living is lower and they receive less than their share of public funding and investment. Their earnings from work are lower, as is the social status attached to the jobs they hold. They are all but absent from the political arena and positions of authority in government. The Arab population is spatially segregated from the Jewish population and Arab communities do not have the infrastructure to support advanced industrial structures. Their development is dependent on and constrained by policies of the central government of Israel. The majority of Arabs today are employed outside their communities of residence, mostly by Jewish employers in Jewish communities. Whether this reflects the integration of the Arab population in Israeli society, or its exploitation, is a point of continuing debate embedded in alternative paradigms applied to the study of Israeli society.

Researchers also agree that the Arab population has remained rural, for the most part, and more dependent on agriculture than the Jewish population. Its age structure is younger, and, recent achievements notwithstanding, it is significantly less educated. However, research into occupational and earnings inequality between Arabs and Jews, found that differences in education, skills, and work experience cannot account for the gaps in earnings, living standards and life chances. Not surprisingly, then, studies have devoted themselves in part to uncovering the ideological factors and institutionalized arrangements which constrain opportunities for Arabs while still maintaining a semblance of an open system.

Notwithstanding the contribution of the studies discussed above, we propose that theoretical models along the lines of control, internal colonialism, or dependency, are not sufficient to capture the complexity of Jewish-Arab relations in the labor market. Specifically, although the control perspective proposed by Lustick provides a useful framework for explaining Arab "acquiescence" in Israeli society by outlining the institutional conditions that produce and reinforce Jewish-Arab inequality, it stops short of analyzing the labor market processes and the differential consequences for Jews and Arabs. Moreover, this perspective is essentially deterministic in that it views all socioeconomic outcomes for Arabs as resulting from political institutional mechanisms. It largely ignores the role of labor market processes and outcomes in determining the position of the Arab minority.

The dependency approach, and in particular the internal colonialism version employed by Zureik, and the class conflict perspective utilized by Rosenfeld, have centered on capital-labor relations. They view the position of Arabs as deriving primarily from their exploitation by Jewish capital. Both

Zuriek and Rosenfeld place the emphasis on employers' need for cheap labor in an expanding Jewish economy. Hence, they focus on the mechanisms that ensure the supply of cheap (Arab) labor. According to these approaches, Jewish-Arab relations are viewed as class relations; that is between Jewish employers and government, on the one hand, and Arab workers on the other, excluding, for the most part, the majority Jewish workers. According to these models, market processes are largely predetermined and hence the study of labor market processes under different structural conditions is irrelevant. It is our contention that the differential resources of the dominant Jewish and subordinate Arab populations, as well as the structural conditions they face, must be taken into account in order to understand the patterns of Jewish-Arab socioeconomic inequality. We propose, therefore, that an understanding of the socioeconomic position of Arabs in Israel can benefit from applying a theoretical framework which underscores competition in the labor market (albeit with different resources) as central to the study of ethnic relations and emergent inequality.[2]

Ethnic Stratification in the Economic Arena

In an endeavor to generate a theoretical framework for the study of ethnic stratification systems, Lieberson (1970) points out that most often, ethnic groups in a multi-ethnic society differ in their occupational opportunities and the rewards they receive from employment, as well as in their power, privilege and influence. To the extent that these differences exist because of their group membership *per se* and are not simply a result of the factors which determine stratification *within* ethnic groups, it is said that ethnic stratification exists. More important for the case under study here is the fact that,

> [T]he most fundamental difference between ethnic and other forms of stratification lies in the fact that the former is nearly always the basis for the internal disintegration of the existing boundaries of a nation-state . . . Ethnic groups are the only strata that have the inherent potential to carve their own autonomous and permanent society from the existing nation without, in effect, re-creating its earlier form of stratification all over again (Lieberson, 1970:173).

According to this view, the differential positions of various ethnic groups in the nation-state serve as a potential source of discontent. Ethnic groups unable to achieve their goals, or better their position within the state, may seek a political course of action which may lead to the undoing of the social-political system. This argument takes on particular significance in the case of Arabs in Israel, where ethnic stratification of Jews and Arabs is embedded in the broader Israeli-Palestinian conflict. Social and economic disadvantages of the Arab minority are often linked to their political subordination, a solution to which may be sought in political separation.

Donald Noel (1968) has suggested that three conditions must be present in order for ethnic stratification to emerge: ethnocentrism, competition, and differential power. Ethnocentrism refers to in-group glorification and the preference of one's own ethnic group and the downgrading of others. While ethnocentrism is a necessary condition for ethnic stratification, it is not sufficient. For ethnic stratification to emerge it is necessary that ethnic groups actively compete for the same resources. The outcome of this competition is likely to be determined by differential group power. In other words, "competition for vital objects will not generate ethnic stratification *unless* they [the groups] are of such unequal power that one is able to impose its will upon the other" (Noel 1968:162). Differential power, whether military force or organizational capabilities, makes it possible for one group to establish dominance and to subordinate another, or several other, groups.

The conditions of ethnic stratification outlined by Lieberson and Noel are strikingly evident in the context of Jewish-Arab relations in Israel. Within both groups there exists extremely high awareness of their distinctiveness, which is both represented and reinforced by ethnocentric ideologies. Zionist ideology, which crystallized a century ago, serves as a cornerstone of the State of Israel and remains central to the identification of Jews as Israelis. Its expressed intent is to provide the rationale for the presence of the Jewish people in Israel, and for the designation of Israel as a Jewish state. This ideology is manifest in Israel's Declaration of Independence which proclaimed the State of Israel to be a "Jewish state in the Land of Israel" which would open its doors to every Jew and grant the Jewish people the status of a nation with equal rights among the family of nations. Corresponding to Zionist ideology, Arab nationalism, which crystallized during the first decades of the twentieth century, provided a focal point for Arab ethnocentrism. Since 1967, when Israel occupied the territories of the West Bank and the Gaza Strip and took control over its 1,200,000 Palestinian residents, the national identity of Israeli Arabs has undergone changes. Renewed contacts with the Palestinians residing in the occupied territories and growing confrontation between Israel and the Palestinians have strengthened Palestinian national identity among Israeli Arabs and radicalized relations between Jewish and Arab citizens of Israel. Hence, even after forty years of co-existence as citizens of the same state, Jews and Arabs maintain clearly identifiable and distinct ethnic identities.

In addition to mutual ethnocentrism, competition for scarce resources has characterized Jewish-Arab relations since the early stages of modern Jewish settlement in Palestine. This competition was primarily over labor and land (Shafir 1989; Kimmerling 1983) but was present in other markets as well (Metzer and Kaplan 1985). During the first part of the twentieth century, competition between Jews and Arabs was marked by sporadic outbreaks of conflict largely contained by the British Mandate authorities. Israel's war of independence in 1948 and its aftermath, however, clearly established the military superiority of the Jewish group over Arabs in Israel. Concomitantly, organizational steps were taken to restrict the Arab minority, thereby hampering their effectiveness as competitors. Superordinate-subordinate relations were set in place.

Although the concepts of ethnocentrism, conflict, and differential power appear to be highly relevant for depicting the conditions for ethnic stratification, the framework as a whole provides a somewhat static *post factum* account. In the present study, we intend to espouse a more dynamic and non-recursive framework. In particular, we focus on stratification as related to labor market competition and examine its mutual relationship with differential power. While ethnocentrism may indeed be present as competition develops, it in turn is altered, reinforced and shaped by the competition process and ensuing ethnic stratification.

Several approaches to ethnic relations have focused on labor market competition between ethnic groups. At the core of these approaches is the notion that in order for there to be competition, the labor force must be split along ethnic lines. A split in the labor market emerges when two or more distinguishable groups are present in society and where there is a discrepancy in their price of labor (Bonacich 1972); that is, one group offers its labor at a lower cost for various reasons (such as differential needs, motivation, or information) which Lieberson (1980) referred to as intrinsic differences among ethnic groups (see also Hodge and Hodge (1965) for a discussion of economic competition among ethnic groups).

The split labor market perspective articulated by Bonacich (1972; 1976) stems from the class conflict paradigm according to which economic processes are seen as more central to the development of ethnic antagonism than primordial sentiments. As a result of employers' quest for greater profit, a quest inherent to the capitalist system, employers are likely to prefer cheaper labor. Hence, three key classes are identified: employers, highly paid labor, and less expensive labor (the latter pertains to a subordinate ethnic group while both employers and high priced labor pertain to the superordinate group). The ethnic group offering its labor at low cost most often does so out of necessity. Its members typically lack the resources to resist employers' offers and have no alternatives. Paradoxically, this very weakness is what makes those ethnic groups providing cheaper labor so threatening to other employees, since business can more thoroughly control them. According to this perspective, the underlying conflict is a class conflict between employers and better paid workers. This conflict is transformed, however, into one between competing worker groups where workers from the better paid group attempt to exclude the lower paid workers from the labor market, or at least from lucrative and more desirable positions in the labor market: "Business, rather than desiring to protect a segment of the working class supports a liberal or *laissez-faire* ideology that would permit all workers to compete freely in the open market" (Bonacich 1972:87).

In contrast to Bonacich, Burawoy (1982) explicitly introduces the state into the split labor market analysis. In his view, the interests of the state must not be confused with those of the individual capitalist. The primary concern of the state is with the reproduction of the conditions for continued growth of the economy or, in other words, the state is responsible for the reproduction of labor power as well as the labor process. Peled and Shafir (1987) point out that regardless which theory of the state is espoused (whether pluralist, functionalist, or conflict-oriented), two conditions must be met in order that the labor market may be split through state action: "First, the state would have to have the capacity to effect such an outcome, and, second, the workers would have to possess sufficient extra-market resources and the ability to use them politically in order to induce the state to undertake the necessary action" (p. 1452). The first condition implies that the state may take certain actions to support the high priced labor. This can be done through direct subsidies or other means, and only the state can distribute the cost of such measures throughout society. In addition, in order to provide "cheap labor" for individual employers, the state turns to boundary-maintaining measures in order to control the subordinate minority. Practices such as geographic segregation, legal closure of employment opportunities, discriminatory labor exchanges, or other forms of discrimination, make it necessary for the subordinate ethnic group to supply its labor at low cost as the only means of competing in the market.

The second condition relates to the ability of higher priced labor to affect state policies. The large numbers of high priced labor (relative to the number of employers from their same ethnic group) and their strategic location in the process of production provide the leverage with which they may influence state policies. Such action, in turn, will reproduce a split labor market by providing ongoing protection to high priced labor from free competition. This may be achieved either through the strategy of exclusion or that of segregation (caste). Exclusion is likely to be pursued by a relatively weak high priced labor whereas segregation and the creation of a caste-like system are more likely when the dominant workers have confidence in their ability to protect their positions through state legislation (Peled and Shafir 1987).

Boswell (1986) elaborates on the role of the state from a split labor market perspective and points out that " . . . initial ethnic differences in the cost of labor will not be continually reproduced under competitive market conditions unless workers continue to be ideologically identified" (Boswell 1986:354). This highlights the point that a discourse of "racism" is critical for the perpetuation of a split labor market, as well as the structural mechanisms by which it is reproduced. The weak market position of the subordinate group is reinforced by the "crowding" brought about by discrimination. When members of the subordinate group are denied access to preferred positions, they are crowded into a relatively small number of less desirable jobs. Market crowding increases the relative supply of members of the subordinate ethnic group and forces them to accept lower wages. This process in turn reproduces the split in the labor market.

The primary purpose of split labor market theory is to provide an explanation for ethnic conflict which, rather than relying on primordialism, is embedded in the reality of economic competition and structural conditions. For proponents of this theoretical approach, an understanding of the circumstances of the evolution and reproduction of a split labor market is a central objective. In line with this objective, Samir Miari (1986) recently applied the split labor market approach to the case of Israel, with specific emphasis on the different degrees of antagonism towards Arabs held by Jews from European or American origin (Ashkenazim) and Jews from Asian or North African countries (Orientals): "While antagonism and prejudice by both ethnic groups towards the Arabs are high, they are higher among the Orientals than among Ashkenazim" (Miari 1986:27). Hence the thesis put forward by Miari sets out to demonstrate " . . . that the status of Arabs in Israel has been influenced by conflicting material interests of the two Jewish ethnic groups" (Miari 1986:29). The argument developed by Miari follows the split labor market framework in its focus on the divergent interests of employers and employees— he equates Ashkenazi Jews with employers, and Oriental Jews with employees, a conceptualization leading to a gross over-simplification of the position of Arabs in Israel and its link to the cleavage within the Jewish population.[3] Nonetheless, we agree with Miari that it would be misleading to attribute the subordination of Arabs in Israel to the broader Israeli-Arab conflict and to national security factors alone. We contend that a closer examination of labor market processes will contribute substantially to the understanding of Jewish-Arab ethnic stratification within Israel.

In our study we contend that the patterns of socioeconomic inequality between Jews and Arabs can be conceptualized within an ethnic competition framework (e.g., Olzak and Nagel 1986; Olzak 1987). Ethnic competition is likely to emerge as two or more ethnic groups try to acquire the same resources. In particular, we are interested in economic competition where two or more ethnic groups compete under unequal conditions for the same jobs and rewards. Such competition is likely to vary over time and is affected by the structural conditions of the labor market. Specifically, integration of low priced labor into a national economy is likely to trigger a competitive process. Contraction of the economy and declining opportunities would intensify economic competition between ethnic groups; and changing ethnic group resources may alter the nature of competition. For instance, increase in the education of a subordinate ethnic group poses a threat to the superordinate group since it intensifies competition. Ethnic competition in turn is likely to result in greater antagonism and economic discrimination against members of the subordinate population.

Traditionally, the notion of ethnic competition was nurtured by the view of labor markets as "clearinghouses" for the supply of, and the demand for, individual workers. However, perfect competition in the labor market does not exist and workers' wages are determined by their ethnic affiliation as well as their productivity. Indeed, a comprehensive discussion of ethnic relations and inequality should take into consideration not only competition as an individualized process but also competition as a collective process. We need, therefore, to broaden our discussion of competition and more explicitly introduce dependency and control as factors which interact with and structure the conditions in which an ethnic split in the labor market is sustained. Our main purpose, then, is to examine how the structural features of this market exert differential impact on Arab and Jewish workers in producing socioeconomic inequality. Moreover, we intend to examine how individual-level characteristics are rewarded under the different market conditions faced by the two groups. By examining the Arab and Jewish labor simultaneously in both Arab and Jewish-dominated labor markets, we expect to go beyond past research on Israeli Arabs and thus to further our understanding of Israeli society.

Our study of Arabs in the Israeli economy is organized around a number of themes. Chapter 2 provides a descriptive overview of the Arab population, its sociodemographic characteristics, family and economic structure, and sub-group composition. It focuses on change over time and provides comparisons with the Jewish population in order to depict the scope of ethnic disparities in Israel. Two factors are especially emphasized: developments in the economic structure of Arab communities, and exploitation in Jewish-dominated labor markets.

These two factors are further developed in Chapter 3 and Chapter 4. In Chapter 3 we provide a brief historical background and overview of the economy in the Arab sector, and seek the sources of constraints on its development. We then discuss the consequences of the current structure in terms of population-labor market mismatch. In Chapter 4 we introduce the distinction between Arab and Jewish local labor markets and proceed with a comparative analysis of the effects of labor market structure on occupational status and earnings.

Chapter 5 is devoted to Arab female employment. Historically, Arab female participation in the market economy has been low and for this reason largely ignored by scholars of Israeli society, in general, and students of gender issues, in particular. Since Arab tradition restricts independent decisions of women and their free movement, we focus on women's employment in the context of local labor markets. We aim to explore the effect of labor market variation on the prevalence of female employment and gender-linked occupational differentiation. In line with the central theme of the book, we also examine the differential consequences for Arab females of working in Arab communities and in Jewish-dominated labor markets, respectively.

In the subsequent two chapters we shift the focus of our attention to the Jewish labor force and explore Jewish-Arab economic relations from yet another vantage point. In Chapter 6 we analyze labor market data in order to examine whether Jewish employees benefit from competition with, and economic discrimination against Arabs and how these benefits are distributed among the Jewish labor force. In Chapter 7 we consider the small number of Jews employed in Arab labor markets and attempt to derive from their demographic and occupational composition an understanding of the nature of such "reverse commuting". Finally, in Chapter 8, we draw on the central findings of our analysis and provide a composite summary of labor market competition and ensuing ethnic inequality. This summary serves as a focal point for our discussion of alternative interpretations of Jewish-Arab relations in Israel in light of the theoretical literature on economic-based ethnic conflict.

Notes

1. Eisenstadt and Ben-Rafael were mainly concerned with the relationship between Jews of European origin on the one hand and Jews who came from Asia or North Africa, on the other. Both scholars extended their models to apply to the Arab minority and to Jewish-Arab relations as well.

2. Arabs in Israel have been alternately, or in combination, considered as a religious, cultural, linguistic, or national minority. In this study we prefer to use the term "ethnicity" to distinguish Jews and Arabs. Throughout the book we apply the term in a generic sense, which refers to " . . . groups defined socially as sharing a common ancestry in which membership is therefore inherited or ascribed" (Bonacich 1972:548). Ethnic groups are typically culturally distinguishable and, as we shall argue, ethnic groups have the inherent potential to become national groups. Hence, defining Arabs in Israel as an ethnic minority neither distorts their situation nor does it entail any loss of generality.

3. It should be noted here that we see the Jewish-Arab cleavage in Israel as fundamentally different from the intra-Jewish cleavage of European and Middle Eastern Jews. Although the distinction within the Jewish population between Jews of European origin and those of Asian or North African descent has been central to the study of Israeli society, and although substantial differences between the groups have been found, we propose that the more significant ethnic split in Israeli society is that between Jews and Arabs. It is true that cultural as well as socioeconomic differences exist in the Jewish population and there are strong feelings of discrimination and deprivation among Middle Eastern Jews (Kraus 1986). Nonetheless, the common Jewish ethnic identity and the unanimous acceptance of the ideology of the "fusion of the exiles" render the intra-Jewish cleavage quite distinct. Whereas relations within the Jewish population may be described as paternalistic co-optation, Jewish-Arab relations are more aptly described as mutual exclusion. Not only do the two groups differ considerably in individual, social and political resources, as well as in the price of labor, they lack a shared ideology and vision of a shared society. For these reasons, and in order for the study reported here to maintain a sharp focus on the situation of Israeli Arabs, we choose to ignore intra-Jewish cleavages. We refer to the Jewish population as a whole, though we are acutely aware that it is far from homogeneous.

2

The Arabs: Profile of
a Disadvantaged Minority

The previous chapter reviewed several explanatory frameworks and laid out the central theme of this book. In this chapter we intend to set the issue of labor market activity of the Arab minority in Israel within the broader context in which Jewish-Arab relations are structured. The primary aim here is to familiarize the readers (especially those not intimately acquainted with the intricacies of Israeli society) with the major characteristics of Arab society in Israel, and their dynamics in recent decades. We will review demographic trends as well as social, political and ecological dimensions of the Arabs' position in Israeli society, since these both constrain the opportunities and the employment patterns of the Arab labor force, and are, in turn, affected by them.

Population Characteristics

Israel, in spite of its short modern history and small size, is remarkably diverse in its social and ethnic composition. Jews from practically every corner of the world have established their home in Israel. The most significant ethnic split in Israel, however, is not within the Jewish majority population but between Jews and the Arab minority population. In 1990, the Arab population comprised about 18 percent of the Israeli population, and they were subordinate to Jews in virtually every aspect of socioeconomic status such as education, occupational prestige, income, political power and standard of living. Furthermore, the residential segregation between Jews and Arabs is extreme. The overwhelming majority of Arabs and Jews do not live in the same communities, let alone the same neighborhoods.

The peculiarity of the status of the Arab population in Israel was clearly stated by Peres (1971:1028):

Arabs in Israel are a recent minority. Until 1948, there was statistically a clear majority of Arabs in Palestine, although they had no sovereign power . . . They are a minority without a political and cultural elite, a village population which had been accustomed to following the leadership of towns such as Jaffa, Nablus, and Beirut. The 1948 war emptied some of these towns and severed the connections with the rest. The resulting lack of trained and accepted leadership increased the vulnerability of the Arabs to Jewish economic and cultural influence.

The Arab minority population of Israel has lived in Palestine for generations. Historically, the Arabs were a rural population with a traditional orientation, minimally exposed to Western culture. Even today the majority of the Arab population of Israel still resides in village communities. They all speak Arabic as their daily language, and local culture is deeply rooted in the broader Arab culture. Nevertheless, the population we refer to as Arab is comprised of three major subgroups: Moslems, Christians, and Druze. The former constitute the largest group and the latter constitute the smallest group. There are several additional non-Jewish groups in Israel, such as the Cherkesse and Shomronites, but these groups are seldom identified separately in official statistics, and their numbers are too small to warrant separate analysis in the present context. The relative order of the groups by size has remained remarkably stable over the years. Moslems constitute about three-quarters of the non-Jewish population and Druze remain approximately 10 percent of the total (See Table 2.1). Although these groups differ from one another in several ways, to be discussed in ensuing sections, we will refer to them throughout the book as "Arabs" or "Israeli Arabs", in order to underscore

TABLE 2.1: Distribution of the Israeli Population in 1961, 1975 and 1990 by Continent of Birth and Religion

	1961		1975		1990	
	N (in thousands)	Percentages	N (in thousands)	Percentages	N (in thousands)	Percentages
Grand Total	2,179.5	100.0	3,493.2	100.0	4,821.7	100.0
Jews Total	1,932.4	88.7	2,959.4	84.7	3,946.7	81.9
Israeli Born Total	730.4	37.8	1,506.3	50.9	2,442.9	61.9
Father Born						
Israel	106.9	5.5	305.5	10.3	880.9	22.3
Asia-Africa	288.5	14.9	718.3	24.3	958.7	24.3
Europe-America	335.0	17.4	482.5	16.3	603.3	15.3
Foreign Born Total	1,201.9	62.2	1,453.1	49.1	1,503.7	38.1
Asia-Africa	480.9	27.4	653.7	22.1	592.2	15.0
Europe-America	721.0	34.8	799.4	27.0	911.5	23.1
Non-Jews Total	247.1	11.3	533.8	15.3	875.0	18.1
Moslems	172.3	7.8	411.4	11.8	677.7	14.0
Christians	50.5	2.3	80.2	2.3	114.7	2.4
Druze and Others	24.3	1.2	42.2	1.2	82.6	1.7

Source: Statistical Abstract of Israel, 1962 Tables 1, 17, 18; 1976 Table ii/18; and 1991 Table ii/22.

the fact that for the most part their being "Arab" (rather than Christian, Moslem, or even Druze) is highly relevant to their position in Israeli society.

In the years following the establishment of the State of Israel in 1948, the Arab minority experienced dramatic changes, not only in its political status, but also in its demographic, social and economic characteristics. It is estimated that in 1947, just prior to Israel's independence, approximately 1.2 million Arabs resided in Palestine (Friedlander and Goldscheider 1984; Al-Haj 1987a). Between 750,000 and 900,000 of these residents were in the territory that was to become the State of Israel, and most of them either fled or were expelled during the war. The exact number of refugees has never been established but various estimates place the figures at 600,000 to 760,000 (see Morris, 1987, Appendix I). Approximately 156,000 Arabs remained and became residents of Israel and, at the outset of the State, comprised almost 20 percent of its population. Large waves of Jewish immigration, however, changed the population composition in favor of Jews so that by the mid 1950s Arabs comprised only 11 percent of Israel's population. Since then the proportion of Arabs has increased steadily to reach 18 percent of the total population of Israel in 1990 (875,000 persons including the Arab population of East Jerusalem). This increase represents an average annual growth of 4.1 percent, a rate very close to the average rate in the Jewish population which stands at 4.3 percent (see Statistical Abstract of Israel, 1990, Table 2.2, p. 39).

Almost half the Jewish population growth (45.7 percent) is due to immigration whereas only 1.6 percent of Arab population growth is accounted for by immigration. The high natural increase of the Arab population reflects the high fertility which has traditionally characterized Arab society, and Moslems in particular, as well as declining mortality.

Figures in Table 2.2 show fertility rates for various Arab populations, with Jewish fertility rates provided for comparative purposes. The total fertility rate (TFR) given in the table is the average number of children to whom a

TABLE 2.2:   Total Fertility Rates for Arab and Jewish Women, by Religion and Continent of Birth, 1955, 1960, 1970, 1980, 1990

	1955[1]	1960	1970	1980	1990
Arabs					
Moslem	7.96	9.31	8.95	5.98	4.70
Christians	4.85	4.61	3.62	2.66	2.57
Druze + others	6.58	7.88	7.46	6.09	4.05
Jews					
Israel	2.83	2.76	3.12	2.76	2.76
Asia-Africa	5.68	5.10	4.07	3.04	3.09
Europe-America	2.63	2.38	2.84	2.76	2.31

[1]The first year for which reliable data are available for the Arab population.

Source: Statistical Abstract of Israel, 1983. Table III/14, p. 99, and 1991, Table III/14, p. 129.

woman is expected to give birth, assuming that at each age she will have the fertility rate characteristic of women of that age in the particular year for which TFR is calculated.

It is apparent that Arab fertility rates were higher than that of Jews throughout the period surveyed, and this is especially true for Moslems. Christian Arab fertility was relatively low already 35 years ago and is now lower than fertility rates among most Jewish groups. Even today, however, the overall Arab fertility rates are approximately 50 percent higher than that of Jews.

Declining mortality has contributed substantially to the natural increase of Israeli Arabs. The crude death rate (CDR) of Arabs in Palestine, which was approximately 20 per thousand during the British mandate (Stendel 1973), dropped to 9.5 per thousand in 1950. This figure was further reduced over the next 40 years, and by 1989 the CDR among Arabs was less than 4 per thousand. The drop in mortality is also reflected in life expectancy which rose from approximately 47 years around 1940 to over 67 years by the mid 1950s.

In the five year period 1955–1959 life expectancy at birth was 67.7 for Arabs in Israel (males and females combined) as compared to 69.7 for Jews. During the next 15 years life expectancy of both groups rose by almost three years: for the years 1970–1974 it was 68.8 years for Arab males and 72.2 for Arab females; the comparable figures for Jews were 70.5 and 73.6 for males and females respectively. By 1989, life expectancy had increased by almost 4 more years for Jews (74.9 for males and 78.5 for females), and slightly less for Arabs. In 1989 life expectancy for Arab males was 73.1 and for females it was 75.5 (three years less than Jewish women).

The persistent inequality in life expectancy is largely a result of an enduring gap between Jews and Arabs in infant deaths. As can be seen from Table 2.3, infant deaths have dropped dramatically over the past 35 years. Currently, the number of infant deaths comprise only one-quarter the number of cases that occurred in the mid-1950s. In 1955 the ratio of Arab-to-Jewish

TABLE 2.3: Infant Deaths (per 1000 live births) among Jews and Arabs by Sex, 1955, 1960, 1970-72, 1980-82, 1987

	1955[1]	1960[1]	1970-72		1980-82		1987	
			M	F	M	F	M	F
Jews	32.4	27.0	10.6	16.8	13.7	11.0	10.2	7.8
Arabs	62.5	48.0	31.1	26.1	23.6	22.4	19.0	15.3
Moslems	--	--	31.4	26.4	24.9	23.4	19.0	15.5

[1]In these years figures appear for both sexes combined and separate information for Moslems is not available.

Source: Statistical Abstract of Israel, 1973. Table III/33, p. 90 and 1990, Table III/31, p. 144.

infant deaths was approximately 2:1. By the early 1970s the ratio rose to 3:1 as a result of a dramatic decline in infant deaths among Jews. By 1987 there were only 7.5 more female infant deaths (per 1000 live births) among Arabs, and 9 more infant male deaths. Nonetheless, the gap has not yet disappeared and the Arab-to-Jewish infant death ratio is still approximately 2:1, indicating greater hardship among the Arab population.

Sub-Groups in the Arab Population

As noted earlier, the Arab population in Israel is divided into several sub-groups, the largest of which are Moslems, Christians, and Druze. Moslems, who make up the majority of Israeli Arabs, constituted 70 percent of the Arab population that remained within the borders of Israel in 1948 and, due to their greater natural increase, they now comprise 77 percent of the Arab population. Virtually all Moslems in Israel are Sunnite Moslems. The majority of Moslems live in rural areas—villages and towns with a population of less than 10,000 inhabitants. Most institutions of the Moslem community, as well as other Arab communities, collapsed during the war in 1948. While the Shari'a judicial system[1] was restored under the State of Israel's legal system, the communal framework has weakened as a result of secularization, as well as the decline of the status of the Shari'a functionaries in a non-Moslem state. Furthermore, a major source of community power—the Moslem Wakf (endowment) property—was considerably weakened when much of its property was expropriated by the Israeli government as absentee property.[2] Among the Moslems, the Bedouin population deserves special note. The Bedouin are nomad tribes now on the verge of sedentarization. Approximately two-thirds of the Bedouin population reside in the Negev in the south of Israel and the remainder in the Galilee. Mounting restrictions on movement and land use have forced a change in the sources of Bedouin livelihood. New occupational opportunities for the Bedouin have also contributed to their settlement and today the Bedouin community is experiencing major residential changes.

The Christians, comprising approximately 13 percent of the Arab population, are the second largest Arab group. They are divided into various sects, all of which try to preserve their distinct identity and their self-directing community life. The largest Christian communities in Israel are the Greek Catholic and the Greek Orthodox. They are concentrated mainly in the north of Israel around the city of Nazareth and in Jerusalem. Indeed, only a minority of Christians are rural dwellers. As with the Moslems, Christians are given extensive autonomy in the organization of religious life and judicial system pertaining to personal status.

Druze comprise about 10 percent of Israel's Arab population. In Israel, as in other countries in which the Druze reside, they constitute a separate socio-religious community. Druze are primarily mountain dwellers and the overwhelming majority of them reside in rural communities: less than 5 percent of all Druze reside in communities with a population greater than 20,000. It took 10 years from the establishment of the State of Israel to grant the Druze community independent religious status, but since then they have become more involved in the life of the State of Israel than other Arab groups. The special treatment of the Druze community was viewed by the governments of Israel as a way to "divide and conquer" the non-Jewish minority and, concomitantly, Druze leaders hoped to enhance the position of their community which is smaller and politically less organized than either Moslems or Christians. In particular, at the request of the leaders of the Druze community, Druze youths are conscripted into the military as are Jewish youths. The expectation was that in this way the Druze community would have claim to a greater share of societal resources and would be integrated into Israeli society. In fact, this has not occurred, and in particular there has been relatively little development and economic change in their communities of residence.

Comparison of the three Arab sub-populations with respect to socio-economic and demographic characteristics reveals considerable differences, the most meaningful of which is between the Christians and the other groups. Christians are more urban than either Moslems or Druze, they attain higher levels of formal education, and they hold occupations and jobs of higher status and prestige. These differences are apparent when the characteristics of the economically active labor force of the subgroups (age 25–65) are compared (Table 2.4). The differences regarding occupational status, earnings and

TABLE 2.4: Mean Characteristics of the Economically Active Labor Force Population of Moslems, Christians and Druze in Israel, 1988

	Moslems	Christians	Druze
Income (Shekels)	19153.9	23864.9	24147.7
Income Per Hour	116.2	144.6	138.5
Occupational Status	34.8	42.1	36.6
Percent in Professional Academic-Scientific	3.3	6.9	2.5
Percent in Technical	13.7	21.3	14.6
Percent in Agriculture	6.1	1.0	4.9
Education Years	7.9	10.5	8.0
Percent with No Education	13.6	2.8	9.0
Percent Academic Degree	6.5	11.4	4.0
Percent Hebrew Speaking	52.2	59.1	60.6
Percent in Major Cities	24.0	30.3	6.5
Percent in Small Rural Areas	11.1	8.7	11.8
Age	36.3	42.1	31.6
Percent Women in Labor Force	10.5	29.3	12.3

Source: 1988, Labor Force Survey of Persons Aged 25-64.

education are especially interesting. Whereas Moslems have the lowest levels of earnings, occupational status and education, Christians have the highest level of both education and occupational status. In fact, more than any other Arab sub-group, Christian Arabs have attained academic degrees and professional and scientific jobs. However, while Druze's educational level is relatively low, their earnings level is higher than any other Arab population group. This may be a result of the greater accessibility of Druze to jobs in Israeli society due to their military service. Indeed, a high proportion of Druze men find employment in security related jobs as policemen and prison guards. In a society where most citizens are required to serve three years in the military, many entitlements are dependent on such service. As we shall point out in the following section, this serves as a major mechanism of discrimination between Jews and most Arabs.

Legal and Political Status

Israel's Declaration of Independence ensures that its citizens will enjoy complete equality in political and social rights irrespective of race, religion or gender. This is manifest in a most straightforward way in Israel's democratic voting system where Arabs are equal participants. Nonetheless, there are various forms of encroachment on the principle of equality which result in discrimination between Jews and Arabs.

Turning first to the political arena, the right to vote and to be elected to public office has been exercised by the Arab minority in Israel since the establishment of the State. Yet, during the early years, the political behavior of Arabs was influenced by the fact that its ". . . leadership in all spheres fled the country during the war of 1948. Along with these leaders, organized parties and political groups formed in the days of the British Mandate have disappeared" (Landau 1969:20; see also Cohen 1990). Throughout most of Israel's existence the political behavior of the Arab community has been characterized by the lack of political parties of its own. Prominent Arabs were typically co-opted into Zionist political parties or headed Arab lists of candidates affiliated with or supported by Jewish parties. This was facilitated by the *hamula* (kinship structure) of Arab communities in which the extended family plays a central role. Political organization was one of the major roles of the extended family and the *hamula* after the establishment of Israel. Often an agreement between a political party and the father of an extended family would suffice so that all family members would cast their vote for that party. This was certainly the case in local elections where lists were frequently based on religious affiliation and *hamula* kinship (Habash 1973, Al-Haj 1987a). At the national level, since the early 1950s, Arabs have been represented by (more or less) 8 members of parliament (6.6 percent of the 120 Knesset members). Not only is this number an underrepresentation of their electoral potential but it is also fragmented among several political parties (Cohen 1990).

Political patterns have changed somewhat since the mid 1970s with the decline of co-optation of Arab leadership. A shift has taken place from instrumental voting behavior to more ideological patterns, with growing support for the Arab Communist Party ("Rakach") and, more recently, the Arab dominated "Progressive List for Peace and Equality". But even as recently as 1988, 40 percent of Israeli Arabs voted for Zionist parties (Ben-Rafael and Sharot 1991) and it is evident that fragmentation along religious, regional and *hamula* lines still hinders Arabs in using the political arena as a lever for social and economic gains.

At the same time that Israeli Arabs have enjoyed the right to equally participate and influence the political arena (albeit with little tangible impact), their legal status, more generally, is unequal to that of Jews in several respects. In his broad and exhaustive review of the legal status of Arabs in Israel, Kretzmer (1987) distinguishes three forms of discrimination: overt, covert, and institutional discrimination. Overt discrimination refers to explicit discrimination anchored in statutory instruments. Instances of such discrimination are rare, but the few laws that do exist are significant, in both symbolic and practical terms. The "Law of Return and Nationality", for instance, provides that every Jew may acquire nationality by virtue of their "return" to Israel, whereas Arabs may acquire nationality only by means of residence, birth or naturalization. A second instance is the law granting special status to Jewish "national institutions", such as the Jewish Agency and the Jewish National Fund. The manifest purpose of these organizations, established prior to the State of Israel, was to facilitate the establishment of a national home in Palestine for the Jewish people. After the establishment of the State, these agencies were granted legal rights to operate alongside government institutions and various laws acknowledge their right to representation in various state agencies (see Kretzmer p. 60). Hence, while these Jewish "national institutions" are entrusted with tasks which are typically of governmental nature, their mandate specifically directs them to operate in the Jewish sector of the Israeli population.

Covert discrimination refers to those instances of disguised discrimination between Jews and Arabs, such as the legal statutes which use military service and geographical region as criteria for entitlements. The Defence Service Law of Israel requires every resident who reaches the age of 18 to serve in the Israeli Defence Force. In practice, however, the State has refrained from recruiting Arabs, except for males of the Druze population and a few Bedouins. Since certain benefits are provided by law only to Israeli residents who have served in the military, this means that the majority of Jews are entitled to the benefits while the majority of Arabs are not. Such entitlements include child allowances (for the third child and any additional children of a person who has served in the military), preference in public sector jobs, occupational training programs and higher education, and enlarged subsidized loans for housing. While some of these benefits may reasonably be argued to be a form of compensation for the period spent serving the country and, therefore, not discriminatory as such, in other cases it is more difficult to make such a claim, and they would appear to be clear instances of covert discrimination. Another instance of covert discrimination is the practice of allocating benefits according to geographical criteria. The extreme ecological segregation of

Jews and Arabs in Israel (to be discussed later in this chapter) makes it possible to draw the boundaries of regions selected for preferential treatment so as to include most Jewish communities and to exclude Arab ones. Various statutes designating development areas and providing tax credits have thus discriminated between Jews and Arabs even though religion or nationality are not mentioned in them. The most notable instance of such a policy is that of development zones (see Lustick, 1980; Zureik, 1979; Khalidi, 1988a).

A third form of discrimination is institutionalized in bureaucratic decisions. Such discrimination is not based on any legal statutes but results from decisions and policies enacted by government agencies. Central to this institutional discrimination are budgetary decisions and resource allocation which differentially affect Jews and Arabs. Later in this chapter we will elaborate on local government funding in the Arab sector and argue that there is considerable discrimination against communities that have a majority Arab population. Other noteworthy areas of discrimination vis-á-vis resource allocations are education, public housing, infrastructure development and the implementation of policies concerning land expropriation and employment.

Socioeconomic Inequality

In recent decades the Arab minority has experienced dramatic changes, not only in its size and political status, but also with regard to educational attainment and the occupational distribution of its labor force. While the growth of education and occupational diversification are to be expected, the contacts between the Arab minority and the Jewish population have intensified and accelerated these changes. It should be noted that a rise in educational levels and a substantial upgrading of the occupational composition of the labor force is also apparent among Jews (e.g. Lewin-Epstein and Semyonov, 1985, 1986). However, the changes have been considerably more pronounced among the Arab minority.

Table 2.5 displays the educational distributions of Jews and Arabs between 1961 to 1990 (population age 15 and over). At all points in time the educational level of Jews by far exceeded that of Arabs. However, the gap between the groups has considerably declined over the years. This decline is mainly a result of the dramatic rise in the educational level of Arabs, as compared to a more gradual rise in the educational level of Jews. More specifically, in 1961, almost 50 percent of the Arab population in Israel was virtually illiterate. By 1990, 13 percent of Arabs were still reported to have no schooling as compared to 4.2 percent among Jews. It should be noted that illiterates (whether Jews or Arabs) are those belonging to the older population groups and, more than any other groups, the younger generations are those that benefitted from the expansion of educational opportunities. The change in educational level is also evident with regard to higher education. For example, in 1961, only 1.5 percent of Arabs had completed more than 12 years of schooling. The comparable figure for Jews was almost 10 percent. In 1990, the proportion of Arabs with some academic training (over 12 years) had increased almost six-fold (to 9 percent). The percent of Jews with academic training increased three-fold

TABLE 2.5: Years of Schooling of Arabs and Jews, 1961-1990 (Persons Aged 15 and Over)

		Years of Schooling								
	Median	16+	13-15	11-12	9-10	5-8	1-4	0	Percents	Thousands
Arabs										
1961	1.2	1.5		7.6		27.5	13.9	49.5	100.0	136.3
1970	5.0	(0.4)	1.7	13.0		35.1	13.7	36.1	100.0	223.2
1975	6.5	1.4	3.1	9.1	12.6	38.0	12.9	22.9	100.0	279.8
1980	7.5	2.2	5.5	13.5	16.0	33.9	10.0	18.9	100.0	344.5
1985	8.6	2.5	5.9	19.2	19.3	32.0	7.7	13.4	100.0	428.2
1988	8.6	2.9	6.0	21.4	16.6	30.6	7.3	15.2	100.0	462.5
1990	9.0	3.0	6.1	23.2	17.4	30.8	6.5	13.0	100.0	502.0
Jews										
1961	8.4	3.6	6.3	34.6		35.4	7.5	12.6	100.0	1,300.9
1970	9.3	4.9	8.1	39.7		31.7	6.3	9.3	100.0	1,809.6
1975	10.3	7.0	10.7	26.1	18.8	25.5	4.3	7.6	100.0	2,708.2
1980	11.1	8.5	12.3	30.4	17.2	21.3	3.9	6.4	100.0	2,315.8
1985	11.5	10.2	14.2	33.6	16.6	17.3	3.1	5.0	100.0	2,511.3
1988	11.8	11.8	15.3	36.7	14.2	14.9	2.7	4.4	100.0	2,558.6
1990	11.9	12.2	16.0	38.0	13.5	13.7	2.4	4.2		

Source: Statistical Abstract of Israel, 1991, Table XXII/1, p. 603-605.

during the same period and reached 28 percent. The change in the educational level of Arabs relative to Jews is clearly reflected in the median years of schooling. Between 1961 to 1990 the median for the Arab population increased from 1.2 to 9 years. During the same period the median years of schooling for the Jewish population rose from 8.4 to 11.9 years. Notwithstanding the impressive gain in the educational level of Arabs in Israel, their average education still lags three years behind that of Jews.

Both the occupational and the industrial composition of the Israeli labor force have also changed over the years. Upgrading of the occupational structure has been evident among both Jews and Arabs. However, the patterns of change have taken different forms in the two populations. Furthermore, at every given point in time, Jews in Israel are overrepresented in higher status (professional, scientific and managerial) occupations, whereas Arabs are overrepresented in farming and manual (skilled and unskilled) occupations.

Since statehood, and even prior to that time, the Israeli economy has been characterized by a large service sector, and small agricultural and manufacturing industries as compared to other nations of equal, or even more advanced levels of development (Ofer, 1976; Ginor 1979). However, the economy of Arab communities within Israel was dominated by agricultural employment (Rosenfeld, 1978). The fact that most of the Jewish population in Israel, unlike the Arabs, consisted of new arrivals, meant lack of traditional patterns of attachment to farmland. Historical patterns of centralized goal setting and control led to the emergence of large bureaucracies and large public sector employment. The continuous and massive external financial aid received mostly by the public sector (e.g. the Israeli government and the Jewish national institutions) resulted in an even greater expansion in this sector without equal increase in the production of exchangeable goods (Ofer 1976).

Throughout the years the occupational and industrial structure of Israel has been transformed in much the same way as other economies that have undergone processes of industrialization and post-industrialization (Single-man, 1978; Bell, 1973). The process of transformation, however, has followed different trajectories in the Jewish and the Arab sectors (see Table 2.6). Among the Arab population there has been a remarkable decline in the labor force employed in agriculture (from almost 50 percent in 1961 to less than 7 percent in 1990). This decline in agricultural employment was accompanied by a substantial increase in the labor force engaged in blue-collar—skilled and unskilled—labor (from about one-third to over half the labor force). This process was not a slow evolutionary one; rather, it was brought about in large part by extensive land expropriation by the State (as will be elaborated in Chapter 3). Consequently, many Arabs have gravitated from the agricultural sector in the Arab communities toward manual jobs in the Jewish dominated economy.

Among Jews, the occupational and industrial transformation was primarily manifest in the rise in professional, scientific and technical occupations. Indeed, between 1961 and 1990, the proportion of the labor force employed in this category more than doubled. At present, professional and scientific occupations comprise a quarter of the Jewish labor force (as compared to 9 percent among Arabs). Clerical and sales occupations (intermediate status jobs) have also grown during this period, albeit at a slower rate. Agricultural occupations have traditionally represented only a relatively small proportion of the Jewish labor force and these decreased even further throughout this period.

At present, Jews are extremely overrepresented in all white collar occupations (higher status as well as intermediate), while Arabs are overrepresented in all manual, service and agriculture occupations. These patterns clearly demonstrate that although Arabs' level of education has considerably increased, they have not been able to narrow the occupational gap. Between 1975 and 1990, for example, Jewish representation in managerial positions increased by 3 percent, while Arabs in managerial positions increased by only 1 percent. Apparently, the growing integration of Arabs into the Jewish dominated economy has not resulted in similar improvement in occupational status. In fact, while Arabs benefitted more from educational upgrading, Jews benefitted more from occupational upgrading; which is to say that Arabs were not successful in converting their educational assets into occupational status.

TABLE 2.6: Arab and Jewish Employed Persons by Economic Branch and by Occupation, 1960-1990 (percent)

	Arabs					Jews				
	1960-1	1975	1980	1985	1990	1960-1	1975	1980	1985	1990
Economic Branch										
Agriculture	48.4	16.4	15.2	10.5	6.3	14.5	5.4	5.4	5.0	3.9
Industry	14.3	17.7	20.2	21.2	22.1	24.6	25.6	24.0	23.2	21.7
Utilities	1.0	(0.5)	(0.6)	(0.4)	(0.3)	1.9	1.0	1.1	0.9	1.2
Construction	14.1	24.2	19.5	19.4	18.6	8.5	6.5	4.9	3.6	3.3
Commerce	*	10.2	10.4	12.9	15.0	*	12.5	11.8	12.4	14.5
Transport	3.3	7.3	5.8	5.6	5.9	6.6	7.2	7.0	6.5	6.3
Finance and Business	7.5	1.9	2.5	3.1	3.9	12.3	7.2	8.9	10.6	10.8
Public and Community Services	7.7	14.7	18.4	19.0	19.5	24.2	28.6	30.8	31.3	31.0
Personal Services	3.3	7.1	7.5	7.9	8.4	7.4	6.0	6.0	6.5	7.3
Occupation										
Scientific Academic, Professional	4.2 {	1.2	2.5	2.5	3.5	12.3 {	7.3	8.0	8.6	9.3
		7.3	10.4	9.1	8.7		13.4	14.6	15.3	17.6
Managers	1.4 {	0.4	1.0	1.9	1.3	14.2 {	3.5	3.8	5.5	5.2
Clerical		3.4	5.0	6.0	6.3		18.8	18.6	18.0	18.6
Sales	5.1	6.0	6.1	7.1	8.6	8.9	8.1	7.6	7.7	8.9
Service	7.0	8.8	9.1	11.3	12.5	12.9	11.9	11.0	12.5	13.2
Agriculture	46.8	16.5	15.0	10.3	7.0	14.4	5.2	5.9	4.9	3.4
Skilled Workers	20.7	41.0	38.8	38.6	42.2	29.6	26.7	26.2	24.6	21.2
Unskilled Workers	11.0	13.4	12.2	13.1	9.8	3.0	5.2	4.3	3.3	2.1

* Included in Finance and Business

Source: Statistical Abstract of Israel, for 1960-1 and for 1991, Tables XII/10, XII/18, XII/19.

Table 2.7 displays the socioeconomic characteristics and family background of the Arab minority and the Jewish majority in the economically active labor force. The data are taken from the 1974 Labor Force Mobility and Fertility Survey—the only large scale representative sample to date that provides information on both respondents' and their fathers' characteristics. Hence, we are able not only to examine the current status of Jews and Arabs in the Israeli labor force, but also to infer their patterns of intergenerational mobility.

The comparison between Jews and Arabs reveals a number of points of interest. First, it is clear that the two ethnic groups differ considerably in their socioeconomic origins as well as in their current socioeconomic standing. The Jews in the survey were born into a much higher socioeconomic status. Their fathers were better educated—6.5 percent of Jewish fathers had some university education while none of the Arab fathers had attained any academic education. By contrast, only 15.6 percent of Jewish fathers were illiterate as compared with 69.7 percent among Arabs. The Arabs were also handicapped in their occupational origins: the majority came from an agricultural background with 64.1 percent born to fathers employed in agriculture. The Jewish fathers, in contrast, were overrepresented in all the white collar and the skilled occupations.

Regarding the socioeconomic status of respondents, Jews were placed

TABLE 2.7: Mean Characteristics of the Arab and Jewish Labor Force Aged 25-64 in 1974

	Arabs	Jews	Ethnic Gap
Mean Income	1298.62	1538.84	240.22
Mean Occupational Status	32.87	41.38	8.51
Mean Educational Level	1.94	3.38	1.44
Father's Occupational Status	29.78	38.61	8.83
Percent Illiterate Fathers	69.74	15.57	-54.17
Percent Fathers Elementary School	27.35	47.30	19.95
Percent Fathers Yeshiva or Religious School	1.86	17.03	15.77
Percent Fathers High School or Teachers Seminar	1.06	12.96	11.90
Percent Fathers Post Graduate Education	.00	6.54	6.54
Percent Females in Labor Force	9.21	29.88	20.67

Source: Mobility and Fertility Survey of 1974.

higher than Arabs in the three variables referring to individual achievement. Jews were underrepresented in the lower levels of educational attainment and overrepresented in the upper levels of education. In the respondents' generation only 12.7 percent of Arabs and 5.2 percent of Jews were illiterate. On the other hand, 10.7 percent of Jews versus 2.7 percent of Arabs had a university education. These statistical facts demonstrate the upward educational mobility that both Jews and Arabs experienced relative to their fathers. Despite this mobility, Arabs still lagged far behind Jews with regard to their educational achievement.

Jews also enjoyed higher occupational status than Arabs, with the average Jew about 8.5 points higher in the occupational hierarchy. Arabs were still more likely to be employed in agriculture (13.2 percent versus 4.2) and as manual laborers (56.4 percent versus 33.3). Nevertheless, Arabs' concentration in agricultural occupations was less pronounced than was the case among their fathers. This mobility from farm origin to mainly manual destinations reflects the extensive proletarization which the Arab population experienced in the course of a generation.

From the comparison of monthly income of the two groups in 1974, it is clear that Jews earned more than Arabs. On average, Arabs earned 84 percent of the monthly income of Jews. A more detailed examination of the income distribution of the two groups (not presented in Table 2.7) demonstrates that Jews were overrepresented in upper income levels and non-Jews in lower ones. Since gender composition of the Jewish and Arab labor force is remarkably different, as can be ascertained from the last row of Table 2.6, and since women in Israel, as elsewhere, receive lower rewards for their work than do men, the income gap observed for the population as a whole was in fact smaller than the gap that would be observed for men only. Furthermore, higher rates of working among Jewish wives and the smaller size of Jewish families also had the consequence of increasing the difference in income between Jewish and Arab households.[3]

The income differences are clearly reflected in the fact that while Arab households constituted only 4.1 percent of all households in Israel in the mid 1970s, they constituted 17.5 percent of the lowest decile of net income per standard person. At the same time they constituted less than one-half of one percent of the top four deciles (Statistical Abstract of Israel, 1980, Table 11/4, p. 272). This figure has not changed much over time, and in 1988, when non-Jewish households comprised 5.3 percent of all households with salaried heads of household, they constituted 20.9 percent of the lowest decile of net monthly income for standard person (Statistical Abstract of Israel, 1990, Table 11.6, p. 302).

The economic disadvantage of Arabs is nowhere more evident than in the official figures on poverty. In 1986/87 (the last year for which comprehensive data are available) 57.2 percent of all Arab families reported incomes that were below the poverty line (National Insurance Institute, 1989). After government (welfare) transfers are taken into account, over one-third (37.5 percent) of Arab families still had a total family income which was below the poverty line. In order to put these figures in perspective, it is noteworthy that during the same year 24.3 percent of all Jewish families were below the poverty line, but only 7.3 percent remained in poverty after the transfer of welfare payments. Hence not only did a higher portion of Arab families receive income which placed them below the poverty line, but it was also the case that government policies did not remedy this situation for Arabs whereas they clearly did so for Jews. Since Arab families are generally larger than Jewish families in Israel, the disparity is even greater when the proportion of the population is considered rather than the proportion of families (National Insurance Institute, 1989, Table 19 and Table 21). Although in this study we intend to focus on the labor market, the above mentioned figures accentuate the point made in Chapter 1, namely that market processes must be examined and interpreted within a social and political context which, in Israel, is structured primarily by agencies of the dominant Jewish group.

Ecological Segregation

Jews and Arabs do not only differ in their social and economic status but also with respect to where they live. The duality of Israeli ethnic structure is mirrored in the organization of communities. Persons are not located in communities randomly, but rather on the basis of their ethnic affiliation. Consequently ecological segregation by place of residence between Jews and Arabs is extreme. Approximately 85 percent of the Arab population reside in village communities and small towns in which they are the sole inhabitants. These communities are typically distant from major urban centers and lack the infrastructure needed to facilitate development.

Furthermore, the Arab population of Israel is heavily concentrated in only a few regions. Approximately half the Arab population of Israel resides in the northern districts as compared to less than 9 percent of the Jewish population. Nazareth—the largest Arab city in Israel—is located in the northern district. In addition, there is a considerable concentration of Arab villages (some have grown to mid-size cities or towns) in the center of the country. This concentration (the area known as the "small triangle") is particularly evident in the Hadera and Sharon sub-districts where over 10 percent of the non-Jewish population and about 7 percent of the Jewish population reside. It is interesting to note that the Arab communities in this area have only recently gained township status and, in actual fact, they are oversized villages with no real infrastructure or solid economic base.[4] Indeed, no town in the center has similar status to that of Nazareth in the north.

In the Jerusalem area, following the 1967 war, the non-Jewish population increased overnight when East Jerusalem, previously under Jordanian rule, was annexed by the government and appended to the western part of Jerusalem, previously Israeli. In 1974, 18.5 percent of the Arab population resided in the Jerusalem district, almost double the percentage of the Jewish population residing there.

In the southern districts of Israel (Negev Desert) there is a concentration of Bedouin tribes. There are very few permanent localities for this nomad population although in recent years the Israeli government has devoted considerable effort and resources to establish several permanent localities (i.e. Rahat, Tel Sheva) for the Bedouin population.[5]

The data in Table 2.8 clearly demonstrate the extent of regional segregation of Jews and Arabs: Arabs are extremely overrepresented in a few administrative districts and extremely underrepresented in all others. The value of the index of dissimilarity for the ethnic distribution in the fourteen districts is 57.0.[6] Translating the index of dissimilarity into a verbal analogy, 57 percent of either the Arabs or the Jews of Israel would have to move to another district of the country for the two groups to be equally distributed. It should be noted, however, that this measure is somewhat conservative since the index of dissimilarity does not capture segregation within region, let alone segregation within cities. Furthermore, regional segregation between Jews and

TABLE 2.8: Percent of Population in Regions by Ethnicity, 1974 and 1990 (percent)*

Region	Jews		Arabs	
	1974	1990	1974	1990
Jerusalem	9.8	10.8	8.5	17.3
Zfat	1.9	1.7	.8	.8
Kinneret	1.4	1.4	2.3	2.3
Yizre'el	3.5	3.5	18.0	16.9
Akko	2.8	3.1	26.1	25.4
Haifa	12.1	10.5	5.3	5.2
Hadera	2.9	2.6	10.7	10.6
Sharon	4.4	4.7	5.9	5.6
Petah Tiqua	4.5	9.0	1.8	1.9
Ramla	3.0	2.7	1.7	2.0
Rehovot	5.6	7.5	.1	.1
Tel Aviv	32.5	27.3	1.6	1.8
Ashqelon	5.9	6.0	.1	.2
Be'er Sheva	6.6	6.7	7.1	8.2

*Figures for the Jewish population do not total 100 percent since a small
 percentage of Israeli citizens are registered as residents of the occupied
 territories.

Source: Statistical Abstract of Israel 1975, 1991 Tables II/7, pp. 49-51.

Arabs has actually increased over the years since Jews are migrating out of the districts and regions where Arabs are concentrated.

Arabs are not only concentrated in a few regions but they are also concentrated in a relatively small number of communities. Indeed, most of the communities in Israel are entirely inhabited by either Arabs or Jews. In fact, there are only seven localities in Israel that are formally defined as mixed localities: Jerusalem, Tel Aviv, Haifa, Acco, Lod, Ramla, and Mallot-Tarshicha. In only three of these towns is there a higher proportion of non-Jews than their proportion in the total population, and in only four does the proportion of Arabs exceed 10 percent. In all other Israeli localities the population is almost entirely Jewish or Arab.

The association between residential segregation and ethnicity in Israel is rooted in historical peculiarities of the state. The Jewish population came to Palestine to establish its own communities rather than to integrate with the Arab population. By 1948 (when Israel achieved statehood) the Jewish population was already well organized in several Jewish cities, towns, and agricultural settlements. Most of this population resided in or near the major urban centers. Extreme residential segregation is reinforced by cultural differences and minimal social integration of the groups; there is no intermarriage and only rarely do friendship networks include members of both groups. Jews and Arabs seem to operate in only partially overlapping social systems. In general it is safe to say that both Jews and Arabs in Israel are committed to maintaining segregation for national and cultural reasons. While much of this segregation is voluntary, in the few known cases where Arabs have tried to move into Jewish communities or Jewish quarters of mixed communities, they have been met with strong and vocal resistance from the local Jewish population.

Not only do Arabs and Jews live in different places, but these places differ greatly in their size and hence in the occupational opportunities associated with size. Arabs are dramatically overrepresented in the small rural localities, and their representation in large cities is negligible (with very few exceptions). In contrast, Jews are overrepresented in large cities, and also in the three major urban centers (see Table 2.9). Indeed, three-quarters of either Arabs or Jews would have to change place of residence in order to create equal distributions by ethnic background across urban communities (Semyonov and Tyree 1981). It should be noted, however, that any segregation measure based on locality of residence does not capture the actual level of segregation, since Arabs who live in the same cities as Jews are concentrated in relatively homogeneous ethnic neighborhoods. Thus, any measure computed here actually understates the residential separation of Jews and Arabs in Israel.

Inequality in Resource Allocation

The extreme spatial segregation of Arabs and Jews in separate communities raises the issue of resource allocation and availability at the local government level. There are two main forms of local government—municipalities and local councils. While the former enjoy greater autonomy both types

TABLE 2.9:   The Percent Distribution of Arabs and Jews by Size of Locality, 1961, 1972, 1983, and 1990

Size of Locality (No. of Residents)	1961 Jews	1961 Arabs	1972 Jews	1972 Arabs	1983 Jews	1983 Arabs	1990 Jews	1990 Arabs
1) Jerusalem			8.6	18.1	9.1	17.8	9.6	16.7
2) Tel-Aviv			13.3	1.4	9.5	1.4	8.3	1.4
3) Haifa	37.2	7.2	7.7	2.7	6.2	2.5	5.7	2.5
4) 100,000-199,999			8.1	0.1	24.3	0.5	27.0	0.7
5) 50,000-99,999	7.5	0.1	17.7	0.2	10.3	0.2	10.5	6.4
6) 20,000-49,999	22.5	14.3	16.8	10.7	18.2	13.2	18.0	11.2
7) 10,000-19,000	9.0	0.9	11.6	8.3	7.6	13.9	6.9	15.3
8) 2,000-9,999	10.8	41.1	6.3	38.0	4.9	37.1	4.5	33.5
9) Less than 2,000	13.0	36.5	9.8	20.5	9.8	13.4	9.6	9.2
Total N (thousands)	1932.4	247.1	2686.7	461.0	3350.0	687.6	3946.7	875.0

Source: For 1961, 1972 and 1983, The Israeli Census Bureau, Statistical Abstract, 1984, Vol. 35, Table B/10.
For 1989, The Israeli Census Bureau, Statistical Abstract, 1991, Table II/12, p. 63.

depend on the central government of Israel for grants and substantial participation in the funding of local development and services. Various indicators
can be used to measure local government funding in the Arab and Jewish
sectors, but they all lead to the same conclusion: throughout the period since
the establishment of Israel, the Arab sector has received a disproportionately
small share of government and public funds, whether for development,
education, housing, or other services (Kretzmer 1987). Data for the decade of
the 1960s compiled by Lustick (1980, Table 8) indicate that the expenditure in
the Arab sector was 0.2 percent of Israel's total budget for development in the
early 1960s, reached 1.5 percent in the mid-1960s, and leveled off at 1.3 percent in the early 1970s. Considering that the Arab population constituted well
over 10 percent of Israel's population during this period, the figures reveal a
clear pattern of institutional discrimination and demonstrate a consistent
policy of under-funding development in the Arab sector. This under-funding
of Arab communities has continued into the 1990s, as was clearly documented in the State Comptroller's report released in 1992.

Figures on local government budgets provide an additional means of evaluating economic disparities between the Arab and Jewish sectors. Klinov
(1989) reported preliminary figures on this issue for the years 1973/1974,
1978/1979, 1983/1984, 1985/1986 based on special reports of the Central
Bureau of Statistics. Her findings revealed substantial discrimination on most
measures examined, although for some indicators of revenue and expendi-
tures there was no discrimination effect when the size of the population in the
community was taken into account. It is also evident from the analysis that
the extent of discrimination declined between the early 1970s and the mid
1980s (though there was an increase in 1986).

In a pairwise comparison of seven Arab localities with seven Jewish communities in the same geographic districts and roughly equal in size, Al-Haj and Rosenfeld (1990) found that the average ratio of the Jewish local councils to Arab local council budgets in 1970 was about 13 to 1. The disparity was even more strongly accentuated in the distribution of central government grants. By the mid 1970s the differences had narrowed, but the ratio still remained strongly in favor of the Jewish localities.

In order to address this issue in a more comprehensive fashion that would not be dependent on the specific localities selected for study, we undertook an examination of the budgets, taxes, and government transfers per capita in all Arab and Jewish communities. The comparison was carried out for the years 1975/1976 and 1985/1986 (the last year for which data are available). For this analysis local governments were grouped into three categories: small local councils, large local councils, and municipalities (see Appendix 2.A). Within each category we calculated the Jewish to Arab ratios of budget components (per capita) for the two time periods.

The figures in Table 2.10 underscore the discrimination against the Arab population. This was consistent across types of local government, budget items, and over time. The ratios varied from 1.98:1 to 10.36:1 in favor of Jewish communities in 1975/6, and from 1.6:1 to 6.19:1 in 1985/6. In no single comparison was the ratio in favor of the Arab sector.

A major obstacle to economic development in the Arab sector has been their exclusion from national development projects coupled with the lack of government-authorized zoning plans. As Haidar (1990) demonstrated in a recent report, the overwhelming majority of large Arab localities "... lack a validated master plan whereas others have a master plan that was validated only in recent years." (p. 10). Zoning plans are essential for designating land for industrial use and housing purposes, and is a prerequisite for setting up the infrastructure needed for economic development. According to Haidar only one-quarter (18 out of 65) of the localities with approved zoning plans have a population that exceeds 2000 residents and most are very small and remote communities. It is precisely the larger communities in the Arab sector, which

TABLE 2.10:   Local Authority Budget Components in 1975/6 and 1985/6. Jewish-to-Arab Ratios, by Municipal Status[1]

	Small Local Councils		Large Local Councils		Municipalities	
	1975/6	1985/6	1975/6	1985/6	1975/6	1985/6
Total Budget (per capita)	5.98	3.87	4.89	4.02	2.60	2.21
Government Tax Transfers	4.89	3.86	7.75	6.19	3.38	2.42
Total Government Transfers	4.31	3.80	4.93	3.57	2.81	1.60
Property Taxes	2.18	4.54	1.98	5.46	2.81	3.60
Total Local Taxes	4.37	4.64	3.79	5.58	2.88	3.40

[1]See Appendix 2.A for details on sources of data, and the classification of localities by type of local authority.

have the potential for developing a viable economic base, that have been unable to obtain the approval of government agencies for their zoning (master) plans.

In terms of variations on this main theme, three points are worth noting. First, the Jewish-to-Arab ratios were considerably larger in the small and large local councils than in the category of municipalities. Yet it is precisely the smaller communities where most of the Arab population resides (while the reverse is true for Jews). Second, the ratios for most categories declined over time. This suggests a relative improvement for the Arab sector, especially with respect to central government participation in funding of local government activities. Third, the situation of Arab localities actually worsened relative to that of Jewish communities with regard to property and municipal local taxes (e.g. business taxes). This is evident from the increase in the Jewish-to-Arab tax ratios between 1975/1976 and 1985/1986 (as shown in Table 2.10).

Traditionally, government bureaucracy and political officials have blamed low tax rates and inadequate enforcement of tax collection in Arab localities for their financial difficulties. While this might have been the case to a certain extent during the early 1970s, it cannot explain the increase in the ratio of Jews-to-Arab property or business taxes between the mid 1970s and the mid 1980s. Al-Haj and Rosenfeld (1990) point out that during this period there was considerable effort to increase the revenues from local taxes in Arab communities. The rise in property tax in the Arab local governments was among the highest in all local councils. It would therefore appear that the increase in the Jewish-to-Arab ratios (of property and business taxes) truly reflects the weak economic base in the Arab communities, and the fact that the population grew more rapidly than either industry or housing.

It is impossible to fully grasp the slow rate at which the economy of the Arab sector has developed, without considering the policies enacted by the State of Israel, since its inception, toward the land base of the Arab population. This issue will be elaborated in the following chapter. At this point suffice it to say that the waning acreage of land in the possession of the Arab population has not only constrained the size of its agricultural sector but has also inhibited industrial development by private entrepreneurs. The land loss experienced by the Arab population of Israel has even greater significance when the substantial growth of the Arab population is taken into consideration. The process has had massive consequences for the structure of the Arab economy and the composition of the Arab labor force. Employment opportunities in the Arab sector (mostly in agriculture) declined rapidly and many Arabs had to seek employment (mostly unskilled and blue-collar jobs) outside the Arab market. This trend was further intensified by the fact that land expropriation was not accompanied by industrial development in Arab communities. At present approximately two-thirds of the Arab work force are employed in the predominantly Jewish communities.

Kinship and Economy

Before concluding this chapter it is important to emphasize that in the present study we will be concerned with two levels of analysis. At the most basic level this is a study of individuals—men and women—in the labor force. Indeed the primary source of data on which our study is based was collected from individuals. At the macro-level we refer to ecological entities—communities and labor markets—and treat them as economic structures within which individuals' decisions and actions take place. This conceptualization, while common in the study of stratification in modern society, largely ignores the role of kinship as the intermediary between the individual and society. The role of kinship, it should be noted, is often viewed as crucial to the study of traditional society.

For Middle Eastern societies, in general, and Israeli Arabs in particular, two dimensions of kinship have been regarded as central—the kinship group and extended family. Societal organization of Israeli Arabs is based on a patrilineage system where the kinship group (*hamula*) is a patrilineal descent group encompassing all those biologically related to a common great grandfather, or those who have related themselves in order to obtain some advantage (Rosenfeld 1973; Al-Haj, 1987a). The *hamula* is the basic source of legitimacy of the individual's position in the community. Of the three major roles provided by the *hamula*—social, political and economic—the two former roles are still dominant, while the latter has become the least prominent. Al-Haj (1987) points out that even under the system of communal land the *hamula* was not truly an economic unit. Its major economic role was reflected in the mutual aid system, but even this role has diminished in recent years. With the advent of modern state institutions such as social security, government agencies and financial institutions, only a small minority continue to rely primarily on family, friends, and neighbors for support.

According to Al-Haj (1987: 35), the extended family unit is "composed of three generations, the father, the mother, the unmarried children, one or more married sons and their wives and children." The extended family was traditionally both the production and consumption unit in Arab society; hence its central economic significance for individuals. In the past half century, however, economic transformation has brought about important changes in family structure. The shrinking size of land holdings and the general decline in agriculture decreased the value of the patriarch's resources and with it, his authority. Proletarization and growing employment opportunities outside the Arab communities further accelerated this process. By the 1980s, less than 20 percent of Israel's Arabs reported living in extended families (Al-Haj, 1987a; Smooha, 1984). While the structure of the extended family appears to have weakened, it still exists in various complex forms, and association and commitment based on extended family ties are still strong. In some cases present-day extended families are structured around a family-owned business which is based primarily on economic considerations, rather than traditional patriarchy, but includes some elements of joint consumption and residence. Other extended families are still based on agricultural work whereby family lands are controlled by the father and family members serve as the labor force, some of whom may even be paid wages. Residence arrangements and consumption patterns vary in accordance with the form of linkage between the nuclear and extended family, and are sufficiently diverse to warrant the conclusion that the extended family is no longer dominant in the economic sphere.

Even though the extended family has a more central role than the *hamula*, its economic (as opposed to political and social) importance has also diminished over the years, especially in the case of wage labor which has come to encompass the overwhelming majority of the Arab labor force. Hence, while our analysis—which will focus on individuals acting in various labor markets—may to some extent underestimate or miss the role of families, we believe it will capture most economic activity. Moreover, given the fact that the overwhelming majority of Israeli Arabs are wage earners or salaried workers, the individual-level data available to us will provide a useful indication of labor market processes and the position of Arabs in Israel's stratification system.

Concluding Remarks

The data presented in this chapter accentuate the disadvantaged position of the Arab population in Israeli society. Although Arabs have improved their education and occupational status over the years and have experienced considerable intergenerational occupational mobility, they still lag far behind Jews in all aspects of social stratification. Their educational level is lower, they are employed mostly in manual, lower status occupations and their economic rewards are lower than those of Jews. Moreover Arabs as a group face a disadvantaged opportunity structure. They are highly segregated from the Jewish majority and are more likely to reside in small communities characterized by a limited economic and industrial infrastructure. Furthermore, Arab communities as a whole have long experienced unequal treatment by the governments of Israel. They have not received an equal share of resource allocation and have suffered from the implementation of adverse policies of economic development.

These processes have far-reaching consequences for the economic position of Arabs in the Israeli labor force. In the following chapter we will first examine the structure of the Arab economy and describe the social-political constraints within which it has developed during the past forty years. In the second part of the chapter we will focus on the growing mismatch between the economic opportunities which the Arab sector provides and the changing characteristics of the Arab population. It will also be argued that the patterns of development in the Arab sector, or lack thereof, have brought about growing dependency of the Arab workforce on the Jewish economy. Following this argument we will examine the extent to which such dependency affects the patterns of socioeconomic inequality between Jews and Arabs in the Israeli labor market.

Notes

1. Under the system adopted, with some modifications, from Ottoman Law, autonomy is granted in Israel to religious communities. Shari'a, the Moslem court system, has sole jurisdiction to deal with all matters of personal status.

2. The institution of the Wakf in Islam is an ancient one. Any holy property is precluded from being sold; its ownership is ostensibly given to God and its disposition is in the hands of the person consecrating it with a holy document called "Wakfia". During the Israeli War of Independence, members of the Council for Moslem Religious Matters and the special committee which administered the Wakf left the country and Wakf property became absentee property to be administered by the Custodian of Absentee Property. Since 1965, part of the Wakf property was released to trustee committees in communities with large Moslem populations. However, the "Absentees' Property" Law does not obligate the Custodian to release all Wakf property to the trustee committees (although it stipulates that such property must be administered for the purpose of the welfare of the Moslem community (see Kretzmer 1987).

3. Arab households, however, may have several breadwinners since sons and daughters of Arab fathers are more likely to contribute to the welfare of the household than do Jews. Jews are more likely to operate as individuals than within the extended family unit.

4. A sizeable number of Arabs reside in some 51 villages that are not formally recognized by the State. These are rural localities which, for political reasons, the State of Israel refuses to acknowledge and to award legal standing. Consequently most of these villages have no infrastructure (roads, sewers, running water), school system, or social services.

5. Although the overwhelming majority of Israeli Bedouins live in the Negev desert, in the 1974 sample there were no non-Jews in the southern regions. This discrepancy may be explained by the fact that the 1974 sample contained only those people who resided in permanent localities and therefore did not include the Bedouins who lead a relatively nomadic way of life.

6. The index of dissimilarity is defined as

$$D = \frac{1}{2} \ \Sigma \mid P_{ai} - P_{bi} \mid$$

where P is the percentage of population in community i from ethnic groups a and b respectively.

Appendix 2.A

Classification of Localities

1. The local governments were divided into three categories of Municipal status: (1) small local councils; (2) large local councils; (3) municipalities.[1] (Regional councils were excluded.)
2. Each category of Municipal status was divided into Jewish localities and non-Jewish localities.
3. These six categories of local government were compared with respect to their mean per capita figures in different components of their budgets in the years 1975/1976 and 1985/1986. The components of the budget are: ordinary budget and extraordinary budget, according to financial sources and destination.

Ordinary Budget—Income

The income of the ordinary budget is composed of current final incomes, including transfers from previous years and loans. There are three kinds of final incomes:

1. Self income—collected by the municipalities themselves from individuals and organizations.
2. Transferred income—transferred by the government according to law or agreement.
3. Government participation—(a) general participation—divided among the municipalities according to certain criteria; and (b) earmarked participation—for special services.

Source: Israel Central Bureau of Statistics, Local Authorities in Israel, Data 1975/6, 1985/6.
[1]In the category of non-Jewish municipalities all the non-Jewish municipalities were included. The category of Jewish municipalities is based upon a sample of municipalities according to size.

TABLE 2.A   *Localities According to Categories*

	1975/1976		1985/1986	
Jewish	*Non-Jewish*	*Jewish*	*Non-Jewish*	

Municipalities

Jewish	Non-Jewish	Jewish	Non-Jewish
1. Dimona	1. Nazareth	1. Even Yehuda	1. Umm al-Fahm
2. Tiberias	2. Shefar'am	2. Tiberias	2. Nazareth
3. Nahariyya		3. Lod	3. Shefar'am
4. Nazareth Illit		4. Nahariyya	
5. Afula		5. Nazerat Illit	
		6. Qiryat Bialik	
		7. Qiryat Gat	
		8. Qiryat Motzkin	
		9. Ra'anana	

Large Local Councils

Jewish	Non-Jewish	Jewish	Non-Jewish
1. Or Yehuda	1. Umm al-Fahm	1. Even Yehuda	1. Abu Sinan
2. Or Aqiva	2. Baka al-Gharbiyye	2. Or Yehuda	2. Iksal
3. Ofaqim	3. Daliyat al-Karmel	3. Or Aqiva	3. I'billin
4. Bet She'an	4. Taiyibe	4. Azor	4. Baka al-Gharbiyye
5. Bet Shemesh	5. Tire	5. Ofaqim	5. Bet Jann
6. Giva'at Shemue'el	6. Tamra	6. Bet Shemesh	6. Jisr az-Zarqa
7. Gedera	7. Yafi'a	7. Bet She'an	7. Jatt
8. Hod Hasharon	8. Kafar Kana	8. Giv'at Shemu'el	8. Daliyat al-Karmel
9. Hazor	9. Kafar Kasem	9. Gedera	9. Taiyibe
10. Tirat Karmel	10. Kafar Kara'	10. Ganne Tiqwa	10. Tire
11. Yavne	11. Mughar	11. Hod Hasharon	11. Tamra
12. Yehud	12. Majd al-Kurum	12. Zikhron Ya'akov	12. Tur'an
13. Yeroham	13. Sakhnin	13. Hazor	13. Yafi'a
14. Karmiel	14. 'Arrabe	14. Tirat Karmel	14. Yirka
15. Mevasseret Ziyyon	15. Qalansawa	15. Yehud	15. Kabul
16. Migdal Ha'Emeq		16. Yoqne'am	16. Kafar Yasif
17. Ma'alot-Tarchiha		17. Yeroham	17. Kafar Kana
18. Nes Ziyyona		18. Mevaseret Ziyyon	18. Kafar Manda
19. Nesher		19. Ma'ale Edummim	19. Kafar Kasem
20. Netivot		20. Ma'alot Tarchiha	20. Kafar Kara'
21. Arad		21. Nes Ziyyona	21. Mughar
22. Pardes Hanna-Karkur		22. Nesher	22. Majd al-Kurum
23. Qiryat Ono		23. Netivot	23. Majd al-Shams
24. Qiryat Tiv'on		24. Omer	24. Makr
25. Qiryat Mal'akhi		25. Arad	25. Nahef
26. Rosh Ha'Ayin		26. Pardes Hanna	26. Sakhnin
27. Ramat Hasharon		27. Qiryat Ono	27. 'Erin Mahel
28. Ra'anana		28. Qiryat Tiv'on	28. 'Isifya
29. Sederot		29. Qiryat Mal'akhi	29. 'Arrabe
		30. Rosh Ha'Ayin	30. 'Ar'ara
		31. Ramat Hasharon	31. Fureidis
		32. Sederot	32. Qalansawa
			33. Rame
			34. Rahat
			35. Reine

1975/1976		1985/1986	
Jewish	*Non-Jewish*	*Jewish*	*Non-Jewish*

Small Local Councils

Jewish (1975/1976)	Non-Jewish (1975/1976)	Jewish (1985/1986)	Non-Jewish (1985/1986)
1. Even Yehuda	1. Abu Sinan	1. Elyachin	1. Basmat Tiv'on
2. Azor	2. Iksal	2. Elkana	2. Bi'ne
3. Be'er Ya'akov	3. I'billin	3. Efrata	3. Buq'ata
4. Bet Dagan	4. Bet Jann	4. Ariel	4. Judeide
5. Binyamina	5. Basmat Tiv'on	5. Be'er Ya'akov	5. Julis
6. Giv'at Ada	6. Judeide	6. Bet Dagan	6. Jaljulya
7. Gan Yavne	7. Julis	7 Bnei Aish	7. Jish
8. Zikhron Ya'akov	8. Jaljulye	8. Binyamina	8. Deir al-Asad
9. Yavne'el	9. Jisr az-Zarqa	9. Giv'at Ze'ev	9. Hurfeish
10. Yesod Hama'ala	10. Jish-Gush Halav	10. Giv'at Ada	10. Dabburye
11. Yoqne'am Illit	11. Dabburye	11. Gan Yavne	11. Deir Hanna
12. Kinneret	12. Deir al-Asad	12. Yavne'el	12. Kafar Bara'
13. Kefar Yona	13. Deir Hanna	13. Yesod Hama'ala	13. Kafar Kama
14. Kefar Shemaryahu	14. Hurfeish	14. Kochav	14. Mas'ade
15. Kefar Tabor	15. Tur'an	15. Kinneret	15. Mi'elya
16. Migdal	16. Yirka	16. Kefar Yona	16. Meshhed
17. Mazkeret Batyz	17. Kafar Bara'	17. Kefar Shemaryahu	17. Ajer
18. Metula	18. Kafar Yasif	18. Kefar Tabor	18. 'Eilabun
19. Menahemya	19. Kafar Kama	19. Migdal	19. Ein Qinya
20. Mizpe Ramon	20. Makr	20. Mazkeret Batya	20. Fassuta
21. Newe Efrayim	21. Makr	21. Metula	21. Peqi'in
22. Nahalat Yehuda	22. Mi'elya	22. Menahemya	22. Shibli
23. Atlit	23. Mashhed	23. Ma'ale Efrayim	23. Sha'ab
24. Omer	24. Nahef	24. Mizpe Ramon	24. Tel Sheva
25. Pardesiyya	25. 'Eilabun	25. Newe Efrayim	
26. Qadima	26. 'Ein Mahel	26. Nahalat Yehuda	
27. Qiryat Haroshet	27. 'Isifya	27. Savyon	
28. Qiryat Eqron	28. 'Ar'ara	28. Emmanuel	
29. Rosh Pinna	29. Fassuta	29. Atlit	
30. Rekhasim	30. Peqi'in	30. Qadima	
31. Ramot Hashavim	31. Fureidis	31. Qatzrin	
32. Ramat Yishay	32. Rame	32. Qiryat Arba	
33. Shave Ziyyon	33. Reine	33. Qiryat Eqron	
34. Shelomi	34. Sha'ab	34. Rosh Pinna	
35. Tel Mond		35. Rekhasim	
		36. Ramot Hashavim	
		37. Ramat Yishay	
		38. Shave Ziyyon	
		39. Shelomi	
		40. Tel Mond	

3

The Arab Economy in Israel

Historical Background

In order to better understand the economic position of the Arab population in Israel a brief review of economic development during Israel's pre-state period is in order.[1] Significant economic relations between Jews and Arabs were initiated some one hundred years ago with the modern settlement of Jews in Palestine. Although the years between the two World Wars are generally viewed as the crucial period of economic consolidation in Palestine, central attributes of Jewish-Arab economic relations were already being fashioned during the first two decades of the twentieth century. In the following pages we will outline the central characteristics of the economy of Palestine and of the Jewish and Arab sectors. We will discuss the process of separation, which was stepped up with each outbreak of armed violence, as well as the changing nature of Arab subordination following the establishment of the State of Israel.

The Arab and Jewish Communities— Economic Characteristics

The first significant economic encounters between Jews and Arabs involved the purchase of land by the Jewish settlers. While land transactions were not a new phenomenon in Palestine, these were different. In the past, it was usually the case that tenants remained on the land unaffected by land transactions and the succession of landlords. The acquisition by the new Jewish immigrants was of a novel nature and in many cases entailed the removal of tenants from their land, since the whole purpose of purchase was to renew land cultivation by Jews after two millennia of exile. For the first time, now, tenants were directly affected by the implementation of the powerful ideology of "working the land" and of self-labor among the Jewish settlers. The displacement not only disposed the tenants of land they considered their own, but also stripped them of their status as peasants, transforming them into a proletariat (Shafir 1989). This served to bolster labor market competition which was to play a central role in the evolving Jewish-Arab relations. At the same time land sales infused capital into the Arab economy (albeit into relatively few hands) and contributed to the emergence of small industrial enterprises and to growing commerce in the Arab sector (Metzer and Kaplan 1985; Owen 1988).

Substantial economic development, however, did not take place until the establishment of the British Mandate toward the end of the second decade of the century. At the start of the mandatory period, in 1918, Palestine was predominantly an agricultural country, but even at this early stage significant differences existed between the Arab sector and the Jewish sector with respect to the industrial structures of their economies and the characteristics of their labor force. At this point in time the population of Palestine numbered approximately 750,000 persons, ten percent of whom were Jews. In 1922, two-thirds of the Arab labor force were employed in agriculture, and agricultural produce accounted for two-fifths of the Net National (Arab) Product. The figures for the Jewish sector at the time showed 23.4 percent of the work force employed in agriculture, with only 11.1 percent of the Net National (Jewish) Product deriving from agricultural production (Metzer and Kaplan 1985). Concomitantly, in the Jewish sector, the proportion of the labor force in manufacturing, and the Net Product derived from manufacturing were five times greater than in the Arab sector.

During the first two decades of the British Mandate (up to 1939), the population of Palestine grew from approximately 750,000 to over 1.5 million. Jews, who constituted just under 11 percent of the population in 1922 (according to 1922 Vital Statistics Tables), comprised approximately one-third of the population in 1939. The population growth was accompanied by important institutional and compositional changes. Ever since the early years of Jewish immigration to Palestine the settlers faced labor market competition from Arab labor which could not be satisfactorily resolved by means of market processes. Shafir (1989) provided convincing evidence of the attempts at labor market segmentation at the turn of the century; but, as pointed out by Shalev (1989), by the First World War this, by and large, resulted in the exclusion of Jewish (high priced) labor since most pre-war immigrant laborers had left Palestine. In 1920, however, the establishment of the Jewish labor organization (Histadrut) as well as the alliance of labor and the Jewish Socialist parties in Palestine with world Zionism (a relationship which began with the establishment of the Palestine Office in 1908) paved the way for economic segmentation with high-priced Jewish labor subsidized by the Zionist movement. By the mid 1920s, the vast majority of Histadrut members were skilled urban laborers, many of whom were recent arrivals from Poland who fitted in well with the emergence of a vigorous urban economy.

During the 1920s leaders of the Jewish labor organization directed most of their efforts towards securing jobs in the Jewish sector for (Jewish) members of the labor organization and at the same time underscored the national nature of the labor market struggle (Shalev 1989). For example, at the convention of the Jewish proletariat party "Achduth Ha-avodah" held in 1924, a political conception was presented to the delegates which was based on the idea of separation of the Jewish from the Arab population. This conception, which was argued in terms of settlement, economic, and state requirements, proposed that future development of the country be based on separate territorial concentrations of Jews and Arabs (Shapira, 1977). Labor leaders such as David Ben-Gurion and Chaim Arlosoroff warned that solidarity with Arabs and the organization of Arab labor would not prevent the undercutting of wages and, more importantly, would not ensure Arab support for Jewish immigration to Palestine. Hence, the strategy advocated was segregation and the development of a Jewish quasi-national economy. This process was aided by Jewish immigration from central Europe (primarily from Germany) in the early 1930s and the capital resources brought by them.

In the mid-1930s only one-quarter of the Arab population was living in towns, in contrast to three-quarters of the Jewish population. During this period the industrial structure of the Arab economy in Palestine underwent considerable changes, but Arab-Jewish differences still remained substantial. According to Kimmerling (1983) agriculture accounted for just over one-half (52.9 percent) of the jobs in the Arab economy in 1939; down from two-thirds two decades earlier. Manufacturing and construction expanded and now constituted 11.6 percent of the jobs in the Arab economy. The tertiary sector—including commerce and services—accounted for 35.5 percent of the Arab economy. While this structure was quite different from the economic composition of the Jewish community (where, in 1939, 53.6 percent of the jobs were in the tertiary sector, and 27.1 percent were in manufacturing and construction), it is noteworthy that the Arab economy in Palestine was now substantially different from that of neighboring countries such as Egypt, Syria, Turkey or Iran (which remained substantially agricultural).

During this period, economic productivity of the Arab population was considerably lower than in the Jewish economic sector. In 1935 the production per capita was LP17 (Lira of Palestine) among Arabs as compared to LP44 per capita among the Jews. This represents a ratio of 2.6, up from 1.7 in 1922. To a large extent these differences were a result of the higher labor force participation rates among Jews and their higher rates of literacy. Due to the age structure of the Jewish population in Palestine and the relatively high labor force participation rate of women, a larger portion of the Jewish population was in the active labor force. This is probably more representative of the urban sector; in rural areas it is more difficult to ascertain the extent of participation of family members, including wives and young children, in agricultural work. As a whole this population was highly educated with a literacy rate of 90 percent among those seven years of age and older. In contrast, only 30 percent of the Arab population were literate (according to the 1931 census).

An additional factor in the productivity gap was, of course, the more advanced technology introduced in the Jewish sector of the economy, and the greater availability of capital. The major impetus to industrialization came from Jewish immigration which was responsible both for the growing number of entrepreneurs as well as the increase in financial resources and machinery. It is not surprising, then, that by 1936, 5,600 of the estimated 6,000 manufacturing establishments in Palestine (small workshops, for the most part) were in the Jewish sector.

Information about the development of Arab manufacturing is sketchy at best. While Jewish economic activity, in principle, could have provided both opportunities for Arab industrialists and barriers to their expansion, it is difficult to determine which outcome prevailed. There is some indication that contact may have been detrimental to the Arab economy. This is reflected by the substantial decline in the number of Arab manufacturing establishments over the years (although some may have simply consolidated into larger firms), and the fact that during the second World War period most major British military contracts went to the more technically developed Jewish firms. A clear indication of the impact of the war period on the Jewish and the Arab economies can be gleaned from data on annual output of handicrafts and industry (Kimmerling 1983, Table 3.4). In 1939 annual output was LP10 million in the Jewish sector and LP4 million in the Arab sector—a ratio of 2.5. In 1943 the figures were LP38 million and LP5.6 million, respectively, for a ratio of 6.7.

The increasing gap in favor of the Jewish sector should not overshadow the fact that the Arab economy was itself growing rapidly and that in terms of income per capita the gap narrowed slightly from a ratio of (Arab/Jewish income) 0.34 in 1936 to a ratio of 0.40 in 1947 (Kimmerling 1983, Table 3.5). Indeed, the last few years of the British Mandate were extremely important for the development of manufacturing and were characterized by a huge mobilization of labor in the Arab sector. It is estimated that in 1945 approximately one-third of the Arab labor force was employed in wage labor. This served as the basis for the emergence of political and economic centers where entrepreneurs, contractors, skilled workers, and the better educated were now concentrated.

In terms of the interpenetration of the Arab and Jewish economies, Owen (1988:14) has noted that ". . . while it is true that the various separate enclaves of Jewish activity did tend to coalesce into something, which, by 1936, could reasonably be called a 'Jewish economy', this entity had many more points of contact with different sectors in the wider Palestinian economy than some writers generally allow." This point is also made by Ben-Porath (1984) who noted that the Mandatory government and the municipalities of the mixed towns forced some organizational cooperation and instances of joint action on economic matters. Nonetheless, these contacts constituted only a small part of economic activity, especially for the Jewish economy, and represented only provisional interdependence.

Treating the two economies as analytically separate, Metzer and Kaplan (1985) applied import-export analysis to study the exchange between the Arab and Jewish economies. According to their research, in 1935 the value of goods and services exchanged by the Jewish and Arab sectors was approximately equal although this represented a smaller proportion of Jewish production since the Jewish community exported most of its produce out of Palestine. Metzer and Kaplan estimated that in 1936 the Jewish sector's purchases from abroad were nearly three times the value of purchases from the Arab sector, and its exports three times the value of sales to the Arab community. Land sales (some 850,000 dunam between 1920–1939) accounted for almost half of Arab sales to the Jewish sector.

Labor was another resource that the Jewish economy "imported" from the Arab population. Although the proportion of labor value in the total balance of payment did not increase between the early 1920s and the second World War, it constituted a substantial portion of the labor force employed in the Jewish economy. When discussing the labor force in Palestine, it is necessary to differentiate between skilled and unskilled workers. Skilled workers were very scarce in both economies (especially in the Arab economy) and they were immediately absorbed in their respective labor markets. The supply of unskilled workers was much greater. Wages for skilled workers were approximately double those for unskilled and, generally speaking, there was a linkage between the wages of unskilled Jews and Arabs, who shared a common market, so that Arab competition tended to undercut the wages of Jewish workers (Sussman 1974).

In 1936 there was a total of 82,000 employees in the Jewish economic sector (according to Sussman, 1974). Of these, 12,000 were Arab employees, constituting 14.6 percent of the labor force. The industrial distribution of the Arabs employed in the Jewish sector was highly concentrated. They constituted 35 percent of the workforce in agriculture, 20 percent of employees in transportation and ports, and only 6.7 percent of those employed in commercial services. It should be noted, however, that Arabs employed in the Jewish economy represented only 2.5 percent of the total Arab labor force in Palestine (Kimmerling, 1983) whereas the overwhelming majority were either self-employed or wage earners in the Arab economy.

Throughout the first half of the twentieth century, economic forces, which wove a web that joined the Arab and Jewish economies, were countered by other pressures, economic as well as ideological, toward separation. The idea of the "conquest of labor", central to the Socialist-Zionist immigrants to Palestine, was a major separatist force. Its proponents aimed to establish a Jewish economy which would rely (solely) on Jewish labor. It has also been argued (Shafir 1989; Shalev, 1989) that while Jewish workers had no chance of driving Arab workers out of the Jewish economy, they were able to segregate them into unskilled, low-paying jobs, thus in effect subordinating them to the needs of the Jewish economy while reducing labor market competition.

Outbreaks of armed conflict probably contributed more than anything else to sever the links between the Arab and Jewish economies. The riots of 1921 and 1929 caused the dissolution of partnerships and the tendency toward geographic segregation, a process completed by the disturbances of 1936–1939 (Flapan 1979). The Arabs used the boycott of Jewish products and employers as a political weapon that did not generally reflect economic interests. In mixed cities Arabs and Jews moved into mono-ethnic quarters, and little contact was maintained between the two communities. For the Jewish sector this had many advantages. It facilitated the goal of Jewish employment, boosted Jewish agriculture, and brought about investment in infrastructure to assure the autonomy of the Jewish economy. For the Arab population too this was a time of rapid urbanization, industrialization, and establishment of an infrastructure, processes which were abruptly brought to a halt when fighting broke out in the war for Israel's independence.

From Separation to Subordination

During the upheaval brought about by Israel's War of Independence in 1947–1948, the majority of the Arab population, including the more educated and wealthy urban dwellers, fled the country. As outlined in the preceding chapter, those Arabs who remained in Israel found they had become a numerical minority (constituting approximately 11 percent of Israel's population) subordinated politically, socially, and economically. Furthermore, the Arab population was both geographically and socially segregated from the majority Jewish population. Indeed, the Arab economy that emerged following the establishment of the State of Israel was clearly shaped by the extreme spatial segregation of the Arab population, and its subordinate position in Israeli society.

From the early days of the establishment of the State, regulations, administrative policies, and lack of action combined to thwart the development of an Arab economy. Even after the existence of the Arab minority in Israel came to be perceived as permanent, Jewish fear and resentment of Arabs persisted. The legacy of the national-economic struggle just described, combined with the bloody war for Jewish sovereignty, produced the fear that Arab citizens would act as a "fifth column" to undermine Israel's security. These fears were reinforced by the continuing conflict with Arab states and Palestinian terrorist activities.

Beyond security considerations, the possible emergence of an economically and politically independent Arab sector was seen as a threat to Israel's character as a Jewish state and to its fragile economy. These views have not changed substantially in the past forty years. It is unnecessary to elaborate here on this issue which has been fairly extensively researched and documented (e.g., Kislev 1976; Lustick 1980; Zureik 1979). Suffice it to say that practices with respect to the Arab sector have included, among others, control by military rule, expropriation of private land, and explicit exclusion of Arabs (or, more generally, non-Jews) from employment in sections of the economy. Exclusion is especially evident with respect to the defence-related industrial sector and other large scale public enterprises. As discussed at length in Chapter 2, the Arab community in Israel has experienced continuing hardships as a result of policies which limited resource allocation (including central government grants, water quotas, and investment in infrastructure) as well as the failure to approve zoning plans and to designate industrial zones in many Arab communities.

It is probably true that no single action (or inaction) accounts for the particular path of economic development experienced by the Arab sector in Israel. Furthermore, the rural and traditional characteristics of the Arab population, which also contributed to the slow development of its economy, cannot be ignored. Without question, however, the outcome has been one of a limited economic base in the Arab sector accompanied by extensive incorporation (utilization) of individual Arab workers into the Jewish owned economic sector (Waschitz 1975).

The Arab economy that remained in the wake of the 1948 war and the establishment of the State of Israel was a village economy catering to its own needs and concentrated in agriculture. Given the rural nature of the Arab sector and the heavy dependence on agriculture as a major source of livelihood, the land policies enacted by Israel's government have doubtless been an important factor in shaping the economy of the Arab sector, in particular by increasing the dependency of the Arab population on the Jewish economy. This issue has been reviewed extensively (although not conclusively) by several scholars (e.g. Khalidi 1988b; Kislev 1976; Lustick 1980; Miari 1986; Oded 1964; Zureik 1976) and a full discussion of the circumstances, legal framework, and consequences of Arab land expropriation is beyond the scope of the present book. It is important, however, to take note here of these policies for three reasons. First, land expropriation substantially diminished the resources of the Arab population and reduced the size of many communities. According to Cohen (1964:520), by the time the war for Israel's independence was over, the Arabs were left with 30–40 percent of the land they had possessed prior to 1948, and not the best quality land at that.

Second, land expropriation policies most clearly represent the use of state legal apparatus to discriminate against Arab residents of Israel with respect to a major resource and primary means of production. Indeed, the land issue has remained the single most painful aspect of the Arabs' relationship with the Jewish state. An array of government agencies has utilized an intricate web of laws and regulations by which to implement a policy which ". . . consistent, systematic . . . tolerant in all other respects, it seems to have one purpose: to strike at the tottering land base of the country's Arab population" (Oded 1964:11).

In addition to the "Emergency Articles for the Expropriation of Uncultivated Lands", passed in October of 1948, and the "Emergency Land Requisition Law", passed in 1949, two laws in particular have regularized expropriation by means of what Kretzmer terms covert discrimination. The Absentees' Property Law, 1950, defined absentees in an extremely broad way and enabled the use of the property of absentee owners for the economic benefit of the State of Israel. The law made no provision for return of the property to the absentee. The Land Acquisition (Validation of Acts and Compensation) Law, 1953, was enacted in order to formalize (validate) steps taken up to that time, whereby tracts of land owned by Arabs had been taken over for military purposes or for the establishment of new Jewish settlements. The law provided that compensation be given for expropriated land, usually in money or, sometimes by other land, but there was no obligation to provide land of similar quality.

According to the Israel Lands Authority, up to the mid 1970s, over 1.2 million dunam (approximately 300,000 acres) of land belonging to Arabs were expropriated from their original owners by government agencies (Kislev, 1976). In the 1970s, the process of land expropriation continued and took on new forms. First, large tracts of land in northern Israel were expropriated from Arabs; and second, control over the use of certain tracts of land was transferred from the jurisdiction of Arab local councils to Jewish regional and local councils (Rekhess 1977). These acts were the direct cause of a general strike on March 30, 1976 (Land Day) and a fatal confrontation with Israeli police forces during which 6 Arab citizens were killed. Land settlements with the Bedouin residents of Israel's desert region in the Negev are still pending, and with the wave of Jewish immigration anticipated over the coming few years, land expropriation continues to be viewed as a real threat by the Arab population.

The third reason for discussion of land expropriation is most directly linked to the topic of the present study. The extent of Arab land expropriation over the years, particularly early on, was such that it altered the structure of the Arab economy significantly and more rapidly than might otherwise be expected. This is clearly illustrated in the story of one village—Taibeh— which is far from being an extreme case. In 1947, prior to Israel's independence, the area owned by the villagers, who numbered approximately 3,500, amounted to 45,000 dunams including common property (Cohen 1964:529). In 1953, 13,000 dunam were expropriated, and by the mid 1970s the 15,000 village residents were left with only 19,000 dunam in their possession (Kislev 1976). It is not surprising, then, that within a period of 25 years the proportion of residents living off agriculture declined from over 50 percent to less than 10 percent.

Although much Arab land was lost in the first few years following the establishment of the State, Arab communities still maintained access to sufficient amounts of land, water, and labor so that agriculture could continue, albeit on a smaller scale. By contrast, during the war and the subsequent flight of Arab refugees, the industrial infrastructure of the Arab economy completely disintegrated. During the first two decades of Israel's statehood, Arab manufacturing and commercial activity was small in scale and concentrated in labor intensive areas such as construction, carpentry, machine repair, and food processing. Zarhi and Achiezra (1963) estimated that in 1961 there were approximately 1,200 small enterprises in Arab localities in which some 1,500 self-employed persons made a living and which provided work for an additional 2,000 employees. The structure of these activities did not significantly alter until the early 1970s at which time the infrastructure (electricity, roads, and communications) as well as a better qualified labor force became widely available. The constraints on the development of the Arab economy on the one hand, and rapid population growth combined with better education on the other, lead one to expect that the Arab community would experience growing mismatch between its population and the labor market. This is likely to be true both in terms of the relative number of overall job opportunities at the aggregate level, and in terms of the extent to which individuals might find jobs that are suitable for their qualifications.

The Changing Economic Base of the Arab Sector

An examination of the economic structure of the Arab sector, and the extent to which it has changed over the years, necessitates data on job opportunities which would typically come from employers' surveys, or from periodical establishment reports. Such information would ideally provide insight into the industrial composition of the Arab economy, size and ownership of establishments, and the ratios of Jewish-Arab employment in these firms. Establishment information, however, is not regularly collected in Israel and the few scattered surveys (Czamanski et al. 1984; Haidar 1990; Khalidi 1988a) provide extremely useful but incomplete data on the Arab economic structure.

In the following, the analysis of the economic structure of the Arab economy, and the degree of mismatch between jobs and population is based on the two latest population censuses of Israel taken in 1972 and 1983. A unique feature of these surveys is that a 20 percent sample was asked to provide detailed demographic and labor force information. Among other things, respondents reported the specific location of their employment as well as place of residence. Due to the extremely high spatial segregation of Jewish and Arab communities, whether the person is employed in the Arab sector or the Jewish sector of the economy may be gleaned from this information. Aggregation of individual level information on jobs for all persons employed in Arab localities provides a good approximation of the size as well as the industrial and occupational composition of the Arab economy in Israel. It should be understood, however, that these figures are ecologically based and thus contain inaccuracies with regard to ethnic ownership and control of production resources. An Arab employed in a majority Jewish community may be working for an Arab employer and, conversely, some Arabs employed in the Arab sector clearly work for Jewish employers. Although the extent of such inaccuracies cannot be ascertained with the data at hand, this limitation notwithstanding, the analysis provides important information on the Arab sector that is not otherwise attainable.

It should be emphasized that we are making a clear distinction between the Arab labor force and the Arab economy. Over 50 percent of Arab workers commute from the all-Arab communities where they reside to their place of employment in Jewish communities. They are part of the Arab labor force, but are not employed in the economy of the Arab sector. The Arab economy is operationally defined here as the industrial and occupational base of Arab communities which could potentially sustain a population and serve as a resource for socioeconomic success.[2]

Table 3.1 presents the industrial composition of the Arab sector and provides a comparison with the Jewish sector for the years 1972 and 1983. Two estimates were derived from the Israeli census, based on the 20 percent sample of persons aged 25 to 65 in the labor force. The first—lower bound— estimate is based on self-reports which specifically identify an Arab locality as place of employment. The second estimate includes, in addition, those who reside in Arab communities, but who did not report a specific place of employment. If we assume that all these individuals consider their community of residence as their regular place of employment, this figure represents an upper bound estimate of the Arab economy. It is evident that both the overall size of the Arab sector and its industrial composition differ considerably, depending on what estimate is used. Strictly speaking, the lower bound estimate more accurately reflects the size and structure of the Arab economy.

TABLE 3.1: Industrial Structure of Labor Markets in the Arab and Jewish Sectors, 1972 and 1983 (based on a 20 percent sample of the census, all persons aged 25-65)

Industry	1972			1983		
	Arab		Jewish	Arab		Jewish
Agriculture	28.0	21.5[1]	5.3	7.2	5.5[1]	3.5
Labor-Intensive Manufacturing	7.6	7.1	13.5	9.8	8.0	10.4
Capital-Intensive Manufacturing	3.8	4.1	10.5	6.7	5.2	12.4
Utilities	0.6	0.7	1.2	0.5	0.5	1.2
Construction	12.1	21.3	8.3	8.1	28.0	4.9
Commerce & Tourism	12.0	10.3	12.4	12.0	8.0	12.2
Transport & Communication	7.1	7.8	7.5	3.2	9.4	6.7
Finance Services	1.2	1.4	5.6	4.0	2.9	9.9
Public Services	23.6	23.0	29.0	43.8	28.9	33.3
Personal Services	3.7	5.2	6.0	4.6	3.6	5.5
Total	100.0	100.0	100.0	100.0	100.0	100.0
N[2]	16510	28135	709040	24830	48420	1006045
Index of Dispersion[3]	0.86		0.91	0.78		0.87
Arab/Jewish Dissimilarity		32.8			33.5	

[1] Includes "place of employment unknown".

[2] Numbers are population estimates.

[3] See endnote 4 for the computation formula of the index.

This is apparent from an examination of the distributional differences associated with the two estimates. The single most important source of disparity is the category of construction, followed, in 1983, by transportation and communication. In both these industries employment is not bound to a specific locality. Rather, place of employment is likely to change periodically in the case of construction and is inapplicable in the case of transportation. In both instances a large share of the economic activity is likely to take place in the Jewish sector, either as entrepreneurial activity (as in the case of owners of taxis and trucks or construction related sub-contracting) or wage labor. Hence, the lower bound estimate more accurately represents the number of jobs available in the Arab economic sector, and their industrial distribution.

A comparison of the figures for 1972 and 1983 reveals a substantial increase in the estimated number of jobs in the Arab sector. When growth of the population and changing labor force participation are taken into account, we find that in 1972 there were 42 job slots for every 100 persons in the labor force (using the lower bound estimate) and this changed only slightly to 44 positions per 100 persons in the labor force in 1983. When using the upper bound estimate there appeared to be an improvement in the relative opportunities from 73 to 88 jobs per 100 persons in the labor force (for 1972 and 1983, respectively). These figures, however, include a large increase in the number of jobs in construction, most of which in fact were carried out in Jewish communities and with Jewish contractors.

Turning to industrial composition, significant changes took place between 1972 and 1983. Most noticeably, the decline in agricultural jobs, which had begun decades earlier, continued at a rapid pace. Whereas in 1972, 28 percent of the jobs in the Arab sector were in agriculture, in 1983 this sector accounted for only 7.2 percent of the jobs (this represents a net loss of approximately 60 percent of agricultural jobs during the period). A second major change in the Arab sector was the dramatic increase in public service jobs. Accounting for less than one-quarter (23.6 percent) of the jobs in the Arab sector in 1972, this sector swelled over the next decade to encompass 43.8 percent of the Arab labor market.[3] These jobs in local government and state agencies, such as education, welfare and health, are totally dependent on central government funding and represent a form of incorporation applied particularly to the more educated segment of the Arab population (the role of public sector employment will be discussed in detail in Chapters 4 and 5). The period since the early 1970s also witnessed an increase in manufacturing jobs in the Arab sector. The number of positions doubled in absolute terms and increased its share of the Arab economy from 11.4 to 16.5 percent.

In the early 1970s, manufacturing in the Arab sector consisted almost exclusively of small workshop production in carpentry, metal-work and machine and car repair shops. Prevalence figures are rather sketchy, but according to one estimate (Harari 1972) there were over 2,000 such workshops in the Arab sector in 1972. At the same time, among metal-works and textile factories, there were between 30 and 60 larger scale enterprises that employed more than 20 workers (Harari 1974).

The most extensive study to date of manufacturing units in the Arab sector was carried out by Czamanski, Meyer-Brodnitz, and colleagues and summarized in several reports (Czamanski et al. 1984; Meyer-Brodnitz and Czamanski 1986a). Although their study focused on Arab communities in the northern region, they provided some estimates for Arab communities in Israel as a whole. According to their figures, by 1983, there were over 400 manufacturing workshops and factories in Arab communities. Eighty four percent of these units were locally owned. Over 160 establishments employed more than 10 workers, and 120 workshops had less than 5 employees. Textile and clothing, and construction materials were the largest branches of manufacturing in the Arab sector, accounting for 75 percent of the manufacturing establishments. Food production and metalwork were also fairly prevalent, accounting for 20 percent of industrial units (for a detailed description, see Meyer-Brodnitz and Czamanski 1986b).

The development of factories in the Arab sector has not generally been assisted by government agencies. Although extensive policies and financial assistance exist with respect to the development of Jewish communities, no comparable practices exist in the case of the Arab sector, with the possible exception of Druze villages. Recently, however, large Jewish controlled companies have established workshops and small factories (many of which are textile workshops) in Arab villages in an attempt to tap the local (primarily female) labor force. Hence, it is likely that in the future, a growing proportion of jobs, even in the Arab communities, will be controlled by Jewish economic interests.

Banking has also grown in the Arab sector, and comprised the majority of what are described in Table 3.1 as financial service jobs. By the early 1980s there were over 80 branches of the major Israeli banks in Arab communities (Hassdaya and Kahana 1982). It should be emphasized, however, that there was no bank owned or controlled by members of the Arab population. While banking activity has expanded and provides a growing number of jobs for educated persons in the Arab communities, it is still the case that banks have a relatively small role in the development of the Arab economy (Czamanski et al. 1984).

Although the Arab economy grew between 1972 and 1983, it is evident from the measures of dispersion presented at the bottom of Table 3.1 that the Arab economy as a whole became more concentrated. The measure of industrial dispersion was constructed so that it would receive a value of 1 if jobs were equally distributed across all industrial categories, and a value of 0 if all were concentrated in one category.[4] Since it is not at all clear what optimal dispersion would look like, or what figure the index would have in this case, the comparison with the Jewish sector serves as a useful means of evaluation. Both the Arab and the Jewish sectors experienced growing industrial concentration between 1972 and 1983, but the change in the Arab sector (which was already less dispersed at the outset) was substantially greater, indicating growing economic concentration. Finally, although substantial changes in the structure of both the Arab and the Jewish economies took place between 1972 and 1983, there is no evidence of conversion, as reflected in the stability of the index of dissimilarity for the two points in time (32.8 and 33.5 in 1972 and 1983 respectively). About one-third of jobs in either the Jewish or the Arab economy would have to be shifted across (major) industrial categories for the two distributions to become equal.

The Changing Occupational Structure

One aspect of particular relevance to understanding the economic transformation which has taken place in the Arab sector over the years is the decline in self-employment and entrepreneurship. Much has been written about the decline of agriculture and the process of proletarization in the Arab sector, beginning in the pre-state period and accelerating as large tracts of land were expropriated by the State (Carmi and Rosenfeld 1974; Kislev 1976; Rosenfeld 1964; Zureik 1979). However, as is evident from the figures in Table 3.2, substantial change took place in the *non-agricultural* component of the Arab sector even during the short period from 1972 to 1983. The figures in Table 3.2 are provided for men only since Arab women are virtually absent from the categories of employers and the self-employed. As recently as 1972,

TABLE 3.2:   Percent of Employers and Self-Employed in the Arab Labor Market (Excluding Agriculture) in 1972 and 1983, by Age Group (based on a 20 percent sample of the census, males aged 25-65)

Age Group	1972		1983	
	Employers	Self-Employed	Employers	Self-Employed
25-35	4.8	38.2	1.2	19.9
36-46	4.8	53.8	5.1	32.5
47-57	6.5	56.5	2.2	40.8
58 and over	3.2	57.3	3.6	35.8
Total	4.7	48.6	2.7	28.5

almost half of all jobs held by males in the Arab sector were characterized by self-employment, and approximately another 5 percent represented ownership positions. By 1983, self-employment declined to slightly over one-quarter of the jobs in the Arab sector while employer positions represented less than 3 percent. When the figures are broken down by age cohorts the decline is apparent in every age category.

Since the data provided in Table 3.2 are for age intervals of 11 years, it is possible to evaluate the changes over the inter-census period with a fair degree of accuracy. We find that during the period each of the cohorts experienced a decline in the proportion of self-employed and employers (except in the case of the cohort of 25–35 years old in 1972 who were aged 36–46 in 1983). The youngest cohort—those aged 25–35 in 1983—had the lowest proportion of self-employed and employers, lower by a factor of 2 compared to the same age group 11 years earlier. Indeed, these findings concur with the figures for manufacturing and business enterprises (as noted earlier) which indicated a significant decline in workshop establishments in the Arab sector, the consolidation into larger establishments (partly financed by Jewish capital) and the growth of the public sector.

Turning now to the occupational composition of the Arab sector, Table 3.3 presents the distribution of jobs across nine major occupational categories in 1972 and 1983. The figures for the Jewish sector are presented for comparative purposes. The reader is reminded that these figures do not represent the occupational distribution of the Arab labor force since, as already noted, many residents of the Arab communities are actually employed in the Jewish sector and are part of the occupational structure of the Jewish, rather than the Arab sector. Indeed, the figures in Table 3.3 represent jobs carried out within the Arab economy, irrespective of who actually performs them. The slight disparity in the total numbers between Table 3.1 and Table 3.3 is due to differences in missing data.

In 1972, 30.6 percent of those employed in the Arab sector were agricultural workers, and an additional 27 percent were employed as skilled blue-collar workers. This reflects the limited entrepreneurial orientation of the Arab economic structure still evident in the early 1970s. At that time, white-collar jobs (including academic, professional, technical, administrative,

TABLE 3.3:   Occupational Structure of Labor Markets in the Arab and Jewish Sectors,
1972 and 1983 (based on a 20 percent sample of the census,
all persons aged 25-65)

Occupational Category	1972		1983	
	Arab	Jewish	Arab	Jewish
Scientific/Academic	2.0	7.1	5.5	9.2
Professional/Technical	13.6	12.1	27.0	16.5
Administrative/Managers	0.9	3.7	1.2	6.2
Clerical	3.6	15.6	6.2	18.2
Sales	9.5	8.6	10.0	7.6
Service Workers	6.8	12.2	8.0	11.2
Agricultural Workers	30.6	5.7	11.8	3.5
Skilled Workers	27.0	28.9	24.0	24.5
Unskilled Workers	6.0	6.0	6.3	3.2
Total	100.0	100.0	100.0	100.0
N[1]	16345	692740	24920	1002355

[1] Numbers are population estimates

clerical and sale jobs) accounted for just under 30 percent of the Arab labor market. The figures for 1983 reflect the remarkable change that took place during a relatively short period: a dramatic decline in agricultural jobs and an equally remarkable growth of professional and technical jobs brought about, as we saw earlier, by the expansion of public services. Scientific/academic and clerical jobs increased as a proportion of the total market and, by 1983, white-collar jobs accounted for 50 percent of all jobs in the Arab sector.

The significance of the change and its magnitude can be put in perspective by contrasting it with changes which took place in the Jewish sector during the same period. White-collar jobs which, already in 1972, accounted for 47.1 percent of jobs in the Jewish economy increased to 57.7 percent by 1983. The change was less substantial than in the Arab sector and had different characteristics. While the proportion of professional and technical jobs was similar in the Arab and the Jewish sectors in 1972 (13.6 percent and 12.1 percent respectively), the increase was relatively small in the Jewish sector, but massive in the Arab economy. At the same time, administrative and managerial jobs grew more rapidly in the Jewish sector. In 1983 administrative and managerial jobs accounted for 6.2 percent of all jobs in the Jewish economy, but for only 1.2 percent of the jobs in the Arab sector. What appears to be at work here is the disproportionate expansion of certain services—most noticeably education and possibly welfare—which are government funded. Such an expansion is often politically motivated, and may well serve as a means of control through co-optation. At the same time, very little headway was made with regard to the development of economic enterprises that might have served as resources for the Arab population. The steep decline in agriculture did not bring about many manufacturing jobs in its stead; the small proportion of managerial positions attests to the lack of large-scale organizations, whether production or services.

Spatial Mismatch

One way of evaluating the occupational opportunities available in the Arab sector would be to compare the occupational distribution of the population residing in the Arab sector with the occupational composition of the Arab labor market.[5] This would provide some estimate of the extent to which persons in particular occupations are likely to find jobs in such occupational categories in the Arab sector. More importantly, a comparison of the estimates for 1972 and 1983 will indicate whether the situation has improved or deteriorated over the years. Figures pertaining to this comparison are presented in Table 3.4. The figures represent the estimated number of persons (or jobs) in a given occupational category, and the ratios should be interpreted as the number of persons working in a given occupational category for every job available in the Arab labor market in that occupation.

The overall population-to-market ratio, according to figures in Table 3.4, was 2.4 in 1972 and 2.3 in 1983, reflecting the fact that the Arab labor market

TABLE 3.4:   Occupational Distribution of the Population and of Jobs in the Arab Sector, 1972 and 1983 (based on a 20 percent sample of the census, all persons aged 25-65)

Occupational Category	1972			1983		
	Population	Market	P/M Ratio	Population	Market	P/M Ratio
Scientific/Academic	440	335	1.3	1680	1380	1.2
Professional/Technical	2725	2220	1.2	7520	6730	1.1
Administrative/Managers	255	145	1.8	425	295	1.4
Clerical	925	580	1.6	2340	1550	1.5
Sales	2135	1550	1.4	3345	2490	1.3
Service Workers	2765	1105	2.5	4510	2000	2.3
Agricultural Workers	7595	5000	1.5	4410	2945	1.5
Skilled Workers	15230	4415	3.4	22785	5970	3.8
Unskilled Workers	6630	995	6.7	9130	1560	5.9
Total[1]	38700	16345	2.4	56295	24920	2.3
Ratio of Highly Educated Persons to Professional and Managerial Jobs			0.95			1.48

[1] Numbers are population estimates.

was able to accommodate less than half of the labor force residing in Arab communities.[6] The ratios, however, varied considerably across occupational categories. They were generally lower in the more prominent occupational categories, and tended to increase as one descends the occupational ladder. For scientific/academic and professional/technical occupations the ratios were close to 1 in both 1972 and 1983. This suggests that practically all residents of Arab communities employed in these occupations worked within the Arab sector of the labor market. By way of contrast, the ratios at the bottom of the occupational ladder were over 3:1 for skilled labor, and 6:1 for unskilled labor. This means that the great majority of Arabs in blue-collar jobs were employed outside of the Arab economic sector.

The ratios presented in Table 3.4 are subject to different interpretations in that one may choose to focus on the availability of jobs, or lack thereof, or on characteristics of the labor force and their qualifications. One obvious explanation, however, for the low ratios in academic, professional, and administrative jobs is that Arabs are unlikely to find employment in these occupations outside their own labor market. The "match" in this case—ratios close to unity—reflects the lack of opportunities for Arabs in these occupations in the Jewish economy, and the fact that they can only find work in jobs available within the Arab sector. In contrast, the very high ratios in service jobs, skilled occupations, and even more so in unskilled jobs, reflect the heavy utilization of blue-collar Arab workers in the Jewish economy, as well as the lack of labor market opportunities for such workers in the Arab economy.

One difficulty with the preceding interpretation is that rather than emphasizing the lack of opportunities for Arabs in the higher skilled and more rewarding occupations outside their labor market, one may argue that only few Arabs have the education and training to fill such occupational positions. According to this interpretation, the low ratios found for the higher level occupations represent lack of qualifications in the Arab population, rather than constraints imposed by the labor market. Since we do not know what specific occupation people had trained for (and in any case for many occupations there is no specific training), it is impossible to contrast the actual number of persons who had qualified for a particular occupation with the number of job positions and to examine how this had changed over time. However, it is possible to examine this issue more broadly using data on the level of education of the Arab population.

In order to examine the availability of persons with the human capital necessary to fill professional and technical jobs in the Arab sector, we calculated the number of persons residing in Arab communities who received more than a high school education (that is 13 years of schooling, or more). We then contrasted that figure with the number of positions in academic, professional, technical and administrative occupations (where the educational norm is at least some post-secondary education) in the Arab economy. As can be observed from figures at the bottom of Table 3.4, in 1972 the ratio of highly educated persons to the number of professional, technical and administrative jobs in the Arab economy was 0.95. That is, the population of the Arab sector included a slightly smaller number of highly educated people than would be required to fill all high status jobs. In this case one might argue that the development of the Arab economic sector may have been hindered by the lack of highly educated and qualified personnel needed to fill professional and managerial jobs. However, the findings for 1983 reveal a ratio of 1.48; that is, almost 50 percent more highly educated persons resided in Arab communities than there were high status jobs in the Arab labor market.

The detailed figures in Table 3.4 indicate that the absolute number of jobs in the Arab labor market increased in every single occupational category. Yet the level of education appears to have been increasing much more rapidly. This has led to labor market mismatch of two forms. First, at the macro level, restrictions on the expansion of the Arab economy limit the availability of certain types of jobs in which the better educated and more skilled persons may engage. Second, at the micro level, the inferred exclusion of Arabs from professional and especially managerial jobs in the Jewish economy, combined with the dearth of opportunities in the Arab sector, result in the entry of Arab workers into low skill, lower paying jobs for which they are over-educated.

Educational and Occupational Mismatch

In order to address the consequences at the micro level, a more refined and elaborate examination of mismatch was undertaken whereby the educational level of individual Arab employees was compared to the educational norm in the occupation in which the person was employed.[7] It was expected that an educational level higher than the norm in the occupation—referred to here as educational mismatch—might emerge as a consequence of limited occupational opportunities in the Arab sector and difficulty in securing employment in the Jewish sector. This mismatch has exacerbated in recent years as a result of rising levels of education among the Arab population. It was assumed here that spatial segregation, limited occupational opportunities in the Arab sector, and employment policies in the Jewish sector (to be outlined in the following chapter), all contribute to the disadvantageous position of Arabs seeking employment outside the Arab sector. In competing for positions in the job queue, Arabs would have to offer higher qualifications. If this were the case, Arab employees would tend to have a higher educational level than the norm in the occupations they hold. Following this logic, we would expect that educational mismatch would be greater among Arabs employed in the Jewish economic sector than in the Arab sector. Educational mismatch was also expected to be higher in 1983 than in 1972 as a result of the rapid expansion of education unaccompanied by similar expansion of jobs in the Arab economic sector.

Educational-occupational mismatch was defined here as attaining an educational level that was at least one standard deviation higher than the mean for the occupation (where the mean for each occupation was calculated over all individuals—Jews and Arabs—and in both the Jewish and the Arab economic sectors). Figures for educational mismatch (Table 3.5) reveal that in 1972 there were relatively small differences in the extent of Arab employee mismatch in both the Arab and Jewish labor markets. Overall the proportion

TABLE 3.5: Educational Mismatch Among Arab Males in the Arab and Jewish Labor Market, by Age Cohort, 1972 and 1983 (based on a 20 percent sample of the census, all persons aged 25-65)

Age Group	1972		1983	
	Arab Market	Jewish Market	Arab Market	Jewish Market
	Over-Educated for Job Held			
25-35	5.7	5.7	9.4	11.8
36-46	2.5	3.3	6.2	7.3
47-57	2.0	3.2	1.4	5.2
58 and over	2.0	1.9	2.2	6.5
	Under-Educated for Job Held			
25-35	16.8	24.3	15.0	14.0
36-46	35.4	38.0	23.6	23.5
47-57	51.3	52.9	42.0	33.6
58 and over	59.8	55.4	42.2	34.1

of mismatch was rather small, although, as might be expected, it was inversely related to age. The extent of mismatch among the youngest cohort (25–35 years old) was greater by a factor of 3 than the proportion of "over-educated" among persons 58 or older.

The comparison of figures for 1972 and 1983 illustrates the increase in mismatch which approximately doubled in each of the age groups. Among Arab persons aged 25–35 employed in the Jewish sector of the economy in 1972, the mismatch was 5.7 percent. By 1983 this figure had doubled to 11.8 percent. Although figures were lower for other age groups, the pattern for those employed in the Jewish sector was identical. A similar pattern was evident for the young cohort of workers in the Arab economy, but for persons 47 years and older there appears to have been no change over the 11-year period.[8] Not only did each of the age groups (with the exceptions noted above) experience higher mismatch in 1983 than in 1972 but, looking at the change within cohorts, we find growing mismatch, especially for Arabs employed in the Jewish labor market. The inverse relationship to age was even more pronounced in 1983, and it is the youngest age group that was most overqualified, particularly in the Jewish sector. The trend then seems to be one of increasing divergence between educational training and occupational attainment.

One obvious outcome of the educational mismatch is that Arab workers, especially younger cohorts, receive lower returns on education in terms of occupational status (Al-Haj 1987b). Findings reported by Semyonov and Yuchtman-Yaar (1992) indicate that both in 1972 and 1983, education (years of schooling) had a stronger effect on the occupational status of Jews than was true for Arabs. This pattern held up for all age groups examined.

Furthermore, the social mechanisms underlying the gap in occupational status between Jews and Arabs changed considerably over time. Whereas in 1972 there appears to have been no "market discrimination" against Arabs in that their occupational status, on average, was not lower than expected based on their human capital characteristics (age and education), by 1983, Arabs of all age groups experienced "labor market discrimination" and their actual occupational status was lower than one would predict based on their market-relevant attributes.

According to Semyonov and Yuchtman-Yaar (1992), the inability to obtain adequate returns for education was most pronounced among Arab workers aged 25–36 in 1983 and accounted for 24 percent of the total gap in occupational status when compared with Jews of similar age. Among those aged 54–65 "market discrimination" accounted for only 6.5 percent of the Jewish-Arab occupational gap, but this was still quite a change from the early 1970s when Arabs in the oldest age groups were actually "over-rewarded" considering their very low levels of education. Indeed, the 1980s have seen growing difficulties for Arab workers, and especially newcomers to the labor market, to convert their human capital resources into socioeconomic rewards. Finding a job to fit qualifications has become difficult in the Arab economy, but poses even more of a challenge for Arabs seeking work in the Jewish sector.

Concluding Remarks

In the brief historical review of the development of the Jewish and Arab economies in the pre-state period we noted that while these economic sectors were linked at various points, the two sectors largely followed separate paths. Every step-up in the intensification of conflict between Arabs and Jews was accompanied by an increase in separation and isolation. The 1948 war and the establishment of the State of Israel was particularly detrimental to the Arab economy. Its manufacturing and trade infrastructure collapsed as the more wealthy and better educated urban dwellers fled the country. Agriculture also suffered due to the shrinking amount of land available for cultivation and the loss of markets for its produce. The subordinate position of the Arab population, as well as specific government regulations, hampered economic development. At the same time, growing demand for labor in the Jewish sector created job opportunities especially in blue-collar jobs outside the Arab localities. By the 1980s over half the residents of Arab localities commuted to work in the Jewish economy.

The analyses carried out on data from the population censuses of 1972 and 1983 provide an estimate of the economic structure of the Arab economy and demonstrate how this structure changed during the 1970s and early 1980s. The most striking feature of this change was the shift of the Arab economy from agriculture to an economy based largely on services, mostly public services. Although manufacturing expanded, it still played a small role in the Arab sector, and most blue-collar workers were employed in the Jewish sector. The change in the Arab economy entailed a substantial decline in self-employment and ownership of means of production. Most of those employed in the Arab sector were either paid by the national or local government, or by larger firms, some of which were owned by Jewish companies.

In terms of our interest in ethnic relations and stratification, the findings presented in this chapter illustrate the constraints on the development of the Arab economic sector and the contribution of labor market characteristics to ethnic disadvantage. The integration of Arabs into the Israeli (Jewish) economy has entailed social and economic disadvantages in that Arab workers have generally been accepted into the lower level occupations only. Our findings show that rapidly growing education in the Arab population, coupled with limited expansion of the Arab economy, has resulted in relatively few adequate job opportunities for better educated, highly skilled, individuals. One consequence of this, examined here, is a growing educational mismatch, particularly among young Arabs. This is accompanied by declining income returns on education for the younger cohorts.

Up to this point we have addressed the socioeconomic position of Arabs in Israel at the macro level. By now it seems clear that the economic base of the Arab minority does not provide the opportunities for individual achievement of rewards, the most important of which is work and the ensuing income. In the following chapter we intend to examine these patterns more closely and to determine the extent to which the ecological segregation and the spatial and occupational mismatch affect the income of Arabs.

Notes

1. This review relies heavily on the following sources: Cohen (1978), Flapan (1979), Khalidi (1988a, 1988b), Kimmerling (1983), Metzer and Kaplan (1985), and Owen (1988).

2. Ideally we would need information on ownership in order to determine the size and composition of economic establishments controlled by the Arab population. Information based on the distribution of jobs only approximates this since some Jewish owned and controlled establishments have been set up in the Arab sector in recent years (accounting for approximately 16 percent of establishments with two or more employees, according to Czamanski et al. [1984]).

3. The change is less dramatic if we calculate the percentage figures from the upper bound estimate of jobs in the Arab economy (23.0 and 28.9 in 1972 and 1983, respectively). But the upper bound estimate probably includes many jobs actually carried out in the Jewish economic sector which considerably increased between 1972 and 1983. Hence, the percent figures for public services based on the upper bound estimates probably underrepresent the role of public services in the Arab sector, particularly in 1983.

4. The measure of dispersion is calculated as:

$$H = \{-\sum_{j=1}^{k} P_{ji} \ln P_{ji}\} \, 1/\ln k$$

where P_{ji} is the probability that a person belonging to ethnic group i will be in occupational category j, and k is the total number of occupational categories. If all persons are concentrated in one category, the index will have a value of zero; there is no dispersion. The index obtains its largest value when a group is equally distributed across all categories (i.e., maximum permeation). The value of the index in such a case depends on k—the number of categories—and is equal to $\ln k$ (see McFarland 1969). Thus, by multiplying the sum by $1/\ln k$, we obtained values that are stated as a proportion of the maximum value achievable, and the measure thus ranges from zero to one. The measure is obviously affected by the definition of category boundaries, for combining two categories into one, for example, changes both the P values and the value k. It was shown, however, that when the number of categories approached 100, boundary decision had minimal effect (McFarland 1969).

5. These are not independently estimated here since labor market composition is derived by aggregation. Since the aggregation includes those who reside outside the Arab sector, but are employed there, hypothetically certain jobs could be available in the Arab market even though none of the residents of Arab communities hold them (and vice versa).

6. The most striking aspect of Table 3.4 is the high stability in the ratios between 1972 and 1983. Yet the reader should recall that market composition is based on occupational classification of those working in Arab communities and therefore it reflects the *de facto* distribution and not necessarily job slots that employers wish to fill.

7. The educational norm was defined by calculating the mean educational level in each occupation defined at the three digit level. The mean scores were calculated for the Israeli labor force as a whole (including Jews and Arabs and not distinguishing between the Jewish and Arab sectors of the economy). Although based on aggregate educational data, it is assumed here that the mean reflects the educational demands in each occupation. The norm was then defined as the mean plus/minus 1 standard deviation.

8. It should be noted here that the extent of mismatch is not particularly high especially when contrasted with the percent of "over-educated" among Jews which reaches 15 percent in some cohorts. What is significant, however, is that the trend for Jews and Arabs is opposite. For Arabs the mismatch grew substantially during the 1970s and early 1980s, whereas for Jews it declined.

Appendix 3.A

Based on information collected by the census it is possible to classify each person in two ways: (1) according to place of residence; and (2) according to place of employment.

1. Place of residence is divided into two sectors:
   (a) Jewish sector (all communities defined as Jewish or mixed communities). The population of this sector includes:

   - residents of Jewish communities with more than 5,000 inhabitants;
   - residents of small communities (less than 5,000 inhabitants) who stated that their religion was Jewish.

   (b) Arab sector-all communities administratively defined as Arab. The population of this sector includes:

   - residents of non-Jewish communities with more than 5,000 inhabitants;
   - residents of small communities (less than 5,000) who stated their religion was not Jewish.

2. The labor market is divided into two sectors:
   (a) Estimates of the Jewish sector based on:

   - Jews and Arabs working in the Jewish sector (even though they may reside in the Arab sector);
   - Jews who work in small (unidentified) communities;
   - Jews whose place of work is unknown.

   (b) Estimates of the Arab sector based on:

   - Arabs and Jews working in the Arab sector (even though they may reside in the Jewish sector);
   - Persons employed in (unidentified) small communities whose religion was non-Jewish;
   - Non-Jewish workers whose place of work is unknown.

4

Community Segregation and Socioeconomic Inequalities

By now it should be clear to the reader that the position of Arabs in the stratification system of Israeli society cannot be reduced to personal attributes or individual attainment *per se.* To be sure, Jews and Arabs differ in many aspects of human resources, and these differences may affect the attainment of socioeconomic rewards. However, group membership plays a central role in the determination of socioeconomic success since Arabs are disadvantaged even when human capital resources are taken into consideration. That is, ethnicity *per se* exerts a significant effect on achievement. Indeed, previous research has shown a gap between Arabs and Jews in the attainment of education, jobs and economic rewards attributable to ethnic discrimination of one form or another (e.g., Ben-Sira 1991; Kraus and Hodge 1990; Semyonov and Tyree 1981). Not only do Arabs face economic discrimination, but they are also more likely to face an inferior opportunity structure.

In the present chapter we intend to go beyond the "ethnicity effect". We plan to build on the findings of the previous chapters which revealed the extent of Jewish-Arab segregation, on the one hand, and the constraints on economic development in the Arab sector, on the other. Together these pose a particular context for structural effects related to ethnicity and may be expected to impact on economic outcomes. Specifically, we intend to examine the socioeconomic attainment of employed Arabs, and the extent to which this is determined by labor market characteristics and organization.

This chapter, then, deals with the impact of spatial segregation on socio-economic achievements of Arabs and Jews. It focuses attention on the way in which individual-level and ecological variables jointly affect inequality between Jews and Arabs in Israel. We will suggest that attributes of the local labor market where persons are employed have considerable impact on both occupational opportunities and earnings. More specifically, we will argue that due to constraints associated with residential segregation between Jews and Arabs, the effect of local labor market characteristics on socioeconomic attainment is more substantial for members of the Arab minority than for the dominant Jewish group.

The literature on local labor markets underscores such features as community size, industrial structure, economic conditions and sociodemographic composition as important determinants of socioeconomic inequality. This view is derived from the notion that the growth of urban centers has brought about diversified economies based on large organizations and an intensive division of labor which, in turn, leads to specialized professional, administrative, trade and service functions (Duncan and Reiss 1956; Duncan et al. 1960; Kasarda 1978). Consequently, large urban centers are expected to enhance achievement via the magnitude of opportunities associated with size and the complexity of their industrial and occupational structure (Blau and Duncan 1967; Bloomquist and Summers 1982; Kasarda 1978).

Economic diversity, though related to size, is likely to exert independent effects on individual-level attainment. Diversity refers here to the number and variety of jobs available in a labor market (Duncan and Reiss 1956). In particular, workers in labor markets with a wide range of employment opportunities are more likely (other things being equal) to find jobs that match their skills. Since workers are generally rewarded according to the job categories they occupy, job diversity enables workers to achieve the highest pay for their human capital. Limited opportunities, by contrast, tend to restrict the opportunities for workers to change jobs (Doeringer 1984). This may affect earnings since (voluntary) job changes are usually accompanied by pay increases.

In addition to the effects of size and complexity *per se*, the particular industrial and social structure of the community has been shown to contribute significantly to the socioeconomic rewards of individuals. When "high wage" industries predominate in a community, this tends to push wages up across the local labor market (Parcel 1979; Parcel and Mueller 1983; Bloomquist and Summers 1982). This "roll-out effect" means that while the presence of core-lucrative industries in a local labor market provides highly rewarding opportunities in a particular economic sector, it also raises the standard for the entire community. Consequently it generates higher wages for all workers in the locale (Bloomquist and Summers 1982; Rogers et al. 1978; Logan 1976, 1978; Summers and Clemente 1976). In contrast, places composed mainly of low status populations typically lack the resources and political power to attract and develop lucrative opportunities, and this has a negative impact on residents' rewards (Lewin-Epstein 1986; Logan 1976, 1978; Nachmias 1979; Semyonov 1981; Tienda and Lii 1987).

In the following sections we will explore the role played by the local opportunity structure in contributing to socioeconomic inequality between Jews and Arabs in Israel. Since, as we have shown, Arabs in Israel reside in smaller places with inferior opportunity structures, part of their socioeconomic disadvantage can be attributed to the characteristics of their local labor market. Community characteristics are thus viewed here as intervening between ethnicity and socioeconomic outcomes. Part of the economic gap, however, can be attributed to the differential effect of labor market characteristics on the economic attainments of members of superordinate and subordinate groups. As demonstrated in Chapter 3, Arab workers face restricted occupational opportunities in the Arab communities. Consequently, they are forced to widen the range of their job search outside their own communities. The limited opportunities and the skewed industrial structure faced by Arabs necessitate high levels of commuting. In 1983, some 62 percent of the Arab work force (67 percent of the male labor force) were employed outside their community of residence as compared with 50 percent of Jews (57 percent of Jewish males). Arabs also commute greater distances than Jews since many of their communities are located in remote areas distant from major urban centers. It is likely, under these circumstances, that they would gravitate to local labor markets with more abundant opportunities.

Community Effects on Earnings

In the present section we examine whether community characteristics exert a differential effect on the income of Jews and Arabs, over and above individual-level attributes. In order to do so, we use ordinary least squares (OLS) regression analysis. In this analysis, income is taken as a function of individual-level attributes, community characteristics, and whether one works in community of residence or elsewhere.[1] The coefficients estimated by means of these equations (presented in Table 4.1) represent the effects of the various attributes on income. The analysis was carried out using the data set from the 1983 census. It was done separately for Arabs and Jews in order that the effects of individual-level and community on income might be compared. Individual-level variables are those traditionally employed in equations predicting income. In addition to ethnicity, they include age, education, gender, hours of work, marital status, and occupational status.[2] Community-level characteristics include size, job availability, and industrial structure.[3]

Our main interest here is to examine the impact of local labor markets on earning differentials. Before doing so, however, let us turn to the effects of personal attributes to examine whether Arabs and Jews are similarly rewarded for their resources. The figures in Table 4.1 are consistent with previous research on this issue. They reveal that Jews enjoy higher returns on every aspect of individual resources. It is important to remind the reader that income was transformed into a logarithmic scale. For the reader not versed in this statistical technique, we note that the interpretation of the regression coefficients is straightforward: each coefficient represents the *percentage* change in income brought about by a unit change in each determinant.

We see that (other things being equal) an additional year of schooling beyond the average increases the income of Jews by 2.87 percent and that of Arabs by 2.29 percent. Even more revealing is the fact that Jews enjoy an additional 1.36 percent on their income for each additional hour of work, whereas the return for Arabs is only 0.49 percent. Among men, the return for Arabs is still half the return received by Jews. Jews also enjoy higher income returns on occupational status and the income returns for a married person are also lower for Arabs. The only personal attribute for which coefficients for Jews and Arabs appear similar is age. But this latter finding conceals the fact that at every given age Arabs are likely to have more labor market experience than

TABLE 4.1:   Unstandardized Regression Coefficients Predicting Income (ln) of Jews and Arabs with Individual-Level Attributes and Labor Market Characteristics (Standard Errors in Parentheses), Age 25-64, 1983*

	Total Population		Men	
	Jews (N=132,245)	Arabs (N=9,087)	Jews (N=72,607)	Arabs (N=7,407)
Age	0.42 (0.02)	0.45 (0.06)	0.37 (0.02)	0.34 (0.07)
Sex (whether Male)	36.36 (0.37)	30.09 (1.63)		
Years of Schooling	2.87 (0.06)	2.29 (0.21)	2.65 (0.08)	2.28 (0.23)
Married	11.00 (0.46)	11.98 (1.72)	26.07 (0.71)	15.72 (2.17)
Weekly Hours of Work	1.36 (0.01)	0.49 (0.04)	0.84 (0.02)	0.44 (0.04)
Occupational Status[1]	1.26 (0.01)	1.01 (0.04)	1.25 (0.01)	0.97 (0.05)
Commuting	8.55 (0.37)	7.65 (1.52)	9.48 (0.48)	6.41 (1.71)
Community Size (ln)	0.30 (0.12)	-5.27 (0.54)	-0.05 (0.03)	-5.71 (0.59)
Persons-to-Jobs Ratio	-2.48 (0.26)	-1.94 (0.55)	-2.62 (0.38)	-2.11 (0.60)
Job Diversity	-106.16 (18.02)	46.83 (3.21)	-48.41 (23.82)	46.23 (3.57)
Agriculture	0.84 (0.22)	-0.22 (0.18)	0.69 (0.28)	-0.21 (0.20)
Labor-Intensive Manufacturing	-0.05 (0.03)	-0.36 (0.12)	-0.03 (0.05)	-0.31 (0.13)
Capital-Intensive Manufacturing	0.29 (0.03)	0.02 (0.11)	0.43 (0.04)	0.06 (0.11)
Commerce and Utilities	0.48 (0.05)	0.53 (0.15)	0.61 (0.07)	0.65 (0.16)
Construction	-0.65 (0.12)	0.20 (0.29)	-0.70 (0.15)	-0.09 (0.32)
Finance & Business Services	-0.04 (0.05)	0.67 (0.17)	-0.21 (0.07)	0.75 (0.19)
Personal Services	0.59 (0.21)	-2.21 (0.50)	0.48 (0.28)	-2.02 (0.54)
Percent Arab in Community	0.05 (0.03)	-0.03 (0.03)	0.07 (0.05)	-0.02 (0.04)
Constant	897.01	859.73	893.93	900.28
R^2 change due to labor market	0.01	0.05	0.02	0.06
R^2 total	0.39	0.26	0.29	0.25

[1] Based on the Socioeconomic Index of Occupations for Israel (Tyree 1981).

* Coefficients are multiplied by 100.

Jews since they have less average schooling and do not serve in the military. Hence, these figures would appear to underestimate Arab-Jewish differences in returns on experience. Commuting, which is a means to expand the realm of job opportunities, enhances the earnings of both Jews and Arabs, although the impact is weaker for the latter group. This is evident from the coefficients for commuting which, in the case of men, are higher among Jews than among Arabs. Whereas commuting adds about 9.5 percent to the income of Jews, it adds only 6.5 percent to the income of Arabs.

Turning now to the impact of community characteristics on income, the most striking finding is that community characteristics considerably improve our ability to predict the income level of Arabs, but have only a modest impact in the case of Jews. This is evident from the coefficient of determination (R^2) values presented at the bottom of Table 4.1. Community-level characteristics add 5 percent to the explained variance in income among Arabs (6 percent for males) and only 1 percent in the model for the Jewish population (2 percent for males). Aside from the unequal explanatory power of community characteristics in the Arab and Jewish populations, they also exert different effects on the income of Jews and Arabs. Community size has a positive effect on the earnings of Jews (not statistically significant for males), but a negative and highly significant effect on Arabs' earnings. The negative effect for Arabs is contrary to theoretical expectations, but may be understood as resulting from economic competition and market discrimination that Arabs face in (the mostly Jewish) large cities (Semyonov 1988). As expected, the person-to-jobs ratio exerts a negative effect on the income of both Jews and Arabs. Interestingly, the effect is weaker for Arabs, which suggests that Arabs may be employed in less desirable jobs; hence, their income is less affected by the overall supply of labor in the market. Job diversity tends to increase the income of Arabs, but to decrease the income of Jews.

The industrial structure of labor markets appears to affect workers' income in intricate ways. Arabs employed in labor markets with a relatively large proportion of labor-intensive jobs tend to earn less than other Arabs. The effect on the earnings of Jews, however, is very weak (statistically insignificant) and for all practical purposes can be ignored. The presence of capital-intensive industries tends to increase the earnings of Jews, but has a negligible impact on the earnings of Arabs. The size of commerce and utilities in the labor market affects income positively, and the effect is somewhat stronger among Arabs. When construction constitutes a large proportion of jobs in the labor market, the earnings of Jews tend to decline, but the earnings of Arabs are unaffected. The presence of finance and business industries has a strong positive impact on earnings of Arabs, and a weak (negative) effect for Jews. Lastly, the size of personal services industry in the labor market exerts a strong negative effect on the income of Arabs and a weak but positive effect on the income of Jews.

Despite the complexity of relationships that emerge between the industrial structure of labor markets and the income of Jews and Arabs, important differences do emerge. In particular, the contrasting effects of capital-intensive and labor-intensive manufacturing on the income of Jews and Arabs, and the strong effects of service industries on the income of Arabs, are worth underscoring. Curiously, when community characteristics are controlled for, the direct net effect of percent Arabs in the labor market is negligible and statistically insignificant. This appears to result from the ecological segregation of Arabs and Jews, coupled with the limited opportunity structure in Arab communities, as indicated earlier. Hence, community characteristics and ethnic composition (percent Arabs) tend to be conflated, and once the effect of economic characteristics is accounted for, the composition effect is captured as well.

Evaluating the Contribution of Community Attributes

In the previous section we demonstrated that specific labor market attributes affect the income attainment of those in the labor force, over and above individual-level characteristics. We would like to gain a more detailed and precise understanding of the contribution of labor market characteristics to the disparity between earnings of Arabs and Jews, especially in view of the fact that the effects of many of these characteristics appear to differ for the two groups. We thus proceed next to examine the overall contribution of community characteristics to income inequality among the population groups. This is done by taking the income gap between the two groups and evaluating the various mechanisms that generate the gap in order to determine the relative portion of the gap accounted for by individual-level and labor market characteristics. To do so we decompose the mean income difference into several components using regression standardization techniques.

For readers familiar with regression analysis, we provide, in Appendix 4.A, a detailed description of the method of decomposition used here. For those who prefer not to be bothered by a technical discussion, we note that the income gap between Jews and Arabs is made up of several mutually exclusive components. For our purposes, it is most meaningful to distinguish between the portion of the income gap due to differences regarding individual-level attributes such as age, education, or hours of work, and differences with respect to labor market characteristics to which the two groups are exposed, such as size, industrial composition and job diversity. Specifically identified are the portions of the income gap due to *mean differences* in individual-level and labor market characteristics, as well as *differential returns* on individual-level and labor market characteristics.

The findings of the decomposition analysis are presented in detail in Table 4.A in Appendix 4.A, and are essentially similar for the total population and for the male population. Less than half the earnings gap between Jews and Arabs is attributable to the unequal individual-level characteristics (human resources) of the two groups. The difference in human resources accounts for 42 percent of the income gap in the population as a whole, and 44 percent of the income difference between Jewish and Arab men. Of particular interest and importance to the present discussion is the fact that labor market characteristics also have a substantial effect on the income gap between Jews and Arabs. Differences in local labor market characteristics account for 18 percent of the income gap in the male population, and 19 percent of the gap in the population as a whole. This means that about one-fifth of the difference in earnings between Jews and Arabs is due to the fact that they work in markets with different characteristics (amount of opportunities, industrial structure, etc.) and that average markets in which Arabs are located tend to provide lower levels of rewards.

A substantial portion of the difference in earnings between Jews and Arabs is due to group membership and differential returns on resources and labor market attributes. The analysis reveals that Jews receive higher returns on individual-level attributes than Arabs, and that this factor constitutes a large portion of the income gap between the two groups (121 percent of the gap in the total population and 100 percent of the earnings gap for men). The higher returns on human capital resources for Jews, as observed here, can be viewed as an indication of economic discrimination against the Arab minority. The rationale behind this notion is that in the absence of discrimination, workers would receive equal rewards for equal levels of human resources. For example, if an Arab worker receives lower earnings for each year of formal schooling than a Jewish worker, this is considered to reflect discrimination. The validity of the estimates of discrimination depends on the inclusion of all relevant variables in the analysis.

The figure for returns on labor market characteristics has a negative sign indicating a greater impact of labor market characteristics on income returns in the Arab population than among Jews. This finding lends further support for our initial proposition according to which the economic outcomes of Arabs would be more sensitive to the characteristics of labor markets than those of Jews as a result of economic discrimination against individual workers. The opposite signs of the individual-level and the labor market effects further indicate that had the strong impact of labor market characteristics on the earnings of Arabs been ignored, the estimate of discrimination in earnings associated with individual-level attributes would have been considerably higher. These findings, then, affirm the proposition that Jews and Arabs are affected differently by the structure of the labor market and that the earnings of Arabs are particularly sensitive to variations in the labor market structure.

Inequality Inside and Outside the Arab Labor Market

The findings observed in preceding pages clearly demonstrate that spatial segregation is an effective mechanism through which Arabs in Israel are denied access to opportunities and rewards, and thus, serves as one of the major determinants of ethnic inequality in Israel. In a relatively free economy an individual can generally avoid the detrimental consequences of a low opportunity environment by changing place of residence and/or place of work. In fact, as described earlier, Arabs in Israel are most unlikely to change place of residence, especially to Jewish communities, and are more likely to commute to work. This apparent integration into the "majority" labor market is quite costly for members of the Arab minority. Aside from the fact that commuting itself is time consuming and entails additional expenses, Arabs are often at a disadvantage when seeking a job from Jewish employers. They tend to be relegated to the end of the job queue and are viewed primarily as a source of cheap unskilled and semi-skilled labor. While the mechanisms salient to this process will be discussed in greater detail toward the end of this chapter, the disadvantage inherent in the economic integration process will be elaborated in the following pages.

A large number of studies (mostly in the United States) have repeatedly demonstrated that the socioeconomic disadvantages (mostly occupational) of minorities tend to rise as their relative size in the community population increases (e.g., Fossett 1984; Semyonov, Hoyt, and Scott 1984; Frisbie and Neidert 1977; Glenn 1964, 1966; LaGory and Magnani 1979; Martin and Poston 1972; Wilcox and Roof 1978; Tienda and Lii 1987). Two complementary arguments have been advanced to explain the relationship between the increase in minority population and growth in social and economic differentials. The first suggests that an increase in the relative size of a minority population poses a threat to superordinates who fear greater job competition (e.g., Williams 1947; Allport 1954; Blalock 1967; Bonacich 1972, 1976). In order to become competitors, the two groups must experience some degree of integration; they must work, or have the potential to work, in the same labor market. According to this view, antagonism, hostility, and motivation to discriminate grow as the proportion of a subordinate population in the community rises.

A second argument contends that an influx of members from a subordinate population into the labor market increases the supply of cheap labor which serves as a target for economic exploitation. Since occupational labor markets are often split along ethnic (or racial) lines, the growing availability of minority members increases the potential pool of candidates to fill the least desirable, low paying jobs (e.g., Glenn 1964; Spilerman and Miller 1977; Semyonov et al. 1984). Concomitantly, members of the superordinate group abandon the low status jobs and "flow" to more prestigious and lucrative occupations. Consequently, occupational and economic differentiation between minority and majority members tends to widen as the proportion of the former in the population increases (e.g., Glenn 1964; Spilerman and Miller 1977; Semyonov et al. 1984). Furthermore, as the relative size of a minority population within a local labor market increases, so does the probability that any two randomly selected workers from that labor market will be of different ethnicity; hence, the opportunity to discriminate also increases. In light of these arguments, it may be suggested that as integration into a bi-ethnic labor market increases, so do the relative disadvantages of a minority population.

The concept "integration" (or "segregation") used here, differs from that implied by conventional concepts of integration as measured by indices of residential segregation within a city. While the latter type of integration reflects the diminishing socioeconomic disadvantages of minorities, integration, as employed here, simply indicates a relatively high probability that two randomly selected persons in the same local labor market will be of different ethnic groups (cf. Semyonov and Tyree 1981). Since this phrase is too cumbersome for repeated use, the term "integration" (or "segregation") will be used instead, but its operational meaning should be kept in mind.

The logic of the framework developed here suggests that, while segregation in separate ethnic-based communities excludes minorities from equal access to opportunities and rewards, it may also provide them with tentative protection from discrimination generated by competition. That is, work in the ethnic labor market may free subordinate members from direct competition with superordinates. As a result, minorities can enjoy job opportunities that otherwise would be denied to them and taken by superordinates (Frazier 1951; Semyonov and Tyree 1981; Lewin-Epstein 1986).

In other words, when a subordinate population reaches a critical mass and is large enough to develop independent mono-ethnic, labor markets, it may be able to mobilize resources and place incumbents in positions usually held by members of the majority population (Frazier 1951; Fischer 1975; Semyonov and Tyree 1981; Lewin-Epstein 1986). This idea has been advocated in the literature on ethnicity in general, and ethnic enclaves in particular (e.g. Light 1972; Portes and Jensen; 1989; Wilson and Portes, 1980) and was clearly articulated by Lieberson (1980, pp. 297–298).

> Among other factors, as a group gets larger it is likely to develop certain internal strengths that will support some occupational activities even if outsiders are totally against their holding the position. Hence, if the black population base is large enough, there will be support for black doctors, black clergy and so on, even if they remain totally unacceptable to others. Likewise, there will develop certain entrepreneurial possibilities and other employment shifts will occur.

The argument does not imply that subordinates actually benefit from segregation, or that minority workers reap absolute occupational advantages in an ethnic labor market. They do not. Segregation is a structural device through which minorities are excluded from opportunities and rewards. The relative cost of discrimination, however, is expected to be greater in bi-ethnic than in mono-ethnic labor markets. The degree of disadvantage that can be forced by a superordinate group on a minority group is a function of the degree of competition between the groups. Integration, to the extent of living and working in the same local labor market, is a conducive, if not necessary, condition to assure such competition. In this respect it is meaningful to distinguish three types of Arab populations in the Israeli labor force: those who live and work in Arab communities (hereafter "segregated"), those who live in Arab localities but work in Jewish localities (hereafter "commuters"), and those who live and work in Jewish or mixed localities (hereafter "resident workers").

Following the logic outlined above, we would expect that Arabs living or working in Jewish communities (bi-ethnic labor markets) will suffer the detrimental consequences of socioeconomic discrimination more than Arabs living and working in Arab localities (segregated labor markets). More specifically, we suggest that resident workers will be most disadvantaged; that segregated workers, who are free of direct competition with Jewish workers, will be least disadvantaged, if not relatively advantaged; and that the commuters will fall between these two groups.

The characteristics of the three subpopulations and of the Jewish population, based on the 1983 data, are compared in Table 4.2. These include the mean socioeconomic, demographic, and residential characteristics. The data demonstrate that considerable differences exist among the groups with regard to most aspects relevant to the labor market. On the whole, Jews are more likely than Arabs to reside in large urban centers where occupational opportunities are abundant and less likely to dwell in rural and small localities where opportunities are generally more scarce. As might be expected,

TABLE 4.2: Characteristics: Means (Standard Deviations) and Category Percentages of Jews
            and Arab Population Groups of Israeli Labor Force Population, Age 25-64, 1983

Variables	Jews Total (1)	Arabs Total (3+4+5)	Segregated (3)	Commuters (4)	Residents (5)
Monthly income	33,760.73 (34,835.56)	21,117.73 (15,083.40)	22,603.71 (14,871.16)	21,065.29 (13,815.33)	19,362.58 (16,198.36)
Occupational status	46.16 (19.08)	38.45 (19.01)	42.92 (21.35)	32.22 (14.85)	37.72 (18.77)
Years of schooling	12.0 (3.5)	9.9 (3.5)	10.3 (3.9)	8.7 (3.1)	10.0 (4.2)
Years of age	40.6 (11.17)	37.3 (9.7)	36.8 (9.5)	36.2 (9.4)	38.8 (10.2)
Hours of work per week	42.0 (14.2)	42.4 (12.4)	40.0 (13.5)	45.2 (10.3)	43.3 (12.5)
Percent in Major Occupational Categories					
Professional managers	32.0	22.1	32.0	9.0	20.0
Clerical and sales	27.0	16.2	17.0	10.0	20.0
Manual and service	41.0	61.7	51.0	81.0	60.0
Percent Women in Labor Force	40.0	17.06	20.0	7.00	21.00
Percent in Locality of Residence by Size					
Less than 10,000	14.0	40.8	60.0	62.0	2.0
10,000-20,000	7.0	14.6	20.0	23.0	2.0
20,000-50,000	18.0	16.5	20.0	14.0	14.0
50,,000-100,000	10.0	0.3	--	--	1.0
100,000 and over	51.0	27.5	--	--	81.0
Population N	211,417	12,727	5207	3,206	4,314

small communities of residence are especially characteristic of commuters, who are heavily drawn from small places in search of employment opportunities. By contrast, residents—Arabs who reside in "mixed" communities—more than any other group of workers, tend to concentrate in large urban centers.

The differences between Jews and Arabs are also evident with regard to socioeconomic characteristics. While Arabs, on the whole, are characterized by lower socioeconomic status than Jews, it is also evident that the Arab population cannot be treated as homogeneous and that there are considerable differences among the three Arab subgroups. The commuters are the least educated group with an average of 8.7 years of schooling, as compared with 10 years, or more, for other Arabs. It would appear that they do not have the human capital to compete with other Arabs for jobs in the Arab sector, and are forced to search for jobs in the Jewish-dominated economy. Consequently, they must settle for the low status, least desirable occupations relinquished by Jews. The income of commuters, nonetheless, is relatively high. Possibly commuting is an exchange of occupational status for higher income. Segregated workers and residents are characterized by higher levels of education relative to commuters. The former, free from direct competition with Jews, are able to attain higher occupational status as well as higher incomes (which is still only two-thirds of the mean earnings for Jews).

Especially illuminating are the findings regarding the occupational structure of the various Arab populations. Both mean occupational status and standard deviation for segregated workers are considerably higher than for either commuters or residents. Recall that the "segregated" workers are those employed in the Arab economy which, as we have seen, was able to produce a similar proportion of professionals and administrative workers within the Arabs labor markets (32 percent) to that in the larger economy. Commuters, however, supply mainly manual and service workers for the Jewish labor markets. Resident workers, despite their high educational level, are somewhat underrepresented among all white-collar (professionals and administrators, as well as clerks and sales) occupations, and somewhat over-represented among manual and service workers.

The figures in Table 4.2 seem to be in line with the theoretical expectations outlined earlier. Segregated workers, though inferior in status to Jews, are superior in status to the two other Arab populations and appear to be some-what protected from economic discrimination. By contrast, residents are the most disadvantaged group. Their occupational status is relatively low in comparison to their education, and their income is relatively low in com-parison to the occupations they hold. The commuters lie somewhere in between these two extremes. It is quite possible that prior selectivity pro-duces somewhat different relations between human resources (e.g., educa-tion) and socioeconomic status (e.g., occupation, income) among commuters. The commuters tend to reside in smaller places where opportunities are scarce. Furthermore, their lower education and lower age hinder their ability to compete successfully, not only with Jews but also with other Arabs. Thus, they are compelled to take manual and service jobs available in Jewish com-munities and trade-off occupational status for income.

Socioeconomic Attainment Across Labor Markets

Although revealing, the differences just observed do not inform us about the relative impact of labor market segregation on socioeconomic inequalities among the various groups. Nor do the descriptive data in Table 4.2 provide a clear indication as to whether the process of status attainment varies for Arabs employed in the different local labor markets. To address this issue we turn once again to a comprehensive multi-variate analysis of the determi-nants of socioeconomic attainment in each of the population groups defined earlier. For each population group—Jews, segregated workers, resident workers, and commuters—we estimated two ordinary least squared regres-sion equations. The results of this analysis are presented in Table 4.3. In equa-tion 1, occupational status is predicted as a function of education, age, and gender. In equation 2, monthly income is taken as a function of age, educa-tion, occupational status, hours of work, and gender.

The regression coefficients in Table 4.3 represent the direct net effect of each independent variable included in the equation on occupational status (equation 1) or on income (equation 2). In the equations for occupational status, each coefficient indicates the extent of change in occupational status due to a unit change in a given independent variable. Since income was trans-formed to the logarithmic scale, the regression coefficients represent the

TABLE 4.3: Regression Equations Predicting Occupational Status* (Eq.1) and Log. Income[b] (Eq.2) for Jewish and Arab Population Groups of the Israeli Labor Force, Age 25-64, 1983

Independent Variables	Jews Occup. Status Equation 1 — 1	Jews Occup. Status Equation 1 — 1[d]	Jews Log. Income Equation 2 — 2	Jews Log. Income Equation 2 — 2[d]	Segregated Occup. Status Equation 1 — 1	Segregated Occup. Status Equation 1 — 1[d]	Segregated Log. Income Equation 2 — 2	Segregated Log. Income Equation 2 — 2[d]	Arabs Commuters Occup. Status Equation 1 — 1	Arabs Commuters Occup. Status Equation 1 — 1[d]	Arabs Commuters Log. Income Equation 2 — 2	Arabs Commuters Log. Income Equation 2 — 2[d]	Residents Occup. Status Equation 1 — 1	Residents Occup. Status Equation 1 — 1[d]	Residents Log. Income Equation 2 — 2	Residents Log. Income Equation 2 — 2[d]
Gender[c] b	-3.632	-3.616	-.379	-.379	4.037	4.036	-.357	-.358	-1.238	-1.237	-.402	-.402	.582	.610	-.245	-.319
s.e.	(.072)	(.072)	(.004)	(.004)	(.558)	(.558)	(.023)	(.023)	(.875)	(.875)	(.039)	(.039)	(.591)	(.599)	(.028)	(.027)
Years of age b	.079	.068	.005	.005	.201	.197	.012	.012	.117	.115	.002	.002	.078	.072	.002	.002
s.e.	(.003)	(.003)	(.0001)	(.0004)	(.025)	(.025)	(.0009)	(.0009)	(.025)	(.025)	(.001)	(.001)	(.023)	(.023)	(.001)	(.001)
Years of schooling b	3.590	3.516	.031	.032	3.989	3.985	.042	.042	2.846	2.845	.014	.014	2.921	2.912	.037	.003
s.e.	(.010)	(.010)	(.0006)	(.0006)	(.059)	(.059)	(.003)	(.003)	(.070)	(.070)	(.004)	(.004)	(.059)	(.059)	(.003)	(.003)
Hours of work per week b	--	--	.016	.016	--	--	.005	.005	--	--	.008	.008	--	--	.009	.009
s.e.	--	--	(.0001)	(.0001)	--	--	(.0007)	(.0007)	--	--	(.0009)	(.0009)	--	--	(.0008)	(.0008)
Occupational status b	--	--	.013	.013	--	--	.011	.011	--	--	.010	.010	--	--	.008	.009
s.e.	--	--	(.0001)	(.0001)	--	--	(.0006)	(.0006)	--	--	(.0008)	(.0008)	--	--	(.0007)	(.0007)
Constant	4.990	1.988	8.833	8.792	-10.386	-10.752	8.742	8.743	4.538	4.684	9.335	9.344	4.762	3.963	8.782	9.276
R²	.41	.42	.38	.38	.52	.52	.32	.32	.39	.39	.17	.17	.41	.41	.29	.25

a Occupational status measured on Tyree's (1981) 100-point scale of socioeconomic status of occupation in Israel.
b Income (converted in logarithmic scale) is gross monthly income in Israeli shekels.
c Men coded 1; Women 2.
d In equations 1[d] and 2[d], a set of dummy variables representing seven categories of community size was added to control for market conditions that may be associated with size of locality.

percentage change. We saw earlier that the population groups tend to be unequally distributed across communities of different sizes. This in turn may affect the opportunities available to each group. Therefore, we also examined models which control for community size (see note d in Table 4.3). The results of the analysis, however, are virtually identical whether or not size of community of residence was included in the regression equation.

Regardless of the population group considered, the most significant predictor of occupational status in equation 1 is education. More years of schooling tend to improve occupational status. The status return on education is highest for segregated workers and Jews, where every year of schooling adds an average of 3.6 status points among Jews and 4 status points among segregated Arabs. Education is beneficial in terms of occupational status among commuters and residents as well, but in these populations every year of schooling adds somewhat less than 3 status points. Age, in equation 1, has a positive impact on occupational status in all groups and its effect is strongest among segregated Arabs. Gender, however, operates differently in the various groups. The negative sign of the coefficient in the equation for Jews indicates that Jewish women are disadvantaged in the attainment of occupational status compared to Jewish men. Conversely, the positive coefficient for gender among segregated Arabs (b = 4.037) means that segregated women are advantaged over men with similar attributes in the attainment of occupational status within the Arab economy. Gender differences in the attainment of occupational status among commuters and residents are negligible and statistically insignificant. This issue, which is of considerable interest, will be examined in detail in Chapter 5.

Equation 2 reveals similar patterns in the determination of income among all population groups, regardless of the locus of the labor market. Education, occupational status, age, and hours of work all exert positive effects on income. That is, income is likely to increase with rising levels of these four independent variables. In contrast to the findings of gender effects on occupational status in favor of women among segregated Arabs, the findings for the effect of gender on earnings are consistent across all groups. Being female, whether Jewish or Arab, in the Arab economy or commuting, entails substantially lower earnings than men and the disparity is proportionately similar in all groups (see the sign and magnitudes of the gender coefficients). Before concluding this section, it is interesting to note that the impact of education on income is especially low for commuters and indeed, more generally, the model for this group exhibits the poorest fit. Our interpretation of these finding is that education, as well as other human resources, are less relevant for the earnings of commuters. Later in this chapter we will elaborate on this point and go into detail of the labor market mechanisms which make the commuters most vulnerable to discrimination.

Decomposing Mean Differentials

The findings reported thus far provide indirect support for the argument that a bi-ethnic labor market subjects the minority population to greater disadvantages, while the segregated labor market mitigates discrimination generated by competition. This thesis, however, needs further examination. The extent to which the various groups of Arab workers (e.g., segregated, commuters, and residents) gain or lose socioeconomic status due to human capital, ethnic membership, or the local labor market must be established. For example, it is not clear to what extent the lower income of resident workers is a function of discrimination in the bi-ethnic labor market in which they operate, or their inferior education, or lower age. Decomposing mean socioeconomic differences, first, between each group of Arabs and the Jewish population, and second, between the Arab groups, can provide appropriate estimates of the extent to which labor markets are socioeconomically beneficial or detrimental to the minority population. The decomposition procedure, the logic of which was described earlier and outlined in detail in Appendix 4.A, will also generate estimates of the sources of socioeconomic inequality across labor markets.

Table 4.4 presents the results of the application of the decomposition procedure (described in detail in Appendix 4.B) to all the pairs of equation 1 reported in Table 4.3. The first three columns pertain to the occupational gap between Jews and each Arab population. The last two columns pertain to the occupational differences between segregated workers and commuters, and segregated workers and residents, respectively. The decomposition procedure identifies three components. The first component is the portion of the gap due to differential returns of the two groups on their human resources, and therefore can be viewed as the gap resulting from market discrimination. The second component reflects the portion of the gap due to different levels of resources possessed by the two groups. The third component is the interaction between resources and returns in each group. The data lend firm support to the argument that Arabs living and working in Jewish localities (bi-ethnic labor markets) suffer the detrimental consequences of occupational discrimination more than Arabs working in Arab localities (mono-ethnic labor markets).

TABLE 4.4: Components of Occupational Status Differentials Between Pairs of Groups, Israeli Labor Force, Age 25-64, 1983

| | Paired Comparisons | | | | |
	(1) Jews vs. Residents	(2) Jews vs. Commuters	(3) Jews vs. Segregated	(4) Segregated vs. Commuters	(5) Segregated vs. Residents
Observed Gap	8.439	13.941	3.240	10.702	5.199
(percent)	100.0	100.00	100.00	100.00	100.00
Market Discrimination	1.884	2.988	-2.402	3.710	4.508
(percent)	22.0	21.00	-74.0	34.7	86.7
Composition Resources	6.030	9.462	8.330	4.451	.675
(percent)	71.0	68.0	257.0	41.6	13.0
Interaction	.525	1.491	-2.688	2.541	.016
(percent)	7.0	11.0	-83.0	23.7	0.3

A considerable portion of the occupational gap between Jews and either commuters or residents (about 70 percent) can be attributed to the composition of resources in the different groups and, more specifically, to the lower level of education and lower age of the Arab population. About 20 percent of the overall gap, according to the model, resulted from different returns on the resources in each of the groups, or what is usually labeled as labor market discrimination. The findings, however, are quite different when segregated Arab workers are contrasted with Jewish workers. While the magnitude of the composition effect is more than twice the size of the overall status gap (257 percent) in favor of Jews, the market discrimination effect appears with a negative sign (−74.0 percent). The findings should be interpreted to mean that based on the lower education and comparative youth of the segregated group, the gap between Jews and segregated workers should have been five points larger than the observed gap. That is, the occupational status of segregated Arabs employed in the Arab economy is actually higher than one would expect on the basis of their human resources. The negative sign of the discrimination component clearly indicates that Arabs are "overpaid" in the local labor market in terms of occupational status. Furthermore, the negative interaction component also indicates that the combination of resources and returns on human resources is advantageous for Arabs in their own ethnic labor market. In sum, occupational attainment of Arabs is enhanced in the Arab economy and hindered in the bi-ethnic labor market.

The results presented in columns 4 and 5 of Table 4.4 provide further evidence and reaffirm the argument that employment in a bi-ethnic labor market has detrimental consequences for the occupational status of the minority Arab population. While over 40 percent of the occupational advantage of segregated workers over commuters is attributable to their superior human resources, most of their occupational advantages over residents is attributable to labor market mechanisms. We interpret these differences to reflect market discrimination faced by the resident group in the bi-ethnic labor market.

We now turn to the examination of differential earning patterns among the groups. Table 4.5 contains results obtained by applying the decomposition procedure to all pairs of equation 2 in Table 4.3. Columns 1, 2, and 3 reveal that only a small portion of the income disparity between Jews and Arabs is attributable to human resources. This ranges from 13 percent in the case of commuters to 30 percent for the segregated Arabs. Even when considering the lower occupational status, lower educational levels, and lower age of Arabs, a considerable portion of the income gap remains attributable to ethnicity and differential returns on human resources (market discrimination). Consequently, the discrimination components account for 82, 77, and 61 percent of the income gaps between Jews and residents, segregated workers and commuters, respectively. Had Arabs' earnings been determined similarly to Jews with similar resources, their earnings would have been considerably higher.

Columns 4 and 5 of Table 4.5 present the results obtained from decomposing mean differences between earnings of segregated workers and

TABLE 4.5:   Components of Income Differentials Between Pairs of Groups, Israeli Labor Force Population, Age 25-64, 1983.

| | Paired Comparisons | | | | |
	(1) Jews vs. Residents	(2) Jews vs. Commuters	(3) Jews vs. Segregated	(4) Segregated vs. Commuters	(5) Segregated vs. Residents
Observed Gap	.487	.332	.296	.035	.191
(percent)	100.0	100.0	100.0	100.0	100.0
Market Discrimination	.400	.203	.228	-.084	.159
(percent)	82.0	61.0	77.0	-240.0	83.0
Composition Resources	.091	.043	.089	.042	.024
(percent)	19.0	13.0	30.0	120.0	13.0
Interaction	-.004	.085	-.021	.077	.008
(percent)	-1.0	26.0	-7.0	220.0	4.0

commuters, and segregated workers and residents, respectively. These results further demonstrate the differential effect of local labor market segregation on the attainment of income. Only 13 percent of the income gap between segregated workers and residents is due to differences in human resources and occupational status. That is, by and large, these two groups display similar market-relevant attributes. The remaining 83 percent of the gap can be regarded as resulting from labor market discrimination. Commuters, by contrast, are overpaid compared to segregated workers. Given their low occupational status, low education, and lower age, commuters' incomes are higher than what they could possibly earn in their local labor markets. This relative advantage is reflected by the negative discrimination component in the Table. Recalling the findings reported in Table 4.4 we may conclude that upon joining the bi-ethnic labor market, commuters trade-off occupational status for higher income; though they surrender occupational status, they compensate for this loss by earning the relatively higher incomes available in Jewish communities.

Discrimination Against Arabs in the Labor Market

The main purpose of this chapter was to examine the role of local labor markets in generating ethnic inequality. The analysis focused attention on the way in which individual-level and ecological attributes jointly determine the income of Jews and Arabs in Israel. Our theoretical exposition suggested that residential segregation has a twofold effect on ethnic inequality. First, spatial segregation implies differential access to opportunities and rewards. Consequently, part of the income gap between ethnic groups is attributable to the inferior opportunity structure faced by the Arab minority. Second, the rules by which income is determined differ by ethnicity, and interact with labor market characteristics. Indeed, decomposition of the difference in mean earnings of Jews and Arabs revealed that a substantial portion of the income gap is attributable to differences in labor market characteristics. Differences in the local opportunity structure accounted for roughly the same portion of the income gap as differences in individual-level attributes. The decomposition further demonstrated that the earnings of Arabs (as compared to those of Jews) are more dependent on the characteristics of the local labor market and less on resources of individuals.

The findings revealed by the analysis are largely in line with the theoretical propositions. Clearly, Arabs and Jews face different opportunity structures. Arabs live in smaller communities where job opportunities are scarce and the industrial base limited. Consequently many Arabs are compelled to work outside their place of residence.

Commuting into the larger labor markets dominated by the majority Jewish population leads to ethnic competition over a relatively fixed pool of jobs. Indeed, we have proposed that the extent of the disadvantages forced on a subordinate group by a superordinate group is dependent in large measure on competition between the groups. Following this logic, it was suggested that bi-ethnic labor markets promote economic discrimination against Arabs in Israel while the mono-ethnic labor market provides them with a measure of protection. In the absence of competition in the mono-ethnic labor market, segregated workers are able to attain occupational positions usually held by Jews. Furthermore, in comparison to Jews, they are able to achieve high status positions with relatively lower education. As noted in Chapter 3, Arab communities are characterized by a high proportion of public sector jobs. Many of these jobs are white-collar professional and semi-professional positions. Consequently, in the segregated labor markets, the Arab population can supply workers not only for low status, low pay unskilled and semi-skilled jobs, but can also produce lawyers, doctors, nurses, teachers, administrators, clerks and mayors.

The analyses presented in this chapter consistently reveal substantial inequality in occupational status and earnings between Jews and Arabs, especially in the case of Arabs who work outside the segregated Arab economy. Since the disparities clearly can not be "explained away" as resulting from systematic differences in personal attributes relevant to labor market processes, we interpret the disparity as reflecting labor market discrimination against the Arab minority. Two issues can be raised with regard to the conclusions derived from the analysis. First, given the macro nature of our analysis and the fact that we did not actually observe discriminatory action carried out by specific employers, could the observed earnings gap reflect legitimate differences not accounted for in the model used? Second, if, as we have argued, discrimination does exist, what are the institutional mechanisms that accommodate such discrimination in face of the basic tenet of Israel's Declaration of Independence that the State will maintain total equality of political and social rights of all its citizens, irrespective of race, religion or sex?

In addressing the issue of discrimination two facets must be distinguished: (a) wage discrimination among those working in similar jobs; and (b) job discrimination where access to jobs is refused to members of a particular group while generally available to others with similar skills and other work-related attributes. Regarding wage discrimination, our analysis revealed earning disparities even when controlling for the socioeconomic status of jobs. It may be argued that status ranking of occupations does not fully capture the variability in jobs and that some of the Jewish-Arab differences in earnings may be explained by job segregation. While this might be true, it is unreasonable to expect that more precise specification would eradicate the entire earnings gap. Indeed, the scant research carried out at the micro level clearly corroborates our findings. In a study of blue-collar workers undertaken by the Institute for Economic and Social Research (Hendeles and Grippel 1988), it was reported that even when Jews and Arabs were employed in blue-collar jobs in the same firms in the food, textile, and hotel industries, Arab men earned 80 percent of what Jewish men earned, and Arab women earned 77 percent of the mean earnings of Jewish women (which, in turn, was only 69 percent of the earnings of Jewish men). Such blatant discrimination appears to be widespread and yet has received surprisingly little public and judicial attention.

In actual fact, Israel has an equal pay law. However, the name of the law—"Male and Female Workers Law, 1964"—discloses its orientation. It specifically states that "An employer shall pay to a female worker a wage equal to the wage paid to a male worker at that place of employment for the same, or substantially the same, work." No mention is made here of such bases of discrimination as religious affiliation, nationality or ethnicity. The only specific reference to these attributes with respect to employment is in a ruling of the National Labor Court which stated that collective agreements which discriminate between employees on the grounds of race, national origins, religion or sex are invalid. Nonetheless, as we have seen, wage disparities between Arabs and Jews are prevalent and this would appear to directly conflict with the notion of economic equality. Yet we have found no legal challenges of employers' policies and no attempts by the courts to define discriminatory behavior with respect to wages.

The concentration of Arab employees—in particular commuters and residents of Jewish-dominated communities—in low status occupations obviates the issues of job discrimination and the segregation of Arab and Jewish workers in different occupational markets. Once again a key factor here consists of employer hiring decisions and the legal framework which sets the ground rules. The only statutory mechanism in this area is the Employment Service Law of 1959 (see Ben-Israel 1989). The government employment service and its labor exchanges constitute a centralized mechanism of locating skilled and unskilled labor upon the request of employers for manpower. The majority of firms in Israel (the figure varies by industry and size) rely on this service when recruiting workers. Article 42 of the law states: (a) "In sending to work, the employment service bureau shall not discriminate against a person on account of his age, sex, religion, ethnic group, country of origin, views or party affiliation, and a person requiring an employee shall not refuse to engage a person for work on account of any of these whether or not that person has been sent to work by the employment service."

As recently as 1986 the prohibition of discrimination in hiring pertained to workers referred by the Employment Service Bureau. Only in 1987 was the law amended to prohibit discrimination in hiring regardless of whether the worker was referred by the Employment Service or otherwise. Article 42, however adds that (b) "It shall not be considered discrimination if the character or nature of the task or consideration of State security prevent a person being sent to, or engage in, some particular work." As we shall discuss shortly, this latter provision has been interpreted very broadly by employers and used as an excuse for not employing Arab workers even when the nature of the product and the location of the facilities rendered security considerations remote.

Before turning to employer practices, two additional points concerning the socio-legal framework are noteworthy. While the Employment Service Law clearly and directly prohibits discrimination on the basis of religion and nationality (as well as other characteristics) the Employment Service Bureaus operate under the principle of local preference. That is, residents of the locality served by the bureau are given preference in the queue when filling employer requests, and only if local workers with the desired skills cannot be found is the request for employees forwarded to other bureaus. In principle, at least, an employee can only register in the bureau serving his place of residence. This procedure is of great relevance in view of the fact that Jews and Arabs are highly segregated residentially. More importantly, we have seen that opportunities in the Arab economy are relatively scarce and many Arab workers must seek jobs in Jewish-dominated labor markets. Under these circumstances, the local preference requirement places them at a considerable disadvantage. Indeed, as we have seen, Arab commuters are more concentrated than any other Arab population of employees in the least desirable jobs.

The second point to note is that although the Employment Service Law appears to directly and comprehensively address the issue of job discrimination, it was apparently considered not sufficiently strong, and, in 1988, the Employment (Equal Opportunity) Law was passed. This law states that "An employer shall not discriminate between his employees, or between persons seeking employment, on account of their sex or their being married or parents . . .". No mention is made here of religion, nationality, or ethnicity and once again it appears that the disadvantaged position of the Arabs (as well as other religious and ethnic minorities) in the Israeli labor market is largely ignored by the legislators.

As a final point of discussion in this chapter we would like to link our findings at the macro-level with more detailed information at the micro-level reported in a study by Wolkinson (1989). Wolkinson provides the first, and to our knowledge the only, attempt to systematically study job discrimination against Arabs at places of work. The study is based on data from 48 manufacturing facilities in four cities located in proximity to Arab populations: Haifa, Petah Tikva, Netanya, and Hadera. Forty five of the 48 plants employed over 100 workers. Only 26 of the 48 plants employed Israeli Arabs. Except for one instance Arabs were virtually absent from all managerial positions and only in 6 plants did Arab employees hold professional or technical jobs. Arabs, however, were clearly central to the production process of these plants, in one-fifth of which they constituted about half the production labor force. From the research findings it was strikingly evident that the overwhelming majority of Arabs were employed as skilled craftsmen or unskilled operatives and laborers. The explanation given by officials of the firms for this concentration typically invoked the lower educational levels of Arabs. In most cases professional and managerial positions require post-secondary education where Arabs fall far behind Jews. This, however, does not explain the absence of Arabs from office-clerical positions. Furthermore, the great difficulty faced by many educated Arabs in finding jobs cannot be reconciled with the explanation given by company personnel focusing on the low education levels among Arabs. Indeed, the author reports that personnel managers in 12 of the 26 firms that employed Arabs expressed their reluctance to employ Arab employees in professional and managerial jobs.

In many cases, according to Wolkinson, personnel officers reported that Arabs were hired only after the firm was unable to recruit Jewish workers. This pattern reflects personal preferences of managers and (largely Jewish) worker councils in their demand that only Jewish workers be hired. Indeed, the principle of local preferences is used by employers to exclude Arabs and maintain a principle of "Jewish work". The few cases where personnel managers resisted attempts by the local labor council to give Jews preference over Arabs, regardless of qualifications, is more the exception than the rule. The preference for Jewish workers expressed by managers represents a widespread attitude in the Jewish population. Data from the mid-1980s (Lewin-Epstein 1989) indicate that two-thirds of the Jewish public supported the view that Jewish employers should give preference to Jewish workers over Arab workers. Concomitant with this position, over half the respondents expressed the view that Arab workers occupy jobs that would otherwise be available to Jews.

It is particularly noteworthy that 22 of the firms surveyed by Wolkinson (almost half) employed no Arabs at all. When this absence of Arabs was questioned, the most common explanation given by personnel managers was security considerations. Although some plants did indeed produce for the military, in other cases the policy was legitimated by arguing that they were located in physical proximity to sensitive industrial facilities (in at least one case the "sensitive industrial facility" itself employed Arab workers). In fact, when employers seek to discourage Arabs from applying for jobs, they invariably use service in the military as a screening device. Since the overwhelming majority of Jews serve in the military and non-Jews rarely do, this requirement effectively excludes Arabs from employment opportunities. It is obviously difficult to ascertain the degree of security risk of employing Arab workers, but it appears that the security rationale is excessively applied. Here again, to our knowledge, there has been no consorted attempt to legally challenge these practices and to force a decision as to what constitutes discrimination.

It should be noted that the Druze who do serve in the military were absent from many of the plants even in the region where they are concentrated, and when employed they still did not reach white-collar or managerial positions.

In light of these findings it is interesting to note the current request by many Christian Arab youths to join the Israeli military even though they have traditionally been exempted. The most common reason for this change, in the words of one youth interviewed in a daily newspaper, is that after completing military service ". . . I may work wherever I please. They will not be able to turn me down on the grounds that I did not serve. I want to fulfill all my [civil] obligations and hope to receive the full benefits" (*Hadashot*, August 4, 1991).

This youth appears to have a determined and rather optimistic view of what are quite complex ethnic-related labor market processes. It is our view that since ethnic competition is a central underlying feature of Jewish-Arab relations in Israel, labor market discrimination is likely to persist. In this respect the emphasis on military service as a requirement from job seekers is largely a pretext, albeit a symbolic one. In its absence, other mechanisms which maintain the dominance of the Jewish majority, are likely to emerge. In fact, representatives of the Druze population repeatedly lament that despite their military service, Druze continue to be discriminated against and they face severe difficulty in the labor market.

Concluding Remarks

In the first part of this chapter we pointed out that the lack of employment opportunities in the Arab sector generated large-scale commuting of Arab workers to Jewish-dominated labor markets. Consequently, the dependence of Arab individuals on the Jewish economy has risen. Our analysis of Census data revealed that Arabs employed outside the Arab sector acquire lower socioeconomic status than Arabs employed in Arab communities. We argued that the observed socioeconomic gap largely represents employer discrimination against Arab workers. This interpretation received substantive support in the latter section of the chapter in which we described processes at the micro-level. Quite clearly what we observed is the presence of two distinct ethnic groups competing for social and economic rewards, albeit with unequal resources. This competition is conducive to the emergence of labor market discrimination. Indeed, the illustrations provided above indicate that Arabs are systematically excluded from many firms, and especially from advantageous positions involving greater degrees of autonomy and authority.

Notes

1. One way of conceptualizing the model used in the present analysis is to view it as ". . . an additive specification that allows for variability in the effect of X_1 [a given individual-level variable] but specifies that the variability is unsystematic—sweeping it into an error component. This is attractive when the variability of $ß_1$ [context specific individual-level coefficient] is not of interest to the investigator" (Mason et al. 1983). Although we could not test these assumptions in the present analysis, the formulation used seems appropriate in view of the fact that we are primarily interested in the effect of community-level variables and their contribution to outcomes, over and above

individual-level variables (rather than their effect on the relationship between individual-level variables and the outcomes).

2. *Income* is measured as the natural logarithm of the gross monthly earnings from employment (in Israeli Shekels). *Age* is measured in years, at last birthday. *Education* is defined as the number of years of formal schooling. *Gender* is coded 1 in the case of men, and 0 for women. *Hours of Work* are measured as the usual number of hours worked per week. *Marital Status* is coded 1 for presently married and 0 otherwise. *Occupational Status* is based on the Socio-Economic Index (SEI) of occupations in Israel given at the three-digit classification level (Tyree 1981). The scale ranges from 0 (low status) to 100 (high status).

3. Population size of the communities studied ranges from small urban locations of approximately 5,000 residents to major cities, each with over 250,000 inhabitants. Our measure of *community size* is the natural logarithm transformation of the total population in each community. *Job availability* is measured by the ratio of the population of working age residing in the community to the total number of jobs in the local labor market. Industrial structure of the local labor market is represented by a set of variables indicating the proportion of jobs in the labor market in each of 8 different economic sectors: *agriculture, forestry and fishing, labor-intensive manufacturing, capital intensive manufacturing, construction, commerce, transport, communication and utilities, finance and business services, public and community services,* and *personal services*. In addition, a measure of *job diversity* was constructed for each community in order to capture the variety of opportunity faced by workers in a particular labor market. *Percent Arab* in the labor market was included to represent the population composition. Finally, a dichotomous variable, *commute,* was introduced to distinguish individuals employed in their community of residence (coded 0) from those employed elsewhere (coded 1).

Appendix 4.A

Several alternative procedures for decomposing mean differences have been reported in the literature (e.g. Duncan 1968; Iams and Thornton 1975; Jones and Kelley 1984). These models typically consider the differences in mean scores (as in the case of income) as deriving from three primary sources: (1) group membership and the distinct rewarding mechanisms that operate in each group, (2) unequal endowments and resources at the disposal of the two groups; and (3) an interaction component representing the joint variation in resources and returns. The latter component represents the difference between valuing the endowments disparity at the lower earning group's rate of return rather than that of the higher earning group.

The model adopted here follows the procedure recommended by Iams and Thornton (1975). This procedure takes advantage of the fact that separate regression analysis was performed for Arabs and Jews and that consequently two sets of coefficients and two sets of mean attributes were obtained. The regression equations can be used to predict the expected income. If we now use the set of coefficients estimated for Arabs to predict the income of both Arabs and Jews, based on each group's mean attributes, we obtain an estimate of the difference in earnings due solely to the difference in attributes. In similar fashion, an estimate of the difference in rewarding mechanisms between Jews and Arabs can be calculated when the earnings of Arabs are predicted, first using the regression model estimated for the Arab population, and a second time using the regression model estimated for Jews. In this model the income gap between Jews (represented by "J") and Arabs (represented by "A") is decomposed in the following way:

$$Y_J - Y_A = a_J - a_A + \Sigma(b_J - b_A)X_A$$
$$+ \Sigma(X_J - X_A)b_A + \Sigma(b_J - b_A)(X_J - X_A)$$

where Y represents the mean income of the group; X represents the means of resources and endowments; a and b are the constant and the regression coefficients, respectively.

The decomposition procedure, then, uniquely estimates three components of the (mean) earnings gap between the two groups. The first component is the portion of the gap that is due to differences in the intercept. The second component is the portion due to differential returns on attributes ("regression effect"). The third component represents the portion of the gap that is due to mean differences in various attributes ("composition effect"), and the fourth is that due to the interaction between level of resources and level of returns ("interaction effect").

In order to address specific issues raised at the outset of this paper, we further decompose the components into individual-level and labor market characteristics:

$$\Sigma(b_J - b_A)X_A = \Sigma(v_{ji} - b_{Ai})X_{Ai} + \Sigma(b_{Jc} - b_{Ac})X_{Ac}$$
$$\Sigma(X_J - X_A)b_A = \Sigma(X_{ji} - X_{Ai})b_{Ai} + \Sigma(X_{Jc} - X_{ac})b_{Ac}$$
$$\Sigma(b_J - b_A)X_J - X_A) = \Sigma(b_{Ji} - X_{Ai}) + \Sigma(b_{Jc} - b_{Ac})X_{Jc} - X_{Ac})$$

where i indicates individual-level attributes and related coefficients, and c refers to local labor market characteristics. This procedure provides us with an estimate of the role of labor market attributes, relative to other factors, in "contributing" to the observed income gap.

The results of this decomposition procedure are displayed in Table 4.A. Rows in the table contain the components of the income gap in absolute values and as a percentage of the total income gap. This is done for the total population (first two columns) and separately for men (the latter two columns).

TABLE 4.A: Decomposition of (ln) Income Differences Between Jews and Arabs for the Total Population and for Men

	Total Population		Men	
		Percent		Percent
Observed Gap	0.36	100	0.57	100
Regression Effect	0.24	67	0.31	54
Interceps	0.37	104	-0.06	-10
Individual-Level	0.44	121	0.57	100
Local Labor Market	-0.57	-158	-0.20	-36
Composition Effect	0.15	42	0.25	44
Individual-Level	0.08	22	0.15	26
Local Labor Market	0.07	19	0.10	18
Interaction	-0.04	-9	0.01	2
Individual-Level	-0.01	-2	0.04	7
Local Labor Market	-0.03	-7	-0.03	-5

Appendix 4.B

The model described in Appendix 4.A can be reformulated to distinguish three main components in line with the logic and procedure recommended by Jones and Kelley (1984):

$$Y_H - Y_L = (a_H + \Sigma b_H X_L - a_L + \Sigma b_L X_L)]$$
$$+ \Sigma b_L (X_H - X_L) + \Sigma (b_H - b_L)(X_H - X_L)$$

The Ys are the mean values of the dependent variables of the H (High Status) and L (Low Status) groups. The X's are the mean values of the antecedent variables included in the equation, b's are the regression coefficients, and the a's are the two respective intercepts. Since several paired comparisons are made, the notation of H and L are used as general terms referring to the relative position of the two groups in each given comparison.

The model identifies three components. The first component $(a_H + \Sigma b_H X_L - a_L + \Sigma b_L X_L)]$ is the unexplained differences between the groups and is due to both group membership and returns on human resources. It can be regarded as representing "market discrimination". The second component $(\Sigma b_L (X_H - X_L))$ is the portion of the gap due to differences in human resources (or composition or endowment). The third component $(\Sigma (b_H - b_L)(X_H - X_L))$ is the interaction effect of jointly changing both mean resources and coefficients over the effect of changing them one at a time.

5

Arab Women
in the Israeli Labor Force

The study of the Arab population in the Israeli labor force would not be complete without a close examination of the distinct employment patterns among Arab women. As noted earlier, females constitute only a small portion of the economically active Arab labor force (just over 15 percent in 1990). Yet their growing participation in the market economy and changing occupational distribution are highly relevant to the socioeconomic position of the Arab minority and to gender inequality within the Arab population. In preceding chapters we proposed that employment patterns and the occupational composition characteristic of the Arab population are shaped to a large extent by the dominant Jewish economy and the subordinate position of the Arab minority in Israeli society. In the present chapter we will examine the structural determinants of female employment and occupational differentiation between Arab men and women in the labor force. We will also explore the role of the Arab economic sector and local labor markets in affecting gender-linked socioeconomic inequality.

The social transformation experienced by Arab women over the last decades has been momentous. Modernization processes affected the traditional family structure, opened new avenues for education, and delayed the age of marriage (Al-Haj 1988). The decline in the importance of land and the employment of Arab men as wage-earners created a need for additional sources of income. Hence, Arab women began to join the market economy. Yet participation of Arab women in the labor force is a complex matter, influenced by traditionalism of the Arab society on the one hand, and by the state of dependence of the Arab economy on the other. Although practically no economic base for the employment of Arab women has been developed in their communities of residence, Arab women are not very likely to commute. Social norms and traditions limit the mobility of women and forbid interaction with men who are not family members. The role of family organization and the kinship system in the Arab society was clearly articulated by Youssef (Youssef 1972:152) who pointed out that

[I]n the Middle East . . . control over women is monopolized by the kinship network and female seclusion is legitimized in terms of family honor and esteem. Institutional mechanisms, therefore, operate effectively to insulate women from alternatives outside of marriage and prevent them from participating in public activities which presuppose contact with the opposite sex.

In his recent study of an Arab urban community in Israel, Al-Haj (1987a) showed that contact with the Jewish community was perceived to have mixed effects on the status of Arab women. Perceptions varied by religious group (i.e., Moslem, Christian, or Druze) and gender. About half the women in the study stated that contact with the Jewish population had not brought about a change in women's status in the Arab community; practically all other women, regardless of religious affiliation, viewed the Jewish population as having a positive effect. In general, the men, particularly if they were Moslem, had a more negative perception of the effect of contact with Jews on Arab society. Indeed, those who emphasized the negative effect felt that contact exposed women to a different culture and that the resulting educational and socioeconomic aspirations contradicted the values of modesty and family honor.

Although values of modernity have not replaced traditional values in the Arab population, among men and women alike, and family structure and cultural norms are still powerful factors affecting women's position, changes have occurred. As we noted in Chapter 2, fertility has declined over the years and the education level of women has considerably risen, especially since the mid 1970s. In 1961, 6.4 percent of Arab women age 14 and over had post-elementary education, and by 1970 the figure had only slightly increased to 8.9 percent. By 1976 the percentage was 20.9 and by 1990 it had increased almost twofold when it reached 40 percent. Concomitantly, expansion of the service sector in the Israeli economy in general and in the Arab communities in particular (as discussed in Chapter 3) created many jobs requiring female workers. Students of female labor force participation have traditionally associated these factors with entry into the market economy (e.g., Durand 1975; Oppenheimer 1970; Wilensky 1968).

Changing Employment Among Arab Women

Over the last 20 years the female labor force participation rate of Arab women has increased from 7 percent in 1970 to over 12 percent in 1990. This figure is still considerably lower than the participation rate among Jewish women which was 45 percent in 1990 (see Table 5.1). It is likely that Arab female participation in the market economy is underestimated in official figures, as is generally true for less developed economies (Acker 1980; Beneria 1982). Women may prefer to deny their employment outside the house for cultural and taxation reasons. This is especially evident when women are employed in household services or agriculture where work is carried out by the family as a unit. Yet any such downward distortion would account for only a fraction of the gap between the participation rates of Jewish and Arab women.

TABLE 5.1:   Persons in the Civilian Labor Force (in thousands) and Labor Force
               Participation Rates for Arab and Jewish Women in Israel, 1970-1989

	Arab Women		Jewish Women	
	Persons in Labor Force	Labor Force Participation Rate	Persons in Labor Force	Labor Force Participation Rate
1970	7.9	7.2	289.9	32.0
1975	11.7	8.4	365.4	34.9
1980	20.3	11.8	460.9	39.2
1985	26.9	12.5	531.9	41.7
1987[a]	24.3	11.0	560.9	43.7
1990	30.7	12.3	638.8	46.4

[a] From 1987 on, the age for calculating the labor force was changed from 14 to 15.

Source: Israel Central Bureau of Statistics, Statistical Abstracts of Israel,
          No. 22, Table 11.2 (for Jewish women), Table 11.10 (for Arab women);
          and Nos. 27, 32, 37, 39, 42, Table 12.8 (for Arab women) and Table 12.1
          (for Jewish women).

Some insight into female employment patterns can be gained from an examination of employment ratios by age, marital status and education. Such detailed information requires large samples and is available only from census data collected in 1983 (the most recent population census carried out in Israel). Figures reported in Table 5.2 reveal some interesting patterns. In all age groups the employment ratio of Jewish women is more than triple that of Arab women. When only "ever married" women (women who are currently married or were married at some time in the past) are considered, the gap is even greater. Number of children, as might be expected, serves to reduce employment activity among Arab and Jewish women alike, especially those with no more than high school education. Of interest here is the fact that for married women with at least some post-secondary schooling, a large number of children does not depress labor market activity (except for the youngest cohort). In fact, among older Arab women it is associated with higher employment ratios. Employment ratios among the highly educated women with children are also much higher than among women with high school education. It would appear that women with higher education are highly motivated to work and presumably hold jobs which they keep even when there are children in the household. Education and fertility, then, clearly play a role in the employment patterns of Arab women and it should be recalled that by western standards, fertility in the Arab community is still relatively high and education, especially among females, still rather low.

In attributing the patterns of female labor market activity, at least in part, to cultural traditions, the issue of group differences within the Arab population is immediately brought to the fore. We noted earlier that Moslems, Christians and Druze differ in many respects, some of which are directly related to economic activity. This is clearly evident from the figures in Table 5.3, from which a complex pattern of interaction between group affiliation, number of children, and education emerges. Christians have by far the

TABLE 5.2:   Employment Ratios of Arab and Jewish Women in 1983 for Specific Marital and
             Education Status, by Age

	A G E			
	15-24	**25-34**	**35-44**	**45 and Over**
Arab Women				
Total	13.2	18.4	13.6	9.1
Ever Married	10.6	14.5	11.5	8.1
Some High School				
No Children	15.5	44.6	44.0	26.0
4 Children or More	6.9	9.5	23.3	30.0
13-15 Years of Schooling				
No Children	64.8	67.7	47.4	37.9
4 Children or More	20.0	68.1	68.4	70.0
Jewish Women				
Total	35.7	64.1	61.5	28.7
Ever Married	53.4	60.8	60.3	28.5
Some High School				
No Children	72.0	78.7	68.9	30.3
4 Children or More	26.1	30.7	40.9	24.6
13-15 Years of Schooling				
No Children	61.1	87.3	89.0	46.9
4 Children or more	38.1	69.2	72.6	23.5

Sources: Israel Central Bureau of Statistics, 1987.
         1983 Census of Population and Housing, Publication No. 13, Table 3A.

highest employment ratios, although the differences disappear among the small group of highly educated women. Christian Arabs are generally more urban, more educated and less traditional in their cultural orientation. Their fertility is also lower which further facilitates female labor market activity. Indeed, number of children clearly makes a difference for employment decisions of women, especially those with some high school education. For women with higher education, however, number of children does not appear to affect employment, regardless of whether they are Moslem, Christian, or Druze.

The small minority of highly educated women, especially among the Moslems and Druze, may well come from those less traditional families that both permitted them to study and had the means to support the still uncommon activity of leaving home in order to attain an education. This less traditional orientation is likely to apply to their family roles as well. In fact, socioeconomic aspirations of the better educated actually necessitate the employment of married women in order to supplement family income. The extended family structure may facilitate this process by providing assistance in child care.

TABLE 5.3: Employment Ratios of Moslem, Christian, Druze and Jewish Women 15 Years and Over
          in 1983 for Specific Marital and Education Status Categories

| | ARAB | | | JEWISH | | |
| | | | | | Parents | |
	Moslem	Christian	Druze	Israeli Born	Asia/ Africa	Europe/ America
Total	10.4	28.2	11.3	44.3	40.0	46.6
Ever Married	8.7	23.7	7.4	56.6	39.9	46.7
Some High School						
No Children	14.4	35.5	17.3	55.6	51.5	33.1
4 Children or More	10.0	20.9	21.4	36.2	35.5	35.0
13-15 Years of Schooling						
No Children	60.7	51.9	75.0	64.9	65.7	53.2
4 Children or More	58.4	79.5	60.0	78.4	66.5	69.0

Source: See Table 5.2.

For purposes of comparison, the figures for Jewish women, by origin, are presented on the right hand side of Table 5.3. Once again it is evident that employment ratios for the total and for "ever married" women are considerably higher among Jews, regardless of origin. For women with post-secondary education, however, differences tend to disappear. Education does appear to make a difference, but it should be noted that the number of highly educated Arab women is rather small and, as we shall argue later in the chapter, a growing population of highly educated women (as well as other women) may find the lack of suitable employment opportunities a serious hindrance to labor force participation. Indeed, sociological literature has long suggested that labor market characteristics such as size, industrial structure and population composition are powerful determinants of female labor force participation (Bowen and Finegan 1969; Durand 1975; Pampel and Tanaka 1986). Given the strong preference in the Arab community that women remain close to home where they can be supervised by male relatives, differential opportunities are likely to affect employment. We propose to focus then, in the following section, on local labor market variation in structure and opportunities, and its effect on women employment, while taking into account other important factors such as religious affiliation, education and household responsibilities.

Community Determinants of Arab Female Employment

Our main interest here is to shed light on the structural conditions that facilitate or hinder Arab female participation in the labor force. The analysis, therefore, is comparative and uses local labor markets as its units of analysis; that is, female employment ratios in the Arab population of Israel are compared across communities. In this way we will be in position to evaluate propositions regarding the role of local labor market structure and social composition in the incorporation of women into the economically active labor force. The analysis reported here is based on data for 42 communities obtained in the population census of 1983. These represent all the communities in Israel with a population of 5,000 or more, and which had at least 200 sample cases of Arab residents. Among those communities, 34 are all-Arab communities, and 8 are mixed Jewish/Arab communities. The analysis, thus, pertains to approximately two-thirds of the Arab population who do not reside in rural localities.

We computed a series of measures to represent structural and compositional features for each of these local labor markets. These included community size, agricultural employment, public service employment, population-to-jobs ratio, fertility, educational level, and percent of Christian Arabs in the community.[1] Female labor force activity, the dependent variable, was estimated using the employment ratio of Arab females (ERAF) and was measured as the number of employed women per 100 women aged 25–64 (employed Arab women 25–64 / all Arab women 25–64) × 100).[2]

As noted earlier, the participation of Arab women in the market economy of Israel is rather low. The average participation rate across the 42 communities included in the study is only 13.7 percent. There is, however, considerable variation around the mean, as reflected in the standard deviation of 8.8 (see Table 5.4). Communities also differ in their size, economic structure and job availability. While agricultural employment is generally limited, in some communities it still accounts for some 30 percent of the economic structure. In contrast, the average size of public services is 24.1 percent. Here too, however, we find important differences across communities. Additional community differences are evident with respect to sociodemographic characteristics. There is some variation in the average level of female education, ranging

TABLE 5.4:   Means, Standard Deviations, and Ranges for Characteristics of Communities in which Arabs Reside, 1983 (N=42)

Variables*	Mean	S.D.	Minimum	Maximum
Employment Ratio	13.68	8.80	1.21	36.27
Community Size	34,759	86,373	5,000	428,700
Community Size (ln)	9.39	1.12	8.52	12.97
Agriculture	5.40	6.44	0.00	30.53
Public Service	24.10	7.31	9.09	38.66
Jobratio	6.20	3.29	0.74	13.56
Fertility	5.84	0.88	3.54	7.49
Female Education	7.55	1.01	5.09	10.09
Christian	18.80	23.69	0.00	78.54

* See Note 1 for a description of the variables.

from an average of just over 5 years, to an average of 10 years of schooling. There is also considerable variation with respect to fertility, and even more so in terms of religious composition. While the average proportion of Christians across all communities is 18.8 percent, the proportion in some communities is as high as 75 percent, and in others there are no Christian residents at all.

In order to examine the effect of the economic structure and the social composition of communities on women's participation in the economy, we estimated a linear regression equation in which the employment ratio of Arab women (ERAF) in the community is taken as a function of community size, industrial structure, jobs per capita, educational level, fertility rate, and percent Christians in the community.[3] The regression analysis revealed that when all community characteristics are introduced and controlled for, the employment ratio of Arab females is significantly enhanced by the proportion of agricultural employment in the community, by job availability, low fertility rate, and the proportion of Christian residents in the community. Community size, educational level, and public services' share of the economic structure do not appear to have a statistically significant effect on employment.

The findings underscore the importance of economic factors in the incorporation of Arab women into the market economy. Labor market structure appears to be a significant determinant of participation. Consistent with propositions put forward by Durand and others (Durand 1975; Boserup 1970; Rosenfeld 1981), a large agricultural sector tends to raise women's labor force participation. Although the zero-order correlation between agriculture and female participation is negative (not shown), the net effect of agriculture on female employment, as estimated by the regression equation, is positive and significant. This probably results from the specific role of agriculture in female employment in the process of changing economic structure. During agricultural decline, men tend to find employment in other sectors of the economy, frequently outside their place of residence, while women tend to stay behind or even to take over jobs vacated by men. Such a process is especially pronounced in traditional cultures. Job availability (JOBRATIO) also has considerable impact on female employment. As we have seen, local labor markets differ not only in the proportion of agricultural jobs, but also with respect to overall job availability. Women face greater hardship in joining the labor force where job opportunities are limited and competition is more intense.

The level of employment of Arab women is strongly affected by differential fertility and by the composition of the Arab communities (the proportion of Christian vs. Moslem and Druze). Fertility, which is remarkably high among Arabs (5.8 children per married woman), is a severe constraint on female employment, and high levels of fertility in a community tend to hinder female participation in the labor market. Finally, percent Christian in the community is negatively correlated with the fertility rate and positively correlated with education. Christians also tend to live in larger communities where job opportunities are more abundant. However, even when these factors are taken into consideration, percent Christians in the community has a direct positive effect on female participation. We attribute this effect to the less traditional culture which is likely to prevail in communities where Christians are concentrated.

Occupational Differentiation

Labor force participation captures one dimension of women's status in the labor market. The reader should also note that the variation in female employment ratios that we have been studying is around a mean of 13.7 percent, which is rather low. Some 80 percent of the variation observed can be systematically related to labor market and population characteristics of communities where Arabs reside. Increased labor force participation, however, does not mean greater equality for women. Even when women are recruited into the labor force, they may still be segregated in a few specific and less rewarding occupations. Thus, a second and significant dimension of women's status in the labor market is captured by the degree of gender-linked occupational inequality.

Assessing the position of Arab women in light of the economic transformation of the Arab community, Rosenfeld has noted that in view of the traditionalism of Arab society, and as a result of the transition of Arab men from employment in agriculture to construction and manufacturing, Arab women have tended to replace men in agriculture in their villages (Rosenfeld 1981). This argument is consistent with the findings observed in the previous section where the size of the agricultural sector was a strong determinant of female employment. It is also in line with the dependency perspective which has been applied to the study of female subordination in the process of economic development (Boserup 1970; Young 1982; Ward 1984). In a similar vein Haidar noted that

> Employed Arab women suffer from twofold exploitation and discrimination; on the one hand because they live in a rural society that restricts their movements and actions and, on the other, because they belong to a national minority that suffers from discrimination in every sense in the labor market (1990:88).

His conclusion was based primarily on the fact that many Arab women employed in unskilled jobs in agriculture and services (e.g., cleaning) are exploited by *ra-ism* (contractors or subcontractors) who "escort" and "protect" Arab women employed in the Jewish economy and mediate between them and Jewish employers.

While this may be true, it captures only part of the change in employment that has taken place among Arab women. Only a small portion of Arab women are presently employed in agriculture. Many hold white-collar or semi-professional jobs (teaching, nursing); others have recently entered jobs in manufacturing. Our aim here is to shed more light on these patterns and in particular to examine occupational differentiation of men and women across communities and its relationship to labor market attributes and female labor force participation.

As a point of departure it is useful to first review the occupational distribution of all men and women in the Arab population regardless of their community of residence. In Table 5.5 we present the percentage distribution of women and men aged 25–64 across nine major occupational categories for the year 1983. The occupational categories are ordered from high to low according to their mean status—professional and managerial occupations on top and unskilled jobs at the bottom. The figures in Table 5.5 reveal that women are highly overrepresented in the semi-professional occupations (e.g., teachers, nurses, social workers), while men are heavily concentrated in the manual occupations (e.g., construction, machinery, food industry). In fact the percentage of Arab women in the semi-professional category is greater than Jewish women (40.3 percent and 23 percent, respectively). Although more Jewish women are in professional and scientific occupations (7.1 percent compared to the 4.6 percent reported in Table 5.5), this difference does not alter the fact that the proportion of Arab women in semi-professional jobs is higher than any other group.

The occupational distribution presented in Table 5.5, however, does not provide a clear and concise indication of the extent of occupational differentiation between Arab men and women. In order, therefore, to evaluate the degree of differentiation and inequality we computed the index of net differences (ND) for the distribution across ranked categories.[4] For this measure a value of 1 means that all Arab women are in occupations ranked higher than occupations in which Arab men are employed. The value of −1 is obtained

TABLE 5.5: Distribution of the Arab Labor Force in Arab and Mixed Communities Across Major Occupational Categories, by Gender, 1983

Occupational Category	Women	Men
Scientific-Professional	4.6	4.2
Semi-Professional	40.3	9.1
Managerial	0.4	1.8
Clerical	10.4	5.4
Sales	3.9	6.4
Services	11.6	8.1
Farm Workers	4.4	7.9
Manual	21.5	41.6
Unskilled	2.9	15.5
Total	100.0	100.0
(N)	1,648	10,775
Overall Net Difference (ND)*	0.44	
Mean Net Difference (ND) for 42 Communities (standard deviation)	0.36 (0.25)	

* See endnote 4 for a discussion of this measure.

when the opposite is true. The measure takes on a value of 0 when members of the two groups have equal probability to be in each of the occupational categories. When computed for the occupational distribution presented in Table 5.5, we obtained a value of ND = 0.44. This positive value indicates that, assuming all possible pairings of Arab men and women in the labor force, women's occupational level will exceed men's level 44 percent more often than will men's occupational position exceed that of women. This finding suggests that while job segregation is clearly evident, it does not necessarily have detrimental ramifications for the occupational status of Arab women. On average, they hold more prestigious, higher ranked positions in the occupational hierarchy than Arab men.

The finding noted above, which might at first seem surprising, can be explained in view of the situation of economically active women in the Arab community of Israel who both come from a traditional culture and belong to a socially subordinate population. That is, the relative advantage of Arab women is related to the traditional nature of the Arab society, in which cultural constraints limit the number of women available to join the labor force. Those women who are somewhat deviant with respect to participation in the market economy cannot be said to represent the total population of Arab women. When compared to others they are better educated and less tied to a traditional way of life. In addition, Moslem culture and its prescribed seclusion of women probably enhances opportunities for women in professional and semi-professional occupations. As Boserup (1970) has pointed out:

> Such modern facilities as schools and hospitals can be introduced without danger to the system of seclusion only on condition that a staff of professional women is available so that contacts between men and women belonging to different families may be avoided (p. 126).

The high concentration of women in semi-professional jobs, then, reflects the selective nature of the economically active women, on the one hand, and the norms defining the type and locus of jobs women are permitted to hold, on the other.

The logic outlined above leads us to expect that increased participation of Arab women would reduce their segregation and their occupational advantage; that is, as more women join the labor force their occupational distribution would become more similar to men's. In the analysis that follows we examine the effect of female labor force participation, as well as the communities' economic structure and social composition, on the degree of gender-linked occupational inequality. To do so we calculate the measure of net differences (ND) for each of the 42 communities. The mean value of net differences across communities (given at the bottom of Table 5.5) is 0.36 with a fairly large standard deviation (0.25). In some communities the probability that a randomly selected Arab woman would hold a higher status job than a randomly chosen Arab man is extremely high and exceeds 0.60, while in others it is quite low. Only in two communities is the sign reversed, indicating a higher probability for men to hold higher status jobs.

In Table 5.6, we present estimates for two ordinary least squares regression models predicting the degree of gender-linked occupational inequality. In the first column occupational inequality is taken as a function of labor market and population characteristics. In the second column, the female employment ratio (ERAF) is added to the model. While the signs of the coefficients in the first equation are generally as expected, only the effect of size of agriculture is statistically significant. The larger the agricultural sector, the lower the occupational advantage of women. This is in line with the argument regarding male labor force replacement in the process of structural change. In fact, the effect of agriculture on occupational inequality may be mediated by the magnitude of women's participation in the economy. This expectation is based on the earlier observation that the size of agriculture has a positive effect on the employment ratio of women. We thus turn to the second equation in which the employment ratio (ERAF) is included.

An examination of the coefficients reported in the right most column of Table 5.6 reveals that gender-occupational inequality is strongly affected by female labor force participation. The negative coefficient lends firm support to the theoretical proposition outlined at the outset concerning the impact of increased female labor force participation on women's occupational status. As the participation of women in the labor force increases, their occupational

TABLE 5.6: Unstandardized Regression Coefficients (Standard Errors) for Models Predicting Gender-Linked Occupational Differentiation (ND) Among Arab Women and Men in 1983 (N = 42)

Independent Variables	Gender-Linked	Occupational Differentiation
Employment Ratio		-0.028# (0.009)
Community Size (ln)	-0.067 (0.045)	-0.059 (0.031)
Agriculture	-0.017# (0.006)	0.011 (0.006)
Public Service	0.005 (0.006)	0.006 (0.005)
Jobratio	-0.015 (0.016)	-0.032# (0.015)
Fertility	0.110 (0.065)	0.039 (0.065)
Female Education	0.094 (0.057)	0.136# (0.054)
Christian	-0.003 (0.002)	0.002 (0.003)
Constant	-0.225 (0.823)	0.146 (0.717)
Adjusted R^2	0.21 $F_{7,34}$	0.35~ $F_{8,33}$

* See text for a description of the variables.

Significant at $p < 0.05$.

~ The two models are significantly different at $p < 0.01$.

advantage relative to Arab men tends to decrease. This finding is particularly interesting since it appears to underscore the selective nature of female labor force activity in the process of integration into the market economy. Participation would appear to begin among a select group of more educated and less traditional women who are qualified for and occupy semi-professional white-collar jobs. While their numbers might be small, their concentration in a few (high status) jobs results in gender-occupational inequality with women more likely than men to hold higher positions in the occupational structure. As more women enter the labor force, there is less selection as well as fewer opportunities in higher status jobs. Consequently many women find their way into a greater variety of jobs resulting in a more diverse distribution—more equal to that of men.

It is important to emphasize at this point that here we are inferring dynamic processes from an analysis based on cross-sectional data where community differences in female employment ratios appear to affect the extent of occupational inequality between women and men. Unfortunately, we do not have quality longitudinal data to test the proposition more fully and explicitly. However, we were able to carry out an analysis using the 1972 and 1983 Population Censuses, and the results appear to confirm our conclusion.[5] Indeed, our analysis indicates that increase in the labor market activity of women between 1972 and 1983 is associated with a decline in their occupational advantage, relative to men.

The economic structure of the community has only a weak effect on gender-occupational inequality. *Ceteris paribus* the occupational advantage of women tends to be less evident in larger communities, in places characterized by high levels of agricultural employment, and where the job ratio is higher (only the latter effect, however, is statistically significant). In this regard, it is important to note that neither the size of public service employment, nor the proportion of Christian Arabs and level of fertility, exert an independent effect on gender-occupational inequality.

Occupational segregation is affected by the educational level of women. The higher the level of education, the greater their relative advantage in the occupational structure. Since the educational levels of men and women tend to be positively correlated in the population, an interesting observation is that controlling for other factors, higher education benefits women more than men. That is, education contributes to the likelihood of women, relative to men, of holding jobs higher on the occupational ladder. This too may reflect the interaction between the subordinate position of Arabs in Israel and their traditional culture. Most Arab men are employed in the Jewish sector where their education is less likely to be rewarded with high status jobs. Most women, in contrast, are employed in Arab communities where they do not generally face competition from Jewish workers. Indeed, employment patterns of the two gender groups are strongly affected by the social and political subordination of Arabs on the one hand, and community segregation, which somewhat buffers exploitation of women, on the other.

Gender Differences Inside and Outside the Arab Labor Market

We have seen that employment patterns of Arab women and men differ considerably and, as we have just noted, this may be due in part to the fact that women tend to work in their place of residence while men tend to commute to the Jewish labor market. We now turn to address this issue more directly and to examine the role of place of employment in affecting gender-linked socioeconomic differentiation. In the following section we shall first compare the characteristics of men and women employed in and outside the Arab labor market, second, estimate the socioeconomic returns (occupational status and earnings) on human capital resources of men and women employed inside and outside the Arab labor market and, finally, evaluate the costs and benefits associated with employment in the local labor market for Arab men and women, respectively.

The logic guiding the following analysis contends that the ethnic labor market plays a major role in producing gender differences in socioeconomic attainment. The proposition derived from this logic suggests that the role played by the ethnic labor market is dependent to a large extent on the group's orientation toward women's labor force participation and economic roles. The greater the restrictions on women's employment outside the family the more protective the ethnic enclave will be of women. One of the functions of the Arab labor market is to provide women with "protected" employment opportunities. It is suggested that the socioeconomic costs of gender subordination are lower inside the ethnic labor market than outside it.

Mean characteristics of Arab men and women employed inside and outside the ethnic labor market are presented in Table 5.7. The figures reveal meaningful differences between workers employed in the Arab and non-Arab labor markets, regardless of gender. That is, within each gender group, workers in the Arab labor market are characterized by higher socioeconomic status than Arabs who work outside the Arab labor market. More specifically, workers in the Arab market completed more years of schooling, they hold jobs of higher occupational status, and their earnings are considerably higher. The higher earning levels are even more pronounced when hours of work per week are taken into consideration. The differences between workers in and outside the Arab labor market are also evident with regard to patterns of employment. First, the former are more likely to be employed in the public sector—the sector that dominates the Arab economy, second, they are more likely to be employed in small communities; and third, Arabs employed in the Arab labor market are less likely to speak the Hebrew language when compared to Arabs employed outside the Arab labor market.

When Arab men and women are compared across the two types of labor markets some meaningful differences are revealed. The most apparent difference pertains to the gender composition of the labor market. Women constitute a considerably greater proportion of the Arab labor force within the Arab labor market than outside it. Specifically, they comprise 20 percent of the labor force inside the Arab market and 14 percent of the Arab labor

TABLE 5.7:   Means (Standard Deviation) and Category Percentages of Workers Inside and
Outside the Arab Labor Markets, by Gender: Arab Labor Force in Israel Aged 25-65,
1983

	MEN		WOMEN	
Variables	Inside	Outside	Inside	Outside
Monthly Income	25,174 (17,127)	21,363 (16,128)	19,732 (13,633)	16,947 (12,014)
Occupational Status	43.70 (21.19)	34.38 (16.45)	52.68 (20.67)	40.72 (21.37)
Years of Age	37.67 (9.658)	37.77 (9.96)	33.58 (8.22)	37.09 (9.77)
Years of Schooling	10.38 (4.10)	9.14 (3.83)	11.69 (3.27)	11.19 (3.81)
Hours of Work per Week	41.59 (13.55)	45.19 (10.95)	32.71 (12.02)	37.40 (13.13)
Percent in Major Occupational Categories				
Professional and Semi-Professional	27.1	10.03	60.8	42.8
Clerical and Sales	22.1	14.2	15.7	15.8
Service	7.0	16.4	10.7	21.5
Manual	42.1	58.1	12.9	25.9
Percent Married	91.1	90.2	69.0	54.4
Percent Christian	24.3	21.2	45.1	58.8
Percent Using Hebrew	51.4	55.6	38.3	53.2
Percent in Locality 100,000 and over	0.8	45.0	1.1	60.0
Percent in Public Sector	38.3	22.1	76.8	50.0
Population N	2639	6345	661	1085

force outside it. Furthermore, women in the Arab labor market are more
likely to be married than women outside it. The differences are also evident
with regard to socioeconomic characteristics. The educational level of Arab
women (especially of those employed in the Arab labor market) is higher
than that of men. This finding once again attests to the selective nature of the
process by which the few Arab women join the economically active labor
force. In most respects these women are not representative of the total population of Arab women in that they are qualified, in terms of education, for
higher status occupations (mostly professional, white-collar jobs) considered
permissible to women in Arab society. Indeed, the occupational status of
women is higher than that of Arab men employed in the same labor market. It
is important to emphasize, however, that despite their higher educational
level and higher occupational status, Arab women are paid considerably less
than men both inside and outside the Arab labor market.

The findings regarding the occupational structure of the gender groups
are particularly illuminating. Arab women, and especially those employed
in the ethnic labor market, are overrepresented in the professional and

semi-professional category. By contrast, Arab men, and especially those employed outside the Arab labor market, are overrepresented in manual, blue-collar occupations. Notwithstanding the differences between men's and women's occupational distributions, it is apparent that within their local labor markets both Arab men and women are more able to place incumbents in high status professional jobs. By contrast, outside the enclave, Arab men and women supply a disproportionate number of workers to low paying, low status blue-collar manual jobs.

Socioeconomic Attainment Inside and Outside the Arab Labor Market

The findings presented in Table 5.7 seem to support the hypothesis concerning the protective nature of the ethnic labor market. Employment in the Arab labor market appears to enhance the occupational status and earnings of both men and women. However, it is not clear from the descriptive data whether and to what extent the higher socioeconomic rewards of workers in the Arab labor market result from higher returns on their human capital resources, or if they simply reflect their higher levels of resources (i.e., education). It is also not clear whether the relationship between human capital resources and socioeconomic outcomes differs across gender groups, and whether the selectivity which characterizes the participation of Arab women produces different relationships between resources and gender outcomes, in the two types of labor markets. Details of the regression equations predicting occupational status and earnings for each population group (i.e., workers in Arab and non-Arab labor markets classified by gender) are provided in Appendix 5.A.

The analysis reveals that regardless of the group considered, occupational status is likely to rise with education, age, urban employment, and public sector employment. Furthermore, the results clearly demonstrate that in both gender groups Arab labor market employees receive higher occupational status returns on their human resources than other workers. More specifically, for both men and women, the occupational status returns on education, age, urban center employment, and public sector employment are significantly higher in the ethnic labor market than outside it. Knowledge of the Hebrew language, however, has a negligible effect on the status of men and only a weak negative effect on the status of women. Evidently knowledge of Hebrew is not essential to the occupational attainment of Arabs given the types of jobs they hold outside the Arab market and it is even less relevant for those employed in the Arab labor market. These findings lend further support to the hypothesis that the ethnic labor market provides tentative protection to members of the minority population.

With regard to earnings, the data suggest that earnings are similarly determined in all population groups. That is, earnings are likely to increase with occupational status, education, hours of work and knowledge of Hebrew. Earnings are also likely to rise with age, but the relationship between age and earnings can best be described as curvilinear. Marital status (being married) exerts a positive effect on earnings, but the effect is significant only among men. Public sector employment increases the earnings of women, but does not significantly influence the earnings of men. Finally, earnings are not affected by urban employment.

The comparison between the earnings equations for employees in Arab and non-Arab labor markets lends only partial support to the hypothesis that earnings returns on human resources are greater inside the ethnic labor market than outside it. Among men, the findings demonstrate that Arab labor market workers receive higher returns on occupational status, education, age and marital status, but lower returns on hours of work, and use of Hebrew. Among women, those who work in the Arab labor market receive higher returns on occupational status, age and public sector employment, but lower returns on education, hours of work and use of Hebrew. The stronger effect of Hebrew outside the Arab labor market can be understood in light of the role of language in the two labor markets: as might be expected, Hebrew is a more important resource outside the Arab labor market.

The findings reported thus far lend general support to the thesis that the ethnic labor market shelters minority workers from discrimination associated with competition. First, the socioeconomic rewards of Arab labor market workers are greater than the rewards of non-Arab labor market employees. Second, socioeconomic returns on most human resources are greater in the ethnic labor market than outside it. However, the complex and, at times, inconsistent patterns make it difficult to assess whether Arab workers gain or lose status due to human resources or due to market conditions associated with employment in the Arab labor market. Furthermore, it is not obvious from the findings whether men and women are differentially affected by local labor market employment. For example it is not clear whether the higher occupational status of women in the Arab labor market is due to their superior human resources (e.g., higher education) or due to the locus of employment. Indeed, the extent to which the socioeconomic gap between groups is a function of different human resources or of the labor market must be established. To do so, we next examine the socioeconomic differentials between pairs of groups (i.e., Arab labor market versus non-Arab labor market workers classified by gender) and decompose these differences in order to obtain more precise estimates of the sources of the socioeconomic gaps between groups.[6]

Comparing Workers
Inside and Outside the Arab Labor Market

Table 5.8 presents the results of the decomposition procedure applied to the equations predicting occupational status (equation 1) and earnings (equation 2) for Arab men and women employed inside and outside the Arab labor market. Readers interested in the technical aspects of the analysis are advised to consult Appendix 4.A and 4.B in Chapter 4, and endnote 6 of the present chapter. The analysis used makes it possible to distinguish between two major components of the occupational and earnings gap. The first component is the portion of the gap due to differential levels of human resources

TABLE 5.8: Components of Occupational Status and Earnings Differentials Between Arab Labor Market (i) and Non-Arab Labor Market (j) Workers for Men and Women. Arab Labor Force in Israel Aged 25-64, 1983.[c]

	Arab Labor Market vs. Non-Arab Labor Market Occupational Status[a]		Arab Labor Market vs. Non-Arab Labor Market Monthly Earnings[b]	
	Men	Women	Men	Women
Observed Gap 100% $Y_i - Y_j$	9.32	11.96	3880	2830
(100 Percent)				
Resource Component	3.38	.95	3604	1673
Percent of Gap	36.3	7.9	92.9	59.1
Process Component	5.94	11.01	276	1157
Percent of Gap	63.7	92.1	7.1	40.9

[a] Measured on Tyree's 100-Points Scale.

[b] Expressed in Israeli Shekels.

[c] Enclave (i) Non-Enclave (j).

(resource component). The second component is the portion of the gap due to differential returns on resources (the process component).

The results displayed in Table 5.8 generally lend support to the thesis that ethnic labor markets benefit members of the subordinate group. Arabs employed in the Arab labor market, especially women, are likely to gain both in occupational status and earnings. The results reveal that a considerable portion of the occupational gap among men (64%) is attributable to differential returns and group membership, and only a small portion (36%) may be attributed to differential levels of human resources. Among women, almost the entire gap (92%) between those employed in and outside the Arab labor market is attributable to differential returns. Clearly employment in the Arab labor market is likely to enhance the occupational status of Arabs in general and of Arab women in particular.

The earnings of persons employed in the Arab labor market are considerably higher than the earnings of those employed outside their local labor market. Results of the decomposition procedure presented in columns 3 and 4 reveal that employment in the Arab labor market especially enhances women's earnings. Employment in the ethnic labor market increases the earnings of women by IS 1,157 (41 percent of the gap). We interpret these findings to mean that employment inside the Arab labor market is relatively more advantageous to Arab women than to Arab men not only in terms of occupational status but also in terms of earnings.

Comparing Men and Women

The logic followed in this chapter contends that for societies in which female labor force participation is restricted, the ethnic labor market serves to provide special protection for women. Thus, we would expect gender-linked socioeconomic inequality to be less pronounced within the Arab labor market than outside it. In order to test this hypothesis the decomposition procedure (discussed in the previous section and in endnote 6) was applied to the regression equations presented in Table 5.A. The results of the analysis of the 1983 data are presented in Table 5.9. The first two columns pertain to the occupational gap, and the last two columns to the earnings gap.

The findings presented in Table 5.9 strongly support the proposition that the ethnic labor market is relatively more protective of Arab women than of men. The results are especially evident with regard to occupational status. Arab women employed in the Arab labor market are occupationally advantaged over men. Their mean occupational status is 9 points higher than that of men. Most of this advantage reflects the fact that women have higher resources (especially education), but 15 percent of the gap is due to women's higher occupational returns on their resources. That is, when compared to men with equal resources, Arab women employed in the Arab labor market are occupationally over-rewarded with an average gain of 1.4 status points. Outside the Arab labor market, women's occupational status is also higher than that of Arab men by an average of 6.4 points. However, based on their higher levels of human resources (e.g., education), their occupational status should have been 7.2 points higher. The gap of -0.8 points indicates that outside the Arab labor market women's occupational status is lower on average than what they would have attained had they been rewarded like men. While the process components in the case of occupational status favors women inside the Arab labor market, it disfavors them outside it. In both cases, however, the process component is rather small. The occupational status gap in both markets primarily reflects the higher education of employed women.

Turning to monthly earnings we find quite a different picture. The decom-

TABLE 5.9: Components of Occupational Status and Earnings Differentials Between Women (i) and Men (j) Employed Inside and Outside the Arab Labor Market: Arab Labor Force Population Aged 25-64, 1983.

	Women vs. Men Occupational Status[a]		Women vs. Men Monthly Earnings[b]	
	Arab Labor Market	Non-Arab Labor Market	Arab Labor Market	Non-Arab Labor Market
Observed Gap[c] $Y_i - Y_j$ (100 Percent)	8.98	6.39	-5351	-4301
Resource Component	7.57	7.23	-435	368
Percent of Gap	84.3	113.1	-8.1	8.5
Process Component	1.41	-.84	-4916	-4687
Percent of Gap	15.7	-13.1	-91.9	-108.5

[a] Measured on Tyree's Scale.

[b] Measured in Israeli Shekels.

[c] Women (i), Men (j).

position procedure reveals that in comparison to men Arab women are severely underpaid both inside and outside the Arab labor market. In the ethnic market, only a small portion of the earnings gap between men and women (8%) can be attributed to human resources (e.g., education, hours of work, and occupational status). The remaining 92 percent of the gap are attributable to differential returns and group membership that may reflect market processes or discrimination. Outside the Arab labor market, women's earnings disadvantage is even more severe. Over 100 percent of the earnings gap between men and women is attributable to differential returns and group membership. Had Arab women outside the Arab labor market been rewarded like Arab men, their income would have been considerably higher. Here too market discrimination is somewhat more severe outside the Arab enclave, but the essential finding is that Arab women earn considerably less than Arab men because they are rewarded at a lower rate for the resources they bring to the labor market.

Comparing Jews and Arabs

The role of the ethnic labor market can be addressed from yet another angle. As suggested in earlier chapters, ethnic labor markets provide relative protection to minority members from economic discrimination generated by competition with members of the majority population. Hence, an essential task in the examination of the thesis is to compare the socioeconomic attainment of Arabs with that of Jews. If the ethnic labor market shelters minority members from economic competition, we would expect that the economic disadvantage of the ethnic minority, relative to the dominant ethnic group, be smaller in the ethnic labor market than outside it. Furthermore, if the ethnic labor market is especially protective of women, we would expect the costs of ethnic subordination to be lowest for women employed in the Arab labor market. To examine these propositions we once again utilize the decomposition technique and apply it to the differences between Arabs and Jews.

Table 5.10 presents the results obtained from decomposing mean differences in occupational status and monthly earnings between Jewish men and Arab men employed inside and outside the Arab labor market, and between Jewish women and Arab women employed inside and outside the Arab labor market.[7] The figures in columns 1 through 4 pertain to occupational status while the values in columns 5 through 8 pertain to monthly earnings.

The results presented in Table 5.10 reaffirm the thesis that the ethnic labor market serves as a buffer and that it safeguards the occupational attainment of the subordinate population employed in it. Employment outside the ethnic labor market, in contrast, has detrimental consequences for occupational status. A considerable portion of the occupational gap between Jewish women and Arab women employed outside the ethnic labor market, and between Jewish men and Arab men employed outside the ethnic market is due to differential human resources (65.4% and 60.4%, respectively). Yet over one-third of the gap can be viewed as resulting from differential returns and group membership (process component or market discrimination).

TABLE 5.10: Component of Occupational Status[a] and Earnings[b] Differentials Between Arabs and Jews Israeli Labor Force Population Aged 25-64, 1983*

	Occupational Status				Monthly Earnings			
	Jews vs. Arabs in Arab Labor Market		Jews vs. Arabs Outside Arab Labor Market		Jews vs. Arabs in Arab Labor Market		Jews vs. Arabs Outside Arab Labor Market	
	Men	Women	Men	Women	Men	Women	Men	Women
Observed Gap (100%)	4.30	-6.47	13.63	5.49	16,080	3664	19,959	6494
Resource Component	7.05	5.03	8.23	3.59	4729	-2348	6867	3233
Percent	163.9	77.7	60.4	65.4	29.4	-64.1	34.4	49.8
Unexplained	-2.75	-11.50	5.40	1.90	11,350	6012	13.092	3261
Percent	-63.9	-177.7	39.6	34.6	70.6	164.1	65.6	50.2

[a] Measured on Tyree's 100-Point Scale.

[b] Expressed in Israeli Shekels.

[c] Jews (i), Arabs (j).

The findings are quite different for the Arab work force employed inside the ethnic labor market. When considering differences in education, age, knowledge of Hebrew, urban setting, and sector of employment, the occupational status of Arab men in the Arab market is actually 2.7 points higher than one would expect on the basis of their resources (as also indicated by the negative sign of the market discrimination component).

The occupational advantage of Arab women employed in the Arab labor market relative to Jewish women is even more pronounced. Indeed, the mean occupational status of Arab women in the Arab labor market is actually higher by 6.5 points than that of Jewish women, which is due to the fact that Arab women in the Arab labor market are better rewarded for their human resources than are Jewish women on average (a difference of 11.5 points). Apparently, Arab women in the Arab labor market are occupationally "over-paid" not only in comparison to Arab men but also in comparison to Jewish women.

The results regarding the earnings disparity between Arabs and Jews reveal that regardless of the type of labor market, Arabs are economically disadvantaged. Among men, only a small portion of the earnings gap is attributable to differential human resources and occupational status (30% and 34% for the Arab and non-Arab labor market workers, respectively). Most of the earnings gap, however, is attributable to differential returns on human resources and ethnic origin which are more favorable for Jews (i.e., market discrimination). Among women, when considering differences in human resources and occupational status, the process components appear to be substantial. That is, had Arab women been rewarded like Jewish women, their earnings would have been considerably higher. The earnings "loss" among Arab women employed outside the Arab labor market amounts to IS3,261, while the earnings "loss" for women employed in the Arab labor market is almost twice as much (IS6,012). It would thus appear that when compared to Jewish women, Arab women in the ethnic labor market trade-off occupational status with earnings: they gain occupational status but lose a considerable amount of income.

Concluding Remarks

The main purpose of this chapter was to examine the extent to which social, cultural, and economic characteristics of local labor markets affect employment of Arab women in the process of economic change shaped by social and political subordination. Labor force participation of Arab women has only recently begun to rise, and is quite low when compared to other (Jewish) women in Israel. As noted in previous chapters, the Arab population tends to reside in village communities and small towns, which are generally distant from major urban centers and lack the infrastructure to provide employment opportunities. Most Arab women are confined to place of residence and are limited to only a few occupational positions. Consequently, their participation is strongly influenced by attributes of their local labor markets.

As a first step toward understanding Arab female labor market behavior, employment ratios of Arab women were compared across communities in order to discern the structural factors that affect the incorporation of women into the market economy. The analysis clearly revealed that participation of Arab women is systematically related to both the economic structure and the social composition of communities. Women's employment levels tend to be higher in places characterized by agricultural employment. Participation tends to be lower in places where job opportunities per capita are limited and when fertility is high. Finally, women's employment is strongly affected by the social composition of locales. Participation is considerably higher in communities inhabited by Christian Arabs as compared with Moslems. This effect, which is evident even after controlling for level of education and degree of urbanization (which tend to distinguish Christians from Moslems), appears to represent a cultural feature. Apparently, the presence of Christians in the community, who are less tradition-bound than Moslems, creates the normative conditions conducive to greater participation of women in economic activities.

Further analysis demonstrated that the occupational distribution of Arab women is considerably different than that of Arab men. While only a small number of Arab women join the economically active labor force, those who do so are overwhelmingly concentrated in professional and semi-professional occupations. In fact, when comparing the occupational distributions of men and women in a ranked occupational structure, we find women to be occupationally advantaged relative to men. Increased labor force participation of Arab women, however, tends to decrease their occupational advantage. This is in line with previous research on developing societies. When women come to comprise a substantial proportion of the economically active labor force, they are more likely to be channelled into the less prestigious female-type occupations and become increasingly economically disadvantaged.

In Israel, as in other societies, the segregated ethnic labor market provides members of the subordinate minority with some measure of protection from economic discrimination generated by competition with the superordinate group. In the absence of competition, Arab workers are able to attain jobs and positions that are typically denied to them outside the Arab labor market. That is, in the ethnic labor market Arabs are able to place workers not only in low status, low paying jobs, but also in high status, professional and managerial positions. The impact of the ethnic labor market on occupational attainment is especially pronounced in the case of Arab women. Our analysis revealed that Arab women employed in the Arab labor market are advantaged relative to Arab women employed outside the Arab labor market. The Arab labor market provides women with unique protection by allocating them to a few occupational positions (mostly professional and semi-professional jobs) considered especially suitable for women. Consequently, the rather select group of Arab women that joins the economically active labor force of the ethnic labor market does not face competition over these high status jobs from either Jewish women or Arab men. Here we may draw the more general conclusion that in traditional societies in which female labor force participation is highly restricted, the ethnic labor market serves to further protect the few economically active women.

Before concluding this chapter, it is important to note that in the past five years an additional pattern, not captured by the census data available to us, has emerged. Large numbers of young Arab women have entered unskilled jobs in factories and workshops recently established in Arab communities and their surroundings. Although there is not much documented evidence of this phenomenon at present, at least one survey of manufacturing in the Arab sector (Atrash 1991) estimated that one-half of the textile and clothing factories and workshops in Arab communities were established after 1986. Concomitantly, over 90 percent of all Arab women employed in manufacturing hold unskilled and semi-skilled jobs in the textile industry.

While this rapidly unfolding employment pattern represents a change from traditional labor force activity of Arab women (at least in magnitude), close examination reveals that, in fact, the main conventions governing Arab female employment are carried over into the new economic setting. First, employment in manufacturing necessitates commuting. Approximately 20–25 percent of women employed in the textile industry commute to their place of employment (Atrash 1991). However, organized commuting, where all women from a certain locale are transported to and from place of work, continues to ensure some measure of community surveillance and control. Second, since the overwhelming majority of women are employed in the "women only" textile and clothing industry, seclusion of women is generally maintained. Hence, gender-linked occupational segregation evolves in new directions as the participation of Arab women in the market economy continues to grow.

The new patterns of employment further demonstrate our proposition that as the number of women entering the labor force increases, new entrants will find the more attractive jobs occupied (and fewer will have the skills to qualify for such jobs), and they will be recruited into the lower skilled, less rewarding occupations. This, in turn, leads to a decline in occupational status advantages of Arab women relative to Arab men, as described in this chapter, and to diminished gender-linked occupational differentiation.

Notes

1. Community size refers to the number of residents at the time of the census. It ranges from small communities with approximately 5,000 residents to the three major urban centers (population size was transformed into the natural logarithmic scale). Agricultural (Agri) and public service employment were measured as the percent of the labor force employed in each of the two sectors. Availability of jobs (Job Ratio) in the community was defined as the ratio of the number of persons of working age in the community to the number of job slots available in the local labor market.

Fertility was measured as the number of children per married women in the community. Educational level was taken as the mean number of years of formal schooling for women in the community. The percent of Christian Arabs (Christian) was used to estimate the population composition of the community. The distinction between Christian Arabs, on the one hand and Moslems and Druze, on the other, is important in this context since, as we have noted, their employment patterns differ considerably and the former are likely to be better educated, more urban, and less traditional than the latter.

2. A second indicator of female participation in the market economy considered was women's share of the Arab labor force. Although the two indicators represent somewhat different aspects of women's participation, they are strongly related (the zero order correlation is $r = 0.93$) and, when substituting one measure for the other, the results of the analysis were virtually the same.

3. The coefficient estimates of the regression predicting the employment ratio are as follows:

Employment Ratio = 22.15 − 0.39 Community Size + 0.22 − Agri − 0.02 Public Service
        (12.55) (0.57)   (0.10)   (0.10)

        − 0.70 Job Ratio − 2.79 Fertility + 1.55 Female Education
        (0.26)   (1.08)   (0.94)

        + 0.18 Christian
        (0.03)

        Adjusted $R^2 = 0.82$ $F_{7, 34} = 28.07$

4. The measure of net differences (ND) was proposed by Lieberson (1975) and is calculated as

$$ND_{xy} = \sum_{i=2}^{n} X_i \left(\sum_{j=1}^{n=i-1} Y_j \right) - \sum_{i=2}^{n} Y_i \left(\sum_{j=1}^{n=i-1} X_j \right)$$

where X and Y represent relative frequency distributions of two different groups, and i and j are counters used to identify rank-ordered categories. The measure indicates which group is more likely to occupy higher rungs on the occupational ladder. It takes on a value of 0 when the distributions are equal, a value of 1 when all individuals in group X are higher than all in group Y, and −1 when the opposite occurs.

5. In this analysis we computed measures of female employment ratios and net differences for communities in 1972, as we had done for 1983. Using the communities as units of analysis, we then regressed the female employment ratios in 1983 on the employment ratios for 1972 and obtained the residuals from this analysis. A similar calculation was performed for the measure of net differences. The residuals obtained in this manner may be viewed as indicators of change in female employment and occupational differentiation within communities. In the final step we correlated these two measures and found a statistically significant correlation coefficient of $r = -0.29$.

6. As indicated in the Appendices to Chapter 4, there are several parallel models for decomposing mean differences between pairs or groups via the use of regression equations (for details see Jones and Kelly, 1984). The model adopted here distinguishes between the portion of the gap due to human resources and the portion of the gap due to differential returns on human resources and group membership. Thus, in the analysis, the gaps in occupational status and earnings between pairs of groups (Arab labor market and non-Arab labor market workers, men and women, Jews and Arabs) are decomposed according to the following equation:

$$Y_i - Y_j = \Sigma(X_i - X_j) b_j + K$$

where Y's represent the mean values of the dependent variable of the i and j groups, X's are the mean values of the independent variables included in the equation, and b's are the respective coefficients of the regression equation. The term $(X_i - X_j) b_j$, thus, represents the portion of the gap due to unequal levels of human resources (hereafter "resource component"). The K term represents the component of the gap between the two groups that is due to differential returns on human resources and group membership (hereafter "process component").

7. The data for the Jewish labor force population were also obtained from the 1983 Israeli Census of Population. The population included in the analysis is the economically active Jewish labor force aged 25 to 64.

Appendix 5.A

Two separate regression models are estimated. The first model pertains to occupational status, and the second model pertains to monthly earnings. In equation 1 occupational status is taken as a function of education, age, knowledge of Hebrew, urban center residence and public sector employment. In equations 2 and 2a monthly earnings are estimated as a function of age (the square of age is added to model the declining contribution of age to earnings as one gets older), education, occupational status, hours of work, knowledge of Hebrew, marital status, employment in an urban-center and public sector employment. The regression coefficients represent the direct net effect of each predictor on either occupational status (equation 1) or monthly earnings (equation 2 and 2a). These effects can be viewed as socioeconomic returns on human resources (e.g., age, education) and on market conditions (e.g., urban center, public sector). The estimates of the regression equations are displayed in metric form with standard errors in parentheses.

TABLE 5.A: Regression Equations Predicting Occupational Status (Eq.1) and Monthly Earnings* (Eq. 2, 2a) for Ethnic Labor Market and Non-Ethnic Labor Market Workers by Gender: Arab Labor Force in Israel, Age 24-64, 1983**

	Men						Women					
	Inside Arab Labor Market			Outside Arab Labor Market			Inside Arab Labor Market			Outside Arab Labor Market		
	(1)	(2)	(2a)	(1)	(2)	(2a)	(1)	(2)	(2a)	(1)	(2)	(2a)
SES	--	314.87 (26.09)	.0106 (.0009)	--	242.65 (16.10)	.0083 (.006)	--	243.36 (38.36)	.013 (.002)	--	134.73 (25.86)	.008 (.001)
Age	.177 (.030)	1869.93 (291.10)	.069 (.011)	.212 (.018)	589.46 (167.36)	.0267 (.0063)	.032 (.073)	1443.27 (538.87)	.096 (.025)	-.145 (.051)	659.60 (340.33)	.054 (.018)
Age^2	--	-18.14 (3.49)	-.0007 (.0001)	--	-5.39 (2.00)	-.0003 (.0000)	--	-13.09 (6.99)	-.001 (.000)	--	-6.79 (4.19)	-.0006 (.0002)
Education	3.280 (1.641)	1126.67 (137.05)	.047 (.005)	2.655 (.049)	538.68 (72.65)	.025 (.003)	3.651 (.213)	256.62 (240.17)	.031 (.011)	3.020 (.145)	770.48 (139.21)	.040 (.007)
Hebrew	-1.413 (.559)	-1979.45 (695.40)	.0689 (.0263)	-1.484 (.368)	-4465.21 (438.35)	-.227 (.016)	.576 (1.222)	-1487.55 (1121.83)	-.098 (.051)	1.986 (.989)	-3497.43 (793.30)	-.192 (.042)
Urban Employmnt	2.450 (3.106)	-1309.20 (3864.27)	-.009 (.146)	.829 (.369)	-2921.04 (438.57)	-.175 (.016)	6.917 (5.677)	-3310.42 (5218.01)	-.294 (.240)	1.731 (1.051)	-1256.79 (836.83)	-.092 (.044)
Public Sector	10.370 (.687)	-3458.22 (909.43)	-.037 (.034)	3.173 (.443)	-97.07 (529.39)	.037 (.020)	11.920 (1.592)	131.82 (1578.85)	.269 (.073)	11.492 (1.089)	1832.88 (918.36)	.110 (.048)
Married	--	2645.68 (1305.35)	.147 (.049)	--	1498.32 (732.94)	.101 (.028)	--	627.31 (1298.23)	.008 (.060)	--	914.79 (827.43)	.055 (.043)
Hours	--	74.55 (27.00)	.002 (.001)	--	123.01 (18.69)	.007 (.000)	--	120.45 (49.02)	.010 (.002)	--	156.00 (31.03)	.012 (.002)
Constant	-.338	-47014.65	7.251	5.146	-10125.26	8.428	-.6824	-32840.56	6.078	4.624	-16951.18	7.253
R^2	.61	.32	.34	.41	.17	.22	.53	.35	.35	.51	.22	.26

* Monthly earnings are expressed in equation 2 in Israeli Shekels and in equation 2a in logarithmic transformation.

** Standard errors in parentheses.

6

Who Benefits from Economic Discrimination?

Conceptual Considerations

The previous chapters were mainly concerned with the socioeconomic status of Arabs in Israeli society. The findings presented thus far clearly reveal that Arabs are overrepresented in the low status, low paying jobs and in marginal industries and that their economic rewards are considerably lower than those of Jews with comparable human capital. At the core of these processes is the Weberian notion of closure—"the process by which collectivities seek to maximize rewards by restricting access to resources and opportunities to a limited circle of eligibles" (Parkin 1979, p. 4). According to the logic embodied in the notion of "closure", Arabs are denied access to lucrative prestigious jobs so that Jews (the superordinate group) can maximize opportunities and rewards. However, it remains to be seen whether and to what extent Jewish workers benefit from economic discrimination against Arabs.

According to the split labor market perspective outlined at the outset, the differential cost of workers from distinct ethnic groups is central to understanding labor market processes as well as the emergent relationships between the groups. If the higher cost workers are to maintain their earnings they must succeed either in raising the earnings of the "cheap" labor group to their level or in developing mechanisms for minimizing the competition between the groups. With respect to the latter, two possible strategies can be identified: exclusion—where members of the low cost group are denied access to labor markets in which members of the superordinate group operate; or segmentation and segregation—in which case the low cost laborers share the same labor market with the superordinate group, but are relegated to certain job categories that are typically less desirable.

From the discussion in the previous chapters we may readily conclude that in the case of Arabs in Israel there has been no serious attempt to raise the earnings level of Arabs to that of Jewish workers even though Arab workers were incorporated into the Histadrut (the central labor organization) several decades ago (see Shalev 1989, for a detailed discussion of this point). On the contrary, the earlier chapters portray a reality of substantial exclusion, with many Arab workers employed in a somewhat isolated Arab economy. Yet,

alongside this separation of economies many Arab workers (in fact a numerical majority) are employed in the Jewish labor market, but their job
distribution is considerably different from that of the Jewish labor force.
Hence exclusion and segregation exist side by side. The term segregation as
used here differs from our use in Chapter 4. In the earlier chapter we underscored the physical aspects of segregation and used the term to distinguish
Arab workers in the Arab labor market. In the present context we focus on the
labor market mechanisms that operate when Jews and Arabs are in the same
labor market. Under these circumstances it is possible to maintain ethnic segregation along occupational lines. We will refer to this in the following pages
as "job segregation". While both exclusion and job segregation of Arabs are
clearly evident, these are by no means unmitigated. In fact some Arabs do
share the same local labor market and occupation with Jews and often work
in the same firms. Hence, for some Jewish workers the threat of competition
is a real possibility. Under these conditions, where segregation is far from
absolute, it is of great interest to examine the effects of the labor market position of Arabs on the labor market outcomes of Jewish workers.

The discussion in this chapter embraces two central issues: first, the effect
of economic discrimination against Arabs on the earnings of Jewish workers;
and second, the effect of the ethnic composition of occupations (the proportion of Arab employees) on the changing earning levels of Jewish workers in
various segments of the economy. Due to the low level of Arab female labor
force participation noted in the previous chapter, and the possible biases
inherent in studying the earnings of the combined labor force of males and
females, the findings presented in this chapter will pertain only to the male
labor force.

Consequences of Discrimination
for the Superordinate Group[1]

Economic Gain of Jews

The two main theoretical positions regarding the issue as to whether
members of the superordinate ethnic group financially gain or lose from
racial discrimination against subordinate ethnic groups are seemingly incompatible. One is derived from neo-classical economics, the other from Marxist
class analysis. Neo-classical economic theory contends that discrimination is
economically irrational since employers underpay minority workers but
overpay majority workers. Hence, while employers who practice discrimination lose out, the beneficiaries of such practices are employees from the
superordinate group (Arrow 1973; Becker 1957). Marxists take issue with this
position. Viewing discrimination as one strategy of the capitalist class to
divide and conquer the working class, they claim that while racial and ethnic
discrimination increases the profits of capitalists, it reduces the earnings of
workers belonging to both superordinate and subordinate population groups
(Reich 1971, 1978; Szymanski 1976).

Previous empirical research, undertaken primarily in the United States, utilized various measures of discrimination and statistical procedures in an attempt to resolve the theoretical controversy on the topic. Thus far, however, this body of literature has produced inconsistent, even conflicting findings (cf. Beck 1980). While several researchers have found empirical support for the neo-classical position (e.g., Glen 1966; Villemez 1978), others provided findings congruent with the Marxist prediction (Reich 1971, 1978; Bonacich 1972; Szymanski 1976, 1978).

The issue of discrimination and its effect on members of the superordinate group is extremely pertinent to the study of Arabs and Jews. The analysis described later in the chapter will be confined to the effects of market discrimination (i.e., income differentials between Jews and Arabs which are not a function of their different levels of human capital) on the economic well-being of the Jewish labor force.

The Concept of Competition and Segregation

The second issue concerning the relationship between ethnic composition of labor markets and the consequences for the superordinate group, concerns the effect of discrimination against Arabs on the income of Jews within specific occupations. In line with the split labor market perspective, we would expect that a flow of "cheap labor" (the subordinate minority) into an occupational labor market would generate competition which, in turn, would depress the income of all incumbents. Thus, the subsequent discussion is cast within the two models known as "competition" and "segregation" (e.g., Snyder and Hudis, 1976).

Over two decades ago, Hodge and Hodge (1965, 1966) and Taueber, Cain and Taueber (1966) proposed two alternative models of the causal mechanisms underlying the negative relationship between the proportion of subordinate population groups in occupational labor markets and the income level of superordinates in the same occupation. Hodge and Hodge contended that the entrance of subordinate groups (i.e., blacks and women) into an occupation's labor force would depress the income of superordinates in that occupation. They referred to this process as the competition effect. Countering this position, Taueber et al. argued that workers in lucrative occupations control access to these occupations, and systematically exclude members of subordinate groups. They labeled this process the segregation effect.

The competition hypothesis is derived from the marginal productivity model and focuses on the differential ability of individual workers or groups to compete in the labor market. Proponents of this approach assert that perfect competition in the labor market does not exist, and that the wages of certain groups of workers are determined not only by their productivity, but also by the sex or race composition of the labor market in which they are employed. They suggest that racial (and gender) discrimination alters the nature of the competition in occupations employing substantial proportions of minorities. Proponents of this view (Bergmann 1971; Hodge and Hodge 1965, 1966) argue that the entry of members of a subordinate group into an occupation engenders competition with superordinate workers, since the former, due to discrimination, are compelled to work for lower wages. They contend that "some groups find the conditions of work less negotiable than others. When such groups supply their labor at a lower cost, they may well lead to the deterioration of the working conditions enjoyed by other groups" (1965, p. 250). According to the competition view, entry of subordinate groups into an occupation's labor force depresses the relative income level of superordinates.

Although the conceptualization of the underlying mechanisms differs somewhat, this explanation is largely consistent with the logic embodied in the split labor market thesis (Bonacich, 1972, 1976) which posits that labor markets tend to be split along racial lines: "To be split, a labor market must contain at least two groups of workers whose price of labor differs for the same work, or would differ if they did the same work" (Bonacich 1972, p. 549). According to this view, antagonism towards minority workers arises because they are "willing" to work for lower wages, thus threatening the income of majority members (see also Labovitz and Hagedorn, 1975; Lewin-Epstein 1989).

In contrast, the job segregation hypothesis suggests that workers in the better paying occupations utilize barriers such as unions, licensing requirements, or specific job prerequisites in order to exclude members of subordinate groups. Through such devices, minority workers are systematically denied access to lucrative and/or prestigious occupations, and are relegated to undesirable occupations. Proponents of the job segregation hypothesis (Taueber et al. 1966) imply that within occupations there should actually be perfect competition among individuals or ethnic groups, and that the social composition of the occupation's labor force should not affect wage differentials between groups (cf. Hodge and Hodge (1966) comment on this issue). Thus, according to the segregation model, the key to explaining the negative relationship between ethnic composition and earnings of members of the superordinate group lies in sorting individuals into occupations rather than in processes taking place within the occupation. Here the emphasis is on job discrimination and segregation rather than wage discrimination. It follows from this logic that the income of superordinates is not affected by the proportion of subordinates in the occupation. Rather, minority populations are increasingly segregated in low paying occupations. Indeed, both the competition and the job segregation perspectives agree that subordinate groups are overrepresented in lower status jobs. They disagree, however, on the causal mechanisms that determine changes in occupational income level and work force composition.

In the analysis that follows, we shall address the question of whether Jewish workers—the superordinate group—actually benefit from economic discrimination against Arabs—the subordinate group. We shall first examine whether the degree of market discrimination against Arabs is related to the economic well-being and income gain of Jewish workers, and whether such gains are equally distributed among Jewish workers. Next, we will examine whether and to what extent the entry of Arabs into an occupational labor market depresses the income of Jewish incumbents, or whether access to better paying occupations is denied to Arab workers.

Examining the Outcomes for Jewish Workers

Measuring Market Discrimination

A measure of market discrimination which takes into account the relevant characteristics (e.g., education) of the superordinate and subordinate groups (e.g., Jews and Arabs, respectively) is necessary for testing the neo-classical prediction. Since our research is confined to the effects of labor market discrimination, it fully and directly addresses the neoclassical position, and deals only with those aspects of the Marxist perspective that pertain to the labor market. We will not deal here with the effects of pre-market discrimination (such as education or residential location).

For the purpose of the present analysis, we identified 33 Jewish communities (or aggregates of adjacent communities) which can be viewed as local labor markets containing a substantial number of Arab workers. The availability of the 1983 census data on individuals as well as at the community level made it possible to estimate both mean characteristics and regression equations predicting income for Jewish and Arab subpopulations employed in each community. In order to derive an estimate of market discrimination, two regression equations, one for Jews and one for Arabs, were estimated in each of the 33 local labor markets (total of 66 equations). In each equation, monthly income was taken as a function of years of formal education (EDUC), age in years (AGE), age squared (AGESQ), and weekly hours of work (HOURS). The regression equations were then used to decompose the differences in mean earnings of Jews and Arabs in each community using the technique described in Appendix B of Chapter 4. The "returns" component calculated with this procedure was then used as the estimate of market discrimination in each community.

Market discrimination is defined here as the portion of income gap between the superordinate and the subordinate groups which does not stem from differences in human capital characteristics (the "legitimate" gap), but rather from group membership and differential returns on relevant human capital resources. Thus, market discrimination measures the portion of income gap between Jews and Arabs employed in the same community attributable to group membership and differential returns on hours of work, education, and age. Market discrimination calculated for each community was then used in the analysis as a characteristic of the local labor market. The magnitude of market discrimination was measured twice: in Israeli shekels, and as a percentage of the total income gap between the two groups.

Estimating Economic Well-Being

Since our purpose in the present chapter is to examine whether the economic well-being of Jewish employees is related to the magnitude of discrimination against Arabs in various labor markets, it is necessary to define a measure of economic well-being. The economic well-being of Jewish workers in each community was estimated by two indicators—income level and income gain. The first indicator is straightforward and similar to those used in previous studies. It is measured by the mean income of Jewish workers in the community. The second indicator focuses on the residual income of Jewish workers in the community, net of their human resources. It represents the portion of income that remains after the variation in human resources of individuals across labor markets is taken into account, and which appears to be determined by differences in community characteristics. This will be referred to as a measure of income gain (or loss) associated with a specific community. While the two indicators represent different facets of well-being, they are not mutually exclusive (the correlation between them exceeds $r = 0.9$).

In order to calculate the income gain coefficient for each community we used Duncan's (1968) model of indirect standardization (see Appendix 5.A). To do so, we first calculated a regression for the total Jewish male labor force, including the same variables as in the community level equations (i.e. education, age, age squared, and weekly hours of work). We then forced the mean socioeconomic characteristics of employed Jewish men of each community through the regression equation predicting income for the total Jewish male labor force. In this way it was possible to calculate the expected income of workers in the community had their income been determined exactly as estimated in the regression equation for the total Jewish male labor force. The deviation of the observed mean income of Jewish men in each community from the expected mean income represents the amount of income workers "gain" or "lose" relative to the total Jewish male labor force.[2] Positive values represent net "gain" of income while negative values indicate relative net "loss" of income associated with employment in the particular local labor market. We will refer to this measure as "income gain", while keeping its operational definition in mind.

The Relations Between Market Discrimination and Income Gain

After estimating market discrimination and the two indicators of economic well-being (mean income and income gain) for each of the 33 communities, we are in a position to examine the relationship between the variables. However, before turning to such an examination it is important to note that the mean income of Jewish workers is substantially higher than that of Arab workers, and that there is considerable variation in the income level of the two groups across local labor markets (see Appendix 6.A). Furthermore, the figures demonstrate that, on average, nearly 40 percent of the income gap between the groups can be attributed to differential returns on human resources and group membership (i.e., market discrimination).

The zero-order correlation coefficients among the variables representing income characteristics of the communities (presented in Appendix 6.A) lend support to theoretical expectations derived from the neo-classical model and do not support the Marxist perspective. Market discrimination is positively related to both mean income and income gain of Jewish workers. The correlation between market discrimination (in Israeli shekels) and mean income is positive and significant (r = 0.461). The correlation between income-gain and market discrimination is also positive and substantial (r = 0.523). The correlation between the second indicator of discrimination (expressed as a percentage of the total gap) and mean income is r = 0.200. The correlation between income gain and market discrimination (as a percentage of the total gap) is r = 0.282. Evidently, Jewish workers enjoy a higher income gain in places where market discrimination against Arab workers is more pronounced.

From a theoretical viewpoint, market discrimination is the key independent variable for explaining income gain of Jewish workers. Nevertheless, as discussed at length in Chapter 4, the sociological literature underscores several other community characteristics that are central for understanding both income level of residents and socioeconomic differentials between ethnic groups. The community attributes most often employed in previous research are size, ethnic composition, and industrial structure (e.g. Frisbie and Niedert 1977; Semyonov, Hoyt and Scott 1984; Villemez 1978). Since we are specifically concerned here with the possible effect of discrimination against Arabs on the well-being of Jews, it is important to estimate the effect of market discrimination on economic gain of Jewish workers while controlling for the relevant community attributes. We thus estimate several models in which ethnic composition, size, and industrial structure of the labor market are included. To recall, ethnic composition is measured by the percentage of Arab workers in the community work force; size of the labor market is the number of persons employed in the community; and industrial structure is defined as the percentage of the work force employed in manufacturing industries.

In Table 6.1 a series of regression equations are estimated. In equation 1 mean income of Jewish men is taken as a function of market discrimination (expressed in Israeli shekels) and all other community characteristics. In equation 2 mean income is estimated as a function of market discrimination (expressed in terms of percent of the gap), and all other community characteristics. In equations 3 and 4 income gain replaces mean income as the dependent variable.

The findings revealed by the regression analysis are consistent with and more precise than those derived from the correlation analysis. In fact, the addition of community characteristics does little to reduce the effect of market discrimination on the economic well-being of Jewish men. Once again, the findings of the regression analysis appear to lend support to the neo-classical view. The results clearly demonstrate that employees belonging to the superordinate group benefit economically from discrimination against workers of the subordinate group. In all equations the effect of the market discrimination variable (whether expressed in Israeli shekels or in percentage of the income gap) is positive and substantial. We interpret this to mean that in labor markets where economic discrimination against Arabs is more

TABLE 6.1:   Regression Results Predicting Two Measures of Economic Well-being of Jewish Workers
              in 33 Israeli Communities, 1983 (standard errors in parentheses)

Variable	Mean Income		Income Gain	
	(1)	(2)	(3)	(4)
Market Discrimination (In Israeli Shekels)	.352*** (.127)		.367*** (110)	
Market Discrimination (% of total gap)		48.2 (36.3)		58.1* (31.1)
% Arabs	-85.9 (107)	-91 (118)	-116 (92)	-125 (104)
Size	.148* (.075)	.173** (.081)	.048 (064)	.050 (.072)
% Manufacturing	-2.5 (48)	-.88 (53)	-.80 (42)	2.2 (47)
Constant	36095	36349	-946	-952
R squared	.352	.222	.327	.157

*   p < .10

**   p < .05

***   p < .01

pronounced, Jewish workers enjoy higher income in both absolute and relative terms.

Considering the Role of Occupational Differentiation

The positive effect of market discrimination against Arabs on the economic gain of Jewish workers may result, to a large extent, from the extreme occupational segregation between the groups. As shown in Chapter 4, Arab workers, especially those employed in Jewish locales, are heavily concentrated in low status, manual, and service occupations. Indeed, Arabs employed in Jewish communities are generally excluded from the high status, rewarding jobs. According to the logic embodied in the "overflow thesis", their presence in the labor market may enable Jews to abandon the least desirable occupations and to "flow" in disproportionate numbers to prestigious and rewarding jobs (e.g., Glenn 1966; Spilerman and Miller 1977; Semyonov et al. 1984). The positive association between economic discrimination and income gain may reflect the relationship of each variable with occupational segregation. Thus, the findings observed in the previous section may be interpreted as resulting primarily from occupational segregation between Arabs and Jews.

Following this line of argument it is important to examine whether the income gain of Jewish workers actually results from occupational segregation between the groups. To this end we reestimated market discrimination while taking into account the difference in occupational status between Jews and Arabs. The new estimates of market discrimination were obtained by applying the decomposition procedure described earlier to regression equations that predict income (of Jews and Arabs) as a function of age, age squared, education, hours of work, as well as occupational status. This procedure was repeated for each one of the 33 local labor markets. These new estimates of market discrimination represent the portion of the income gap between Jews and Arabs attributable to group membership and differential returns on human resources *as well as on occupational status.*

These new estimates of adjusted market discrimination between Jews and Arabs, whether measured in Israeli shekels or in percentage of the total income gap, were positively correlated with both the average income and the income gain of Jewish workers. The correlations between the variables range between r = 0.527 to r = 0.183 (see Appendix 6.A). That is, even when controlling for the variation in occupational status between Jews and Arabs, the income of Jewish workers tends to be higher in labor markets characterized by higher levels of market discrimination against Arabs.

Table 6.2 displays a series of regression equations predicting average income (equations 1, 2) or income gain (equations 3, 4) of Jewish workers. In equation 1 and 3 the adjusted measure of market discrimination is expressed in terms of Israeli shekels. In equations 2 and 4 the measure is expressed as the percent of the income gap between Jews and Arabs. The results of the regression analyses lend further support to expectations derived from the neo-classical model. In all equations the effect of market discrimination on the income level of Jewish workers is positive and substantial. That is, the income of Jewish workers tends to be higher in places in which market discrimination is greater. The income gain of Jewish workers cannot be explained away simply by the dissimilar occupational distribution among Jews and Arabs. Indeed, Jewish workers seem to gain from economic

TABLE 6.2:   Regression Results Predicting Two Measures of Economic Well-being of Jewish Workers in 33 Israeli Communities, 1983 (standard errors in parentheses)

Variable	Mean Income		Income Gain	
	(1)	(2)	(3)	(4)
NEWMD -[a] (In Israeli Shekels)	.416*** (.132)		.417*** (115)	
NEWMD -[a] (% of total gap)		58.5 (36.0)		64.0** (31.9)
% Arabs	-117 (107)	-134 (122)	-146 (91)	-169 (108)
Size	.147* (.072)	.176** (.080)	.024 (.063)	.053 (.071)
% Manufacturing	-3.42 (47)	-1.12 (52)	-.42 (42)	2.16 (46)
Constant	35967	36230	-996	-895
R squared	.391	.244	.358	.176

*   p < .10
**   p < .05
***   p < .01

[a] Differences in occupational status were also included in the estimation procedure of NEWMD (market discrimination); see text for further details.

discrimination against Arabs even when the occupational gap between the groups is taken into account.

Market Discrimination and Income Inequality

The findings presented thus far demonstrate that, on average, Jewish workers enjoy an income gain in places where economic discrimination against Arabs is more pronounced. This finding, consistently repeated in our analysis, raises an interesting question as to whether all Jewish workers gain equally from such discrimination. Specifically, it is both of theoretical and practical importance to know if Jewish workers at the top of the economic distribution gain more from the economic discrimination against Arabs than those at the bottom of the distribution. Given the nature of occupational and ethnic stratification, we might expect that as one ascends the occupational hierarchy, competition from the subordinate ethnic group will be less prevalent whereas at the lower end of the occupational ladder, stronger competition from the subordinate group will tend to decrease the wage differential.

In order to examine the relationship between market discrimination and the relative gain of workers at the top and the bottom of the income distribution of Jews, we computed two measures of income inequality among Jewish workers. The first measure was calculated as the share of (Jewish) income received by the top 5 percent of Jewish workers in each local labor market (TOP5). The second measure represented the share of income received by the bottom 20 percent of Jewish workers in the locality (BOTTOM20).[3] We would expect market discrimination to exert a positive effect on TOP5 and negative effect on BOTTOM20 were highly paid workers to gain disproportionately more from economic discrimination against minorities. We would expect market discrimination to affect TOP5 negatively, and BOTTOM20 positively were low-paid workers to gain disproportionately from discrimination. Finally, we would expect no association between market discrimination and either indicator of income inequality if all Jewish workers were to gain equally (proportionately) from market discrimination against Arabs.

In Table 6.3 we examine the impact of market discrimination against Arabs on the income inequality of Jewish workers. In equations 1 and 2, TOP5 is taken as a function of market discrimination with other community characteristics entered as controls. In equation 3 and 4, BOTTOM20 is taken as a function of market discrimination with the same controls present.[4]

The regression analysis reveals that the impact of market discrimination on TOP5 is positive, significant, and stronger than any other term in equations 1 and 2. The effect of market discrimination on BOTTOM20 is negative and significant. Indeed, in all four equations the effect of market discrimination on income inequality is over two times the size of its standard error. These findings consistently support the view that highly paid workers, as compared to the low paid workers, gain disproportionally from market discrimination against minority members. It would appear that in labor markets where discrimination against Arabs is more pronounced, the income share of Jewish employees at the top of the income distribution is larger while the

TABLE 6.3:   Regression Results Predicting Share of Income Received by Jewish Workers at the Top 5% and the Bottom 20% of the Income Distribution in 33 Local Israeli Communities, 1983 (standard errors in parentheses)

| | TOP5 | | BOTTOM20 | |
Variable	(1)	(2)	(3)	(4)
NEWMD (in Israeli Shekels)	.310*** (.082)		-8.34*** (2.52)	
NEWMD (% of total gap)		58.8** (22)		-23.0*** (5.8)
% Arabs	-28.8 (65)	-58.4 (75)	-5.81 (20)	10.2 (20)
Size	.065 (.045)	.086* (.049)	-4.34*** (1.38)	-4.90*** (1.3)
% Manufacturing	-26.1 (29)	-24.9 (32)	10.9 (8.92)	10.9 (8.43)
Constant	14954	14690	7854	8142
R square	.418	.299	.500	.553

*   p < .10
**   p < .05
*** p < .01

income share of Jews at the bottom of the distribution is smaller. This finding is consistent with studies carried out in the United States which found that income gains are not equally distributed; workers at the top are likely to gain more than workers at the bottom (Villemez and Wiswell 1978; Freeman 1973).

The implication of these findings is that while, on average, Jewish workers in Israel gain economically in labor markets where economic discrimination against Arab workers is more pronounced, economic discrimination against Arab workers also amplifies income inequality among Jewish workers: while it increases the income share of Jewish workers of the upper levels of the income distribution, it tends to decrease the income share of workers at the lower end of this distribution. Though these data are in line with the neo-classical position, they also demonstrate that the relationship between market discrimination and the income of superordinates is more complex than suggested in previous research. Ironically, those who benefit most from economic discrimination against Arab workers in Israel are the workers least likely to compete with them. Indeed, a more elaborate analysis (not presented here) in which the income distribution of Jews was further subdivided into the top 5 percent, the next 15 percent, and quintiles thereafter, leads to similar conclusions. While most Jews gain from discrimination against Arabs, the gain declines as one descends the income distribution (except for the lowest quintile) and those who benefit most from discrimination were Jewish workers at the top of the income distribution (Tyree and Semyonov 1992). The findings suggest, therefore, that when more than one group of workers stand to benefit from economic discrimination against minorities, those at the top of the social system benefit more than those at the bottom.

Testing Competition and Job Segregation

In order to further explore the effect of economic discrimination against Arabs on the income of Jews, the analysis in the second part of this chapter will focus on the occupational structure. To be sure, we are still concerned with the portion of the economy shared by Jews and Arabs. While the previous section focused on the effects of earnings discrimination and examined variation across community labor markets, this section addresses the dynamic relationship between changing ethnic composition and earnings within occupational labor markets.

To address the dynamic nature of the processes of competition and job segregation (discussed at the outset of this chapter) and their pertinence to labor market structure in Israel, we make use of the 1972 and 1983 census data sets. Employing the three-digit occupational classification, we were able to aggregate the data and to create occupational level files consisting of 323 occupational categories that can be viewed as distinct labor markets. This procedure was repeated for the 1972 and 1983 data so that comparisons of the size of occupations as well as their ethnic composition and other characteristics could be performed.

For purposes of this examination, we define the superordinate group in this case more narrowly as Jewish male workers of European or American origin. In this way we can introduce into the analysis more complex demographic changes in the labor force composition. Specifically, these changes pertain to the rapid growth of the Jewish population from North Africa or Middle Eastern origins, and the substantial increase in female labor force participation. We are thus in a position to examine the effect of compositional changes involving the proportion of Arabs in various occupations while taking account of other compositional changes that occurred. For each occupation, then, we determined the mean income in Israeli shekels (converted into the logarithmic scale) of European/American Jewish males as an indicator of the reward structure of the superordinate group (INCM), and the proportion of Arab males (ARAB) in both 1972 and 1983. Hence we were able to evaluate the relative change in income levels of European/American males by occupation as well as changes in the ethnic composition during the eleven-year period.

In addition to the two main variables, several other occupational attributes were derived in order to serve as controls. These include the mean age of persons employed in the occupation (MAGE), mean number of hours of work (HRSW), mean number of weeks of employment in the past year (WEEK), proportion of incumbents in each occupation who lived in major cities (CITY), proportion of Asian/African Jewish males (ASAF), and proportion of women (WOMN). These variables were included in a two-wave regression model (Kessler and Greenberg, 1981) to test the competition versus segregation effects. (Readers interested in a detailed description of the model are referred to Appendix 6.B. Readers less interested in the technical aspects of the model should take note that the two-wave regression model estimated here includes two simultaneous equations. In the equation which tests for a competition effect (equation 1), income of the superordinate group is the dependent variable and percent Arab is an independent variable. In equation 2, which tests for segregation, percent Arab in the occupation is the dependent variable and income of Jews is a predictor variable.)

According to the logic underlying the model, if the job segregation hypothesis were to prevail one would expect a negative direct effect of income level at the initial point in time on the proportion of subordinates in the occupation at a later point in time. This is so since the incumbents of highly rewarding occupations would presumably have both the incentive and resources to maintain relative closure which would be reflected in a disproportionately small growth of the subordinate labor force in the occupation. By contrast, a negative direct effect of proportion of subordinates at the initial point in time on income level of superordinates at the later time is taken as support for the competition hypothesis since this would mean that the greater the competition the lower the wage gain of the superordinates. Indeed, in both cases these effects represent the direct impact of either income level or proportion of subordinates on *change* in the alternate variable.[5]

In equation 1 of Table 6.4 the effect of labor force composition (percent Arab males) on relative change in income of the superordinate group (i.e., European/American males) is examined. The data provide firm support for the notion of competition. That is, European/American Jews employed in occupations with higher concentration of Arabs at the initial point in time experienced a relative decline in income level, or, in other words, the effect of percent Arabs in 1972 on change in the income level of European/American men is negative and significant. It is also interesting to note that the effects of both percent women and percent Asian/African Jewish men on the income of European/American Jewish men is similar to that of percent Arabs, and also support the notion of competition.

Equation 2 in Table 6.4 estimates "job segregation effects". The findings reveal that the income level of European/American males in the occupation has virtually no effect on change in the proportion of Arab males in the occupation. Finally, the correlation between the two residual terms of equations 1 and 2 is not significant and indeed negligible, indicating no simultaneous relationship between the variables.

The data presented in the two-wave regression model, thus, support the notion of competition and lend no support for the notion of differential change in job segregation linked to occupational income ranking. At this point we can only speculate that the lack of a "job segregation effect" in the case of Arabs is a result of institutional mechanisms which preserve high and stable occupational segregation between Arabs and Jews. This is reflected by the high stability coefficient for the relationship between percent Arabs in the occupation at the two points in time.

Economic Competition and Segregation in a Dual Economy

Data in Table 6.4 reveal the mechanisms underlying "competition" and "job segregation" across the entire occupational spectrum. The extensive

TABLE 6.4:   Standardized and Unstandardized Estimates of Two-Wave Regression Models
(Standard Errors in Parentheses) Predicting Income of European/American Men (Equation 1),
and Percent Arab (Equation 2) Across 323 Occupations, 1983

	(1) INCM83		(2) ARAB83	
	(β)	(b)	(β)	(b)
INCM72	.40	.44* (.05)	-.03***	-.92 (1.71)
WOMN72	-.11	-.002** (.0008)	.03	.02 (.03)
ARAB72	-.13	-.006* (.002)	.65	.89* (.05)
ASAF72	-.43	-.01* (.001)	.15	.11* (.03)
MAGG72	-.15	-.01* (.003)	.01	.03 (.11)
CITY72	.02	.0005 (.001)	-.05	-.04 (.03)
WEEK72	-.02	-.003 (.006)	-.09	-.41** (.20)
HRSW72	.03	.002 (.004)	-.08	-.19 (.12)
Constant		7.42		37.83
Correlations between Residuals***		--		.04
R^2		.72		.62

*   p < .01
**   p < .05
***   = correlation between the residual term of equation 1 with the residual
        term of each equation

INCM = log transformation of income of superordinate group; WOMN = proportion female; ARAB = proportion
Arab; ASAF = proportion Asian/African; MAGE = mean age of employees; CITY = proportion employed in large
cities; WEEK = mean number of weeks of employment during the year; HRSW = mean number of hours of work per
week.

literature on dual economy leads us to expect differential mechanisms of discrimination across economic sectors (Beck et al. 1980; Kaufman 1984). The competition-segregation discourse and the dual economy literature derive from different, though not necessarily incompatible, approaches to the labor market. Competition and segregation processes are viewed as taking place in a market structured along occupational lines in which the major actors are workers belonging to different membership groups (race, ethnicity). In this context labor market outcomes are perceived to be determined either by competition between dominant and subordinate groups, or through segregation—the process by which ". . . incumbents of higher paying occupations systematically exclude [Negro] minority workers, thereby channelling them into jobs which are already lower paying" (Snyder and Hudis 1976, p. 212).

The dual economy approach has shifted the emphasis of labor market processes from employees to firms and industries. Dual economy theory views the industrial structure as composed of two distinct sectors—the core and the periphery—a distinction which derives from the nature of modern industrial capitalism. Although population groups are unequally represented in the two sectors of the economy, the relationship between group membership (often referred to as primary and secondary labor force) and economic sector is far from perfect. Indeed, members of the Arab minority in Israel are employed in both the core (especially public) and the peripheral sectors.

Firms in the periphery tend to be small and labor intensive. They operate under conditions of intense competition and have relatively low profits. Consequently, jobs in the peripheral sector entail relatively low wages and offer little opportunity for skill development and training: "Once in the periphery (however) there may be less overt discrimination. Since these jobs have lower wage rates and involve less on-the-job training, there is less opportunity for discretionary discrimination in wages" (Beck et al. 1980, p. 115). We propose that the structural characteristics in the periphery facilitate competition among population groups since it is in the interest of employers to struggle to reduce labor costs and constantly seek "less expensive" employees. In this context, the influx of minority workers into an occupation is likely to trigger competition with members of the dominant group and result in lower wages.

Firms in the core operate under conditions of long-term planning and high profits; they have considerable control over their product market and seek economic stability (Averrit 1968). In this segment of the economy employee wages are relatively high, there is extensive on-the-job training and employers seek to minimize labor turnover. From this perspective, competition or job segregation, as employee-induced processes, may be irrelevant since organizational rules and internal labor market structures predominate. We suggest, however, that the structure and organization of work in the core are likely to facilitate "segregation" through selective recruitment, that is, exclusion of subordinate population groups (cf. Beck et al. 1980; Kaufman 1984). Although some selective recruitment may characterize the core as a whole, we expect that barriers will be more substantial in more privileged high paying occupations. This is so since stability is of central importance in the core, and entry of subordinate population groups would pose a threat and a source of uncertainty to workers of the superordinate group. These theoretical expectations are supported by the qualitative data discussed in Chapter 4 where it was pointed out that the pretext of security has played a prime role in excluding Arab workers from large-scale firms. These firms, which enjoy large and fairly secure government contracts, are in position to pay the high cost of labor resulting from the elimination of competition. Finally, unionization is extensive and powerful in the core, typically representing the interest of majority group workers, but also contributing to stability of firms (Bibb and Form 1977; Wallace and Kalleberg 1981). This latter factor has particular importance in Israel where unionization is substantial and powerful. Hence, we propose that "job segregation processes" will be facilitated in the context of the core: occupations in which Jewish employees are most privileged will be more restrictive and will more successfully limit the entry of Arab workers.

Using Stier and Lewin-Epstein's (1988) classification of industries into economic sectors (for Israel), we distinguished between the labor force employed in core industries and that employed in peripheral industries. Using census data at the individual level we were able to compute aggregate attributes for occupational labor markets for each sub-sample. The 118,837 individuals employed in the core in 1983 are distributed across 267 occupations, and the 70,919 individuals working in the periphery are sorted into 231 occupational labor markets. Indeed, most occupations can be found in both sectors; only a small number of occupations are sector specific. In the analysis that follows the two sets of occupational attributes are utilized to estimate competition and segregation in the core and peripheral sectors.

Table 6.5 contains coefficients of the two-wave regression model for the labor force employed in the periphery. In equation 1, the effect of labor force ethnic composition (percent Arabs) on change in income (competition) is

TABLE 6.5: (Standardized and Unstandardized) Estimates of Two-Wave Regression Models (Standard Errors in Parentheses) Predicting Income of European/American Men (Equation 1), and Arab Men (Equation 2) in 231 Occupational Categories in the Periphery: 1972-1983

	(1) INCM83		(2) ARAB83	
	(β)	(b)	(β)	(b)
INCM72	.41	.54* (.08)	-.03	-.96 (2.39)
WOMN72	-.09	-.002** (.001)	.00	-.002 (.03)
ARAB72	-.17	-.008* (.002)	.64	.84* (.07)
ASAF72	-.33	-.009* (.002)	.24	.18* (.04)
MAGG72	-.12	-.01* (.005)	-.02	-.06 (.13)
CITY72	-.03	-.001 (.002)	-.02	-.01 (.04)
WEEK72	.01	.002 (.009)	-.06	-.27 (.26)
HRSW72	.02	.003 (.007)	.02	.05 (.19)
Constant		6.12		20.74
Correlations between Residuals***		--		-.15*
R^2		.62		.60

*   p < .01
**   p < .05
*** = correlation between the residual term of equation 1 with the residual term of each equation

INCM = log transformation of income of superordinate group; WOMN = proportion female; ARAB = proportion Arab; ASAF = proportion Asian/African; MAGE = mean age of employees; CITY = proportion employed in large cities; WEEK = mean number of weeks of employment during the year; HRSW = mean number of hours of work per week.

estimated. In equation 2, the effect of income level on change in the ethnic composition of the occupational labor force is evaluated (job segregation).

The findings presented in Table 6.5 are consistent with our theoretical expectations. The data provide firm support for the competition thesis, but no support for the proposition of job segregation. That is, income level of occupations had virtually no effect on change on the proportion of Arabs. By contrast, the proportion of Arabs had a negative effect on the income level of European/American men (equation 1). This competition effect was supplemented by a simultaneous relationship between the change in ethnic composition and change in income (as implied by the negative correlation between the residual terms). Occupations that experienced disproportional growth in the number of Arab workers also experienced a remarkable decline in the income level of European/American Jewish men.

The model presented in Table 6.6 examines competition and job segregation across occupational labor markets in the core sector of the economy. The

TABLE 6.6: Standardized and Unstandardized Estimates of Two-Wave Regression Models (Standard Errors in Parentheses) Predicting Income of European/American Men (Equation 1), and Arab Men (Equation 2) in 267 Occupational Categories in the Core Sector: 1972-1983

	(1) INCM83		(2) ARAB83	
	(β)	(b)	(β)	(b)
INCM72	.49	.61* (.06)	.04	1.19 (2.07)
WOMN72	-.06	-.001 (.001)	.12	.05 (.03)
ARAB72	-.13	-.006* (.002)	.68	.88* (.06)
ASAF72	-.31	-.007* (.001)	.26	.16* (.04)
MAGG72	-.14	-.01* (.003)	.09	.22** (.11)
CITY72	.07	.002 (.009)	.11	.07** (.03)
WEEK72	.06	.01 (.007)	.03	.16 (.25)
HRSW72	-.00	.0001 (.003)	-.09	-.20 (.12)
Constant		5.01		-24.76
Correlations between Residuals***		--		-.003
R^2		.76		.58

*   p < .01
**   p < .05
*** = correlation between the residual term of equation 1 with the residual term of each equation

INCM = log transformation of income of superordinate group; WOMN = proportion female; ARAB = proportion Arab; ASAF = proportion Asian/African; MAGE = mean age of employees; CITY = proportion employed in large cities; WEEK = mean number of weeks of employment during the year; HRSW = mean number of hours of work per week.

data reveal that percent Arabs exerted a significant, negative impact on change in the income level of European/Americans thus lending support for the notion of competition. Level of income, however, had no significant impact on change in percent Arabs ($ß = 0.04$, $b = 1.19$ in equation 2), providing no support for the job segregation effect. Contrary to our expectations, then, within the core sector of the economy, changes in the relative concentration of the Arab labor force across occupations was not systematically related to the level of income in these occupations. This may reflect wide-ranging job segregation irrespective of income level, but it may also indicate that job segregation as an institutional mechanism is weakening. Of these possible interpretations the former seems more in line with the data presented so far.

Concluding Remarks

Although the analysis carried out in this chapter was rather complex, the findings appear to be straightforward. Firstly, economic discrimination against Arab exists in all local labor markets where Arabs are employed alongside Jewish workers. Secondly, to the extent that local labor markets differ in the magnitude of discrimination so does the gain of Jewish workers—the greater the discrimination the higher the relative gain. Thirdly, Jewish workers do not benefit equally from the discrimination against Arabs—those at the top of the occupational hierarchy appear to gain most.

Consistent with the notion of differential benefits for Jewish workers from the presence of Arabs in the labor market, we examined the relationship between the earnings of the highest status group in Israel (employed men of European or American origin) and the increased participation of Arab workers in occupational labor markets. Our findings here followed a pattern consistent with the competition hypothesis which states that members of the superordinate group employed in occupations with a high proportion of Arabs will experience a decline in earnings relative to members of the superordinate group employed in other occupations. Our findings revealed that the competition process exhibited itself in both the peripheral and core sectors of the economy, although the process was less salient in the latter sector.

The results of the analysis underscore the importance of ethnic composition for determining economic rewards. The social mechanism which seems to be operating is what we termed the "competition process". The implication of competition in this context is that the increased presence of Arab workers triggers a competitive process with unequal resources. We do not know exactly how the process operates, but the literature on ethnic and racial minorities in the labor market, and particularly the split labor market thesis (Bonacich 1972, 1976), suggest that in order to gain access to jobs, members of the subordinate groups render themselves more attractive for employers. They receive lower wages than those of superordinates who are otherwise more desirable. In other words, competition is dependent on the existence of some degree of closure in the labor market. It emerges under particular conditions when a group is faced with limited employment opportunities coupled with ethnic typing. This process, evident throughout the entire labor market, is particularly dominant in the periphery.

Finally, the competitive process appears to be detrimental even to some members of the European/American group. The findings indicate that competition depresses the *relative* income of those Jews who remain in occupations which have high proportions of Arab employees. Unlike Snyder and Hudis (1976) who, in their study of racial composition and economic rewards of occupations in the United States, concluded that neither the effects of segregation nor competition were significant, we did find support for the competition effect in the case of Israel. Consequently, we conclude that the ethnic composition of an occupational labor market has significant implications for income differentials and socioeconomic inequality.

The findings of the preceding section might appear, at first glance, to be at odds with the conclusions of the first section of the chapter which stated that, on average, Jews gain from economic discrimination against Arabs. A close examination of this issue, however, reveals no contradiction. It appears that the income of Jews employed in occupations with a large concentration of Arabs (mostly low-paying occupations) is likely to exhibit a *relative* decline, even though most Jews actually benefit from Arab occupational segregation. Thus, while workers in general may profit from discrimination against Arabs, the relative gain (if not an absolute loss) of those at the bottom of the social ladder is considerably smaller than that of those at the top.

Notes

1. This section is based in part on research conducted by Moshe Semyonov and Yinon Cohen (1990).

2. The computation of the indicator of income gain was performed according to the following equation:

$$\text{Gain} = \bar{Y}_i - \hat{Y}_i = \bar{Y}_i - [-80801 + 3298\,\text{AGE}_i - 33\,\text{AGESQ}_i + 2740\,\text{EDUC}_i + 263\,\text{HOURS}_i]$$

where $\bar{Y}$ and $\hat{Y}$ are observed and expected mean incomes of workers in the i_{th} community and (AGE), (AGESQ), (EDUC) and (HOURS) are the mean value of those variables in the i_{th} community. The difference between actual and expected income represents the amount of income gained or lost by Jewish males in the community net of their human capital resources relative to other workers in the Jewish male labor force.

3. Since the data are confined to employed men and exclude the self-employed and unemployed, the top 5 percent are mostly salaried professionals and managers, and the bottom 20 percent are mostly unskilled workers.

4. Although market discrimination is viewed here as a determinant of inequality, the possibility that inequality may influence market discrimination cannot be rejected. Since our main interest, however, is to explain inequality, it is treated here as the dependent variable. The determination of the causal order between these two variables is beyond the scope of this analysis.

5. Since income at time two is estimated within a lag model, controlling for income at the initial point in time, the coefficients of predictor variables in the model should be interpreted as effects on the relative (rather than absolute) change in income level.

Appendix 6.A

Means, Standard Deviations, and Correlations Among Variables Included in the Analysis: 33 Local Labor Markets, Israeli Labor Force 1983[a]

Variable	Mean (S.D.)	1	2	3	4	5	6	7	8	9	10	11
1. Mean Income (Jews)	38656 (3730)	--										
2. Mean Income (Arabs)	22834 (3479)	.079	--									
3. Income Gain (Jews)	811 (3167)	.894	.080	--								
4. Market Discrimination (in Israeli shekels)	6565 (4524)	.461	-.611	.523	--							
5. Market Discrimination (% of total gap)	39.19 (17.36)	.200	-.410	.282	.858	--						
6. NEMD (in Israeli shekels)	6467 (4245)	.1477	-.551	.527	.980	.862	--					
7. NEMD (% of total gap)	39.37 (18.28)	.183	-.198	.249	.705	.916	.783	--				
8. TOPS	16.4 (2.4)	.424	-.258	.387	.552	.409	.560	.359	--			
9. BOTTOM20	7.3 (.8)	-.511	.131	-.382	-.447	-.420	-.489	-.443	-.629	--		
10. % Arab	7.14 (5.79)	-.184	-.073	-.201	-.044	.161	.142	.363	-.092	.056	--	
11. % Manufacturing	27.82 (13.0)	-.140	-.091	-.086	.012	.076	.054	.155	-.200	.262	.347	--
12. Size	6303 (8029)	.403	-.167	.172	.126	-.005	.095	-.074	.326	-.527	-.215	-.272

[a] See text for definition of variables.

Appendix 6.B

The analysis is performed within the framework of a two-wave regression model (Hiese 1970; Kessler and Greenberg 1981). The basic model is quite straightforward and was utilized by Snyder and Hudis (1976) for testing the "segregation vs. competition" hypothesis. According to Figure 6.B, the paths I_2I_1 and P_2P_1 (lagged effects) represent the stability in the income structure and ethnic composition of occupations, respectively. The cross-lagged path P_2I_1 represents the effect of income structure on the change in ethnic composition, and the cross-lagged path I_2P_1 stands for the effect of ethnic composition on change in the income level of occupations. The path e_ie_p represents the correlation between the two residual terms (i.e., the correlation between the remaining unexplained variation in income and in ethnic composition of occupations). The correlation between the error terms may be interpreted as meaning that there is simultaneous change in the proportion of subordinates and the income level of superordinates in the occupation. There may be other statistical reasons explaining why the error terms are correlated in the model. First, there may be no simultaneous effects but common unmeasured causes of income and composition that were not included in the model. Second, there may be no simultaneous effects but correlated errors. Although there is no way for choosing among explanations, we have no reason to believe that either of these explanations applies to the models displayed. Indeed, correlation between residual terms have long been viewed as indicators of simultaneous changes (e.g., Bohrnstedt, 1969), and we are inclined to accept this explanation for both theoretical and methodological reasons.

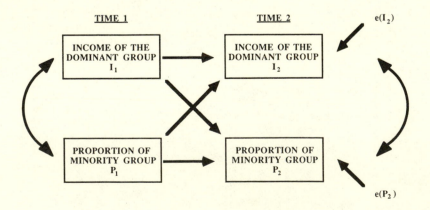

FIGURE 6.B   Two-Wave, Two-Variable Model Representing Competition and Segregation

According to this model, change is defined in relative terms rather than in absolute values. It is measured by deviations from the values predicted on the basis of the distributions at the initial point in time. These values indicate the extent to which income of superordinates, or the percentage of a particular group in an occupation, grew or declined relative to the extent expected. This procedure overcomes problems associated with inflation and change in currency rates. Indeed, the analysis is not concerned with actual income levels of occupations but only in relative change over time. It is important to emphasize that the model entails certain assumptions, the most important of which is that the lag period approximates the measurement period. For a more detailed discussion of this topic, see Snyder and Hudis (1976) as well as Kessler and Greenberg (1981).

7

Jews in Arab Labor Markets

In the preceding chapters we followed two interrelated themes. One theme revolved around the competitive process in the labor market and focused on the Jewish economy and the market discrimination faced by Israeli Arabs participating in it. The jobs held by Arabs are generally of lower status; they rarely cross the blue-collar/white-collar divide into jobs that entail authority and higher prestige and their earnings are low even when compared to the earnings of Jews with similar levels of human capital resources. A central premise of the competition perspective is that the labor market is split along ethnic lines and that members of distinct ethnic groups earn unequal wages for similar work (or that they would receive unequal earnings had they been employed in the same jobs). This raises the issue of the differential price of labor and how it comes about. This issue was the focus of the second theme, which addressed the Arab economy, the constraints on its development, and its inability to provide sufficient opportunities for the Arab labor force.

Combining the above two themes led to a multi-faceted view of the Arab population and the Arab economy in Israel. Specifically, we were able to consider Arab employment in both Arab and Jewish labor markets. It also led to an examination of the consequences for Jews of Arab employment in Jewish dominated communities. Indeed we found that Jewish workers as a whole appear to benefit from the economic discrimination against Arabs, although these benefits are not equally distributed. Workers at the upper levels of the occupational structure are likely to benefit more than those employed at lower income levels. Indeed, the relative position of Jewish workers at the bottom of the occupational ladder—those in direct competition with Arab labor—has deteriorated over time.

In order to complete the discussion of this mosaic-like imagery of economic sectors and population groups, one additional labor market situation must be explored, namely that of Jews employed in the Arab economy. At first thought this might be considered a null-situation given the superordinate position of Jews and the limited resources of the Arab economy. There are, however, small numbers of Jewish workers employed in Arab labor markets who "commute against the stream" to places generally characterized by limited industrial and occupational opportunities. By examining this phenomenon we hope to shed light on Jewish-Arab relations in the economic arena from yet another vantage point.

The split labor market perspective, which typically assumes the existence of one labor market dominated by one ethnic group, entered into by members of a different and low priced ethnic group, is not directly applicable to the situation examined in this chapter. Here we address the issue of two related, but highly segregated economies in which members of the socially and politically dominant population are employed in the labor markets of the subordinate ethnic group.

Several approaches have addressed the situation of a multi-ethnic system and multiple labor markets where ownership and entrepreneurship are not solely in the hands of the superordinate group. One possible approach to exploring the status of Jews in the Arab labor market may be derived from the "middleman minority" theory (Blalock 1967; Bonacich 1973). According to this model, middleman minorities are specific populations in the work force who are familiar with and connected to both minority and majority populations and serve as a bridge between segregated elements of the economy. Middlemen are characterized by their highly adaptive nature, and by their familiarity with local traditional cultures. Simply stated, "A middle minority occupies an intermediate marginal status position and performs go-between economic functions of value both to the groups above and below it" (Davis 1978, p. 79).

In the case of Israel, the foundation of the State with a large Arab minority, coupled with the ensuing processes of development, created a demand for individuals who could serve as intermediaries between the Arab and Jewish economies by providing business contacts and services (such as entrepreneurs, traders, distributors, contractors, etc.). Since the Jewish and Arab communities are highly segregated, the middleman function would be to create entrepreneurial opportunities that would facilitate the flow of goods and labor between the Arab sector and the broader Israeli economy. Based on the middleman minority approach, we might expect that among Jews employed in the Arab economy, the percentage of self-employed and, more generally, the concentration in commerce would be especially high. It is further postulated that Jews from Asian/African origin would be more likely than others to enter into middlemen positions. This expectation is based on extensive research on the ethnic structure of Israel which has led to a popular view of a tripartite ethnic order, with European/American Jews on top, Asian/African Jews in the middle, and Arabs at the bottom. In the Israeli stratification system the position of Jews of Asian/African decent is advantaged relative to Arabs in all dimensions of socioeconomic status, but is disadvantaged when compared with European/American Jews.

While Asian/African Jews cannot be viewed as a middleman minority as conventionally defined in the sociological literature, they might be expected to seek benefits as a middleman group. Furthermore, Asian/African Jews came to Israel from Arab countries and thus they are intimately familiar with Arab culture and language (Patai 1953). These Jews, then, are candidates for middleman positions which serve to link Jewish and Arab segments of the

Israeli economy. If commuting of Jews to the Arab segment of the economy is governed by needs associated with "middleman" functions we might expect a disproportionate number of Asian/African Jews among the commuters.

A related explanation for the employment of Jews in the Arab labor market, also deriving from the super-subordinate relations of Jews and Arabs and the relative segregation of the two economies, contends that members of the superordinate group may choose to work in the subordinate market for purely economic reasons. We label this the "protected labor market" approach. According to this perspective, those who commute expect to escape economic competition in their own market and to achieve higher returns on their human capital resources in a market where they might have a relative advantage. Simply stated, this approach suggests that some Jews work in Arab labor markets in order to obtain the income level or the occupational position they could not achieve in the Jewish sector. The commuters reap socioeconomic benefits by participating in an economy that requires relatively lower qualifications. According to this explanation, we would expect Jews in Arab labor markets to receive higher socioeconomic rewards than Jews with comparable characteristics employed in Jewish labor markets.

The two perspectives outlined above focus specifically on labor market processes and largely disregard the broader sociopolitical context. A third approach adds considerations pertaining to ethnic control. It views the ethnic structure as hierarchial, not only in terms of socioeconomic status, but also in terms of superordinate-subordinate power-relations. From this perspective, the economic relationship between Jews and Israeli Arabs is viewed within the broader context of control, or management of communities, in a deeply divided society. In Israel, market processes and resource competition have combined with the intervention of Jewish-administered state apparatus to further political goals. Hence the need for "control" or "management" of ethnic communities is embedded within the unique historical political and social circumstances of Jewish-Arab relations.

Milton Esman (1973) in his article, "The Management of Communal Conflict", regards communal conflicts as discrepancies over the distribution of scarce resources such as economic opportunities, power and cultural symbols. Esman contends that usually, due to the deep-rooted nature of these disputes, ethnic communal conflicts cannot be permanently resolved; rather they can only be managed through ongoing government intervention. "The main purposes of conflict management in the context of communal pluralism are the authoritative allocation of scarce resources and opportunities among competing communal actors and the prevention or control of overt hostility and violence" (Esman 1973:55). According to this view, the government acts as a neutral force exogenous to the conflicting groups in relation to which it takes on the role of mediator and arbiter.

The perspective that more closely corresponds to the situation in Israel, and which contains a possible explanation of the employment of Jews in Arab labor markets, is that of control through institutionalized dominance. Institutionalized dominance is practised by those regimes dedicated to maintaining the dominance of the superordinate communal group and preserving the inferior status of the subordinate group. Various constraints are placed on members of subordinate groups: limited access to collective political expression, and limited opportunities for educational, economic, political, and symbolic attainment. In this case, the state functions as the legal and organizational agent of the superordinate group and works toward its continued supremacy with the "... bureaucratic apparatus of the state staffed overwhelmingly by personnel from the superordinate segment" (Lustick 1980: 325).

The attempt to build a Jewish state based on the existing pre-state infrastructure, coupled with a need to limit economic competition and to utilize the Arab labor force, led to the particular structuring of the superordinate-subordinate relationship prevailing between Jews and Arabs in Israel. One way of ensuring domination is through the allocation of resources and through maintaining positions of control and surveillance. According to this approach, and given the patterns of spatial concentration of Arabs in separate communities, it would be expected that most Jews who "commute against the stream" into the Arab labor market would be found in the public sector and in management and supervisory positions.

In the analysis carried out in the present chapter "commuters against the stream" (hereafter Jewish commuters) refer to those Jewish workers employed in the 34 Arab urban communities. The Jewish commuters constitute a very small fraction of the Jewish labor force—an estimated 1200 workers out of the entire Jewish workforce. From a theoretical point of view, however, as well as for a better understanding of Jewish-Arab relations in Israel, this is an extremely interesting and important group.

In Tables 7.1 and 7.2, Jewish commuters are compared with several subpopulations in order to explore their relative status in the Israeli labor market. The variables used in the comparison are monthly earnings, educational level, age, and Jewish ethnic origin, as well as the occupational and industrial distributions. The comparison is made separately for men (Table 7.1) and for women (Table 7.2).

As a group, Jewish men employed in Arab markets are characterized by educational levels and occupational status higher than any other subgroup. On average they have slightly over 12 years of schooling, and their mean occupational status score is 49.6. Nevertheless, their earnings are lower than the earnings of the Jews employed in Jewish communities. In contrast to the expectation derived from the 'middleman' thesis, Jews of Asian or North-African origin are not overrepresented among the "commuters". Forty six percent of the Jewish men employed in the Arab labor markets are from Asian or North African origin, exactly the same as among Jews employed in the Jewish labor markets. Almost fifty percent of Jewish male commuters into the Arab sector (46.6%) find employment in public and community services. The large representation of Jews in this economic branch is somewhat less exceptional when we take into account the irregular structure of the Arab sector. In fact, an even greater percentage of Arab workers (52.7%) than Jews find employment in the public and community services (a percentage more than double that of either Arabs or Jews employed in Jewish communities).

TABLE 7.1:   Male Employees - Human Capital Variables and Income Means (Standard Deviations),
Economic Branch and Occupational Distribution, Persons Aged 25-64, 1983

	Jews in Arab Markets	Arabs in Arab Markets	Arabs in Jewish Markets	Jews in Jewish Markets
Means				
Gross Monthly Income in Israeli Shekels	38,830 (13041)	25,711 (16905)	21,551 (16283)	41,482 38365)
Weekly Work Hours	47.57 (11.05)	39.81 (12.63)	45.25 (10.40)	46.70 (11.55)
Age	40.68 (10.48)	35.78 (9.10)	36.51 (9.43)	41.43 (11.55)
Years of Schooling	12.10 (3.71)	11.36 (4.22)	9.17 (3.84)	11.97 (3.80)
Occupational Status*	49.58 (21.15)	49.43 (22.35)	34.94 (16.80)	48.95 (20.09)
Public Sector**	.48 (.50)	.56 (.50)	.25 (.43)	.30 (.46)
Ethnicity***	46% A/A 54% E/A	n/a	n/a	46% A/A 54% E/A
Sample	N=151	N=1435	N=4299	N=59052
Economic Branch				
Agriculture, Forestry & Fishing	3.0% n=4	3.1% n=52	1.7% n-93	0.8% n=545
Industry (Mining & Manufacturing)	28.6% n=38	10.1% n=170	28.7% n=1564	31.1% n=21,792
Electricity & Water	1.5% n=2	0.8% n=12	1.3% n=71	2.4% n=1699
Construction (Building & Public Works)	3.7% n=5	10.7% n=180	12.5% n=683	6.8% n=4702
Commerce, Restaurants & Hotels	3.0% n=4	9.1% n=153	15.1% n=822	10.9% n=7646
Transport, Storage & Communication	3.1% n-4	4.5% n=75	6.9% n=373	7.6% n=5297
Financing & Business Services	4.5% n=6	5.2% n=87	3.9% n=216	10.9% n=7680
Public & Community Services	46.6% n=62	52.7% n=883	22.5% n=1227	25.6% n=17,885
Personal & Other Services	6.0% n=8	3.8% n=64	7.4% n=401	3.9% n=2738
Sample	N=133	N=1756	N=5450	N=69,984

TABLE 7.1 (Continued)

	Jews in Arab Markets	Arabs in Arab Markets	Arabs in Jewish Markets	Jews in Jewish Markets
Occupations				
Academic and Scientific Workers	11.6% n=17	10.3% n=174	3.9* n=207	10.9% n=7689
Liberal Professions, Technicians, etc.	8.3% n=12	28.1% n=476	7.0% n=376	11.2% n=7877
Administrators	17.8% n=26	1.9% n=32	1.0% n=55	10.5% n=7315
Clerical Workers	9.6% n=14	9.4% n=160	7.0% n=374	15.5% n=10,896
Salespeople and Agents	1.3% n=2	7.1% n=120	5.5% n=296	5.7% n=4061
Service Workers	18.5% n=27	7.8% n=132	16.8% n=900	7.5% n=5271
Agricultural Workers	1.4% n=2	4.3% n=73	3.7% n=199	1.2% n=826
Skilled Industrial Workers: Construction, Transportation, Quarry and Others	27.4% n=40	23.9% n=405	41.6% n=2230	33.4% n=23,492
Other Industrial & Unskilled Workers	4.1% n=6	7.2% n=122	13.5* n=724	4.1% n=2849
Sample	N=146	N=1694	N=5651	N=70,276

*   Measured on Andrea Tyree's (1981) 100 point scale for occupational status in Israel.
**   Percentage of workers found in the public sector.
***   Percentage of Asian/African origin and European/American origin.

A closer examination of the occupational distribution of the various sub-populations is most illuminating. Jewish commuters are overrepresented in administrative positions, as well as in service occupations (and to some extent in clerical occupations). Claims of an ethnic hierarchical labor market are reinforced by a further look at the occupational distribution of service workers. Although there is a similar percentage of service workers among both Arab commuters to Jewish communities and Jewish commuters to the Arab economy, the Arab commuters are predominantly found in sanitation, tourism and food and beverage services (9.8%—or more than half the Arab service workers), while the Jewish commuters are primarily concentrated in security services (12.3%—or two-thirds of the Jewish service workers). A closer examination of the detailed 3-digit occupational classification (not presented here) reveals that over ten percent (10.3%) of the Jews working in Arab localities are employed as administrators in government and municipal services and national institutes, and that 12.3% are employed as police officers and other police personnel. For comparative purposes it should be emphasized that no other population group (Jews in the Jewish sector, or Arabs, irrespective of where they are employed) has more than 2.4% of its workers in either occupational category.

The industrial and occupational distributions of the Jewish commuters serve to reject the middleman explanation. Only 3 percent of the group are in

TABLE 7.2: Female Employees - Human Capital Variables and Income Means (Standard Deviations), Economic Branch and Occupational Distribution, Persons Aged 25-64, 1983

	Jews in Arab Markets	Arabs in Arab Markets	Arabs in Jewish Markets	Jews in Jewish Markets
Means				
Gross Monthly Income	36,745 (58552)	19,837 (13636)	17,206 (12433)	23,533 (24098)
Weekly Work Hours	34.84 (11.10)	32.03 (11.46)	37.61 (12.60)	33.89 (12.01)
Years of Age	39.01 (10.24)	32.75 (7.79)	36.16 (9.32)	38.60 (10.11)
Years of Schooling	13.46 (3.15)	11.80 (3.15)	11.25 (3.81)	12.55 (3.40)
Occupational Status*	55.35 (22.68)	55.52 (19.33)	42.74 (21.35)	47.29 (19.07)
Public Sector**	.72 (.45)	.83 (.37)	.52 (.50)	.55 (.50)
Ethnicity	26% A/A 74% E/A	n/a	n/a	39% A/A*** 61% E/A****
Sample	N=82	N=514	N=814	N=48,990
Economic Branch				
Agriculture, Forestry & fishing	1.2% n=1	1.5% n=10	0.9% n=10	0.5% n=293
Industry (Mining & Manufacturing)	9.9% n=8	10.7% n=69	24.1% n=262	13.5% n=8542
Electricity & Water	- n=0	- n=0	0.4% n=4	0.5% n=310
Construction (Building & Public Works)	- n=0	0.1% n=1	0.8% n=9	1.1% n=709
Commerce, Restaurants & Hotels	2.5% n=2	7.9%* n=51	10.4% n=113	12.1% n=7679
Transport, Storage & Communication	3.7% n=3	0.3% n=2	2.3% n=25	2.8% n-1777
Financing & Business Services	6.2% n=5	2.3% n=15	4.5% n-49	13.7% n=8613
Public & Community Services	71.6% n=58	76.0% n=492	49.3% n=536	50.2% n=31,732
Personal & Other Services	4.9% n=4	1.2% n=8	7.3% n=79	5.6% n=3569
Sample	N=81	N=648	N=79	N=63,224

TABLE 7.2 (Continued)

Occupations	Jews in Arab Markets	Arabs in Arab Markets	Arabs in Jewish Markets	Jews in Jewish Markets
Academic and Scientific Workers	25.6% n=21	1.8% n=12	5.0% n-53	9.2% n=5753
Liberal Professions, Technicians, etc.	31.7% n=26	60.9% n=399	32.1% n=339	25.8% n=16,210
Administrators	- n=0	- n=0	0.7% n=8	2.8% n=16,210
Clerical Workers	22.0% n=18	8.3% n=54	13.4% n=141	30.9% n=19,419
Salespeople and Agents	1.2% n=1	6.7% n=44	3.2% n=34	7.2% n=4463
Service Workers	11.2% n=9	9.5% n=62	20.7% n=219	15.2% n=9573
Agricultural Workers	2.4% n=2	2.1% n=14	0.8% n=8	0.3% n=197
Skilled Industrial Workers: Construction, Transportation, Quarry and Others	6.1% n=5	10.1% n=66	19.1% n=202	n=1754 n=4474
Other Industrial & Unskilled Workers	- n=0	0.6% n=4	5.0% n=53	1.4% n=909
Sample	N=82	N=655	N=1057	N=62,767

*   Measured on Andrea Tyree's (1981) 100-point scale of occupational status in Israel.
**   Percentage of workers who are found in the public sector.
*** Of Asian/African origin.
**** Of European/American origin.

commerce; considerably lower than the representation of commerce in all other groups. The same is true for transport and construction, and is also evident in the small proportion of workers in sales and even professional jobs. As for industrial workers, 27.4% of the Jewish commuters are skilled industrial workers. This figure is greater than the figure for Arabs who work in the same markets (22.9%), but 6% less than Jews in Jewish markets (33.4%) and 13.2% less than Arabs who work in Jewish markets (41.6%).

Overall, these figures appear to be at odds with the middleman minority approach both in terms of the (Jewish) ethnic composition of the commuters and their occupational and industrial composition. The figures also do not provide support for the protected labor market view, since the income of commuters is rather lower when compared to Jews in Jewish markets. At the same time, the mean schooling and hours of work of the former are slightly higher. The findings, however, do appear to support the ethnic control explanation in as much as the occupational composition of commuters are in line with postulates derived from this approach. That is, Jews who enter the subordinate market seem to occupy administrative and supervisory positions in which they perform control functions for both employers and the state.

When Jewish women who commute to Arab markets are compared with other female sub-populations, patterns emerge different from those observed for men. The most striking feature is the high income of Jewish women commuters in comparison to that of the other subgroups of women presented in Table 7.2. This finding is most significant in light of the lack of difference in average occupational status between Jewish and Arab women employed in the Arab markets. Apparently, Jewish women commuting to Arab markets benefit economically from their employment in the Arab sector. Their earnings are considerably higher than what they could possibly attain in other labor markets, given the same occupations and human capital resources.

When compared to men, women, regardless of the location of their labor market, are overrepresented in public and community services. In the Arab market, about three-quarters of the employed women (whether Jewish or Arab) are found in this category. In Jewish markets, about fifty percent of women (whether Jewish or Arab) are employed in public and community services. A closer examination reveals that some Jewish women in the Arab labor market are employed in education services and many are health service workers. When compared to Arab women, the representation in health services is over six times the rate of Arab women. It is especially interesting to note that a full 12 percent of the Jewish women employed in the Arab labor market are physicians as compared to the mere 1 percent of female (all Jewish) physicians in the Jewish labor market. The overrepresentation of Jewish women in health-related occupations dovetails with patterns observed for Arab women presented in Chapter 5. As noted earlier, the extreme seclusion of females in Arab culture creates unique occupational opportunities for women. In order to avoid contact between the sexes in such settings as medical clinics, there arises a demand for female physicians, nurses and the like. Evidently, when such positions cannot be filled by Arab women, opportunities emerge for Jewish women.

Following on from the information presented thus far, it is important to examine, somewhat more systematically, whether Jewish commuters gain or lose from employment in Arab markets, that is, whether their earnings or occupational status are higher or lower than those that would be expected in the Jewish markets. Duncan's indirect standardization technique (described in detail in Appendix 7.A) was employed in order to arrive at answers to this question. Expected earnings in this case were estimated by using Jewish men and Jewish women employed in Jewish markets as the standard populations and calculating what the earnings of Jewish commuters (men and women, respectively) would be had they been determined according to the same mechanisms determining earnings in the standard population.

According to the figures in Table 7.3, Jewish men employed in Arab labor markets gain neither occupational status nor income by entering the Arab economy. In fact, they would have received higher levels of income (expected earnings = IS 41,150) and similar occupational status (expected occupational status = 49.14 points) had they been rewarded on their human capital resources at the same rates as Jews in Jewish labor markets. The earning "loss" in this case is (−)IS 2,770. Jewish women who enter Arab labor markets, however, receive significantly higher returns on their human capital resources (as compared to other Jewish women) in terms of both occupational status and

TABLE 7.3: Actual Versus Expected Occupational Status and Earnings of Jewish Commuters to Arab Markets, Persons Aged 25-64, 1983

	Men Commuters	Women Commuters
Actual Occupational Status	49.58	55.35
Expected Occupational Status	49.14	50.58
Occupational Gain = Actual-Expected	.44	4.77
Actual Earnings (IS)	38,380	36,745
Expected Earnings (IS)	41,150	27,168
Earnings Gain = Actual-Expected	-2,770	9,577

income. Their income gain is dramatic (almost IS 10,000) and their gain in occupational status is also substantial (about 5 points on Tyree's scale). Although we do not know very much about the characteristics and motivations of the Jewish women who commute "against the stream", it is evident that they increase their earnings and occupational status potential by entering the Arab market. In this respect the findings reveal a protected labor market situation where (a few) Jewish women are able to gain from employment in the subordinate segment of the economy.

The data reveal different patterns for male and female "Jewish commuters". The male commuters do not appear to operate according to a strict economic rationale. In fact, male commuters leave behind markets with higher average returns for human capital resources and enter less favorable labor markets. They also do not seem to operate as a "middleman minority" and to benefit from the intermediary position between the Jewish and Arab economies. Rather, Jewish men employed in Arab communities seem to perform social and economic control functions within the Arab sector. In fact, almost 50 percent of all male commuters to the Arab markets serve in state and government capacities. The relative odds that a Jew would be employed in public and community services is six-times greater in the Arab economic sector than in the Jewish sector of the economy. Additional support for the control theory, as an explanation for the "reverse commuting" phenomenon, is derived from an examination of the occupational distribution of Jewish commuters. Jews working in Arab markets are highly represented in positions of authority as well as in security related occupations. An illuminating example of this practice was provided by Al-Haj in a personal communication with regard to the assignment of Jewish teachers and educators to the Arab school system in the first decade of Israel's statehood. According to Al-Haj, these teachers were expected to perform three major tasks: teach the Hebrew language; mediate between the school system and state institutions; and "keep an eye" on what went on in the school community.

Data presented in this chapter suggest that, at least in the case of men, Jewish commuters do not gain occupationally or economically from their employment in the Arab sector. They also do not hold jobs typical to the "middleman minority". Rather, most Jewish commuters hold jobs in the public sector. It would appear, then, that many of those who commute to, and are employed in the Arab sector, do so as part of their career trajectory and job requirements. The position of Jewish commuters "against the stream" highlights from a somewhat different angle the way in which political and social facets of Jewish-Arab relations in Israel are intertwined with labor market activity.[1]

Notes

1. This chapter was written in collaboration with Susan Feit-Stern and is based on data analyzed in her M.A. thesis (Feit-Stern 1990).

Appendix 7.A

The standardization technique was used twice: once for evaluating earnings, and a second time for evaluating occupational status. In both cases it involved similar calculations and included several steps. In the first step, an Ordinary Least Squares (OLS) regression equation was estimated for two "standard" populations: Jewish men employed in the Jewish labor market and Jewish women employed in the Jewish labor market. The variables included in the regression equations were age and years of schooling in the case of occupational status, and age, years of schooling, hours of work, public sector, employment and occupational status, in the case of earnings. Four sets of coefficients were derived (occupational status and earnings for men and women separately).

In the second step, the mean values of commuter characteristics (i.e., education, hours of work, etc.) were "forced" through the standard population equations predicting occupational status and earnings for the appropriate gender group. In effect, this procedure estimated what the occupational status and income of commuters (men or women) would be had they been determined in the same way as occupational status and income for the standard population. This is the "expected" mean income or status of the group. In the third step, the expected mean was compared with the observed (actual) mean. When the latter is higher it represents a net gain for commuters. When the observed mean is lower than the expected, this represents a net loss.

8

An Israeli Dilemma

Since Jews began migrating to Palestine over a century ago economic competition and political conflict have pervaded Jewish-Arab relations. Although our study has focused primarily on recent decades, essential attributes of Jewish-Arab economic relations were already being fashioned during the first half of this century. When the State of Israel was established in 1948, Jewish-Arab conflictual relations were reinforced by their structuring along the lines of Jewish superordination and the subordination of the Arab minority. Competition remained inherent to the relationship but now the Arab ethnic group was clearly handicapped vis-à-vis the Jewish majority.

Labor market relations between Jews and Arabs, we have contended, should be viewed in the context of this fundamental ethnic group competition. While the Jewish and Arab economies in the pre-state period were linked at various points, the two sectors largely followed separate paths which led to growing separation and isolation. The establishment of the State of Israel was particularly detrimental to the Arab population. From a numerical majority operating in a relatively segregated economy, only loosely related to the Jewish economy through market processes, the Arab population came to be treated as an ethnic (not national) minority which became highly dependent on and dominated by the Jewish state apparatus. Indeed the rules of competition between Jews and Arabs changed considerably. The subordinate position of the Arab minority hampered economic development which, in turn, increased Arab dependency on the Jewish economic sector. This growing dependency further reinforced the socioeconomic inequality between the two population groups. It is from this vantage point that we chose to examine economic competition and the resulting patterns of socioeconomic inequality between Jews and Arabs in the labor market.

The data presented throughout the book demonstrate that since the establishment of the State of Israel the non-Jewish population has experienced substantial demographic and social changes. Currently, the non-Jewish minority accounts for approximately 18 percent of the total population of Israel. Historically, Arabs have been characterized by low levels of education, relatively low occupational status and meager income in comparison to Jews. Although the educational level of Arabs has considerably risen in recent years and many have experienced upward intergenerational occupational mobility, they still lag far behind Jews in all aspects of social stratification. Indeed, Israeli Arabs remain extremely disadvantaged when competing with Jews in the labor market.

Not only do Arabs possess lower levels of human capital resources, but they also face a disadvantageous opportunity structure. Jews and Arabs are extremely segregated; Arabs are likely to reside in small communities characterized by limited industrial infrastructure and scant economic opportunities. Furthermore, Arab communities have long experienced unequal treatment by the governments of Israel—a major difficulty in a society where decision-making and resource allocation are highly centralized. They have not received an equal share of funding and resources, and have suffered from the implementation of adverse policies of economic development. This has reinforced the growing dependency of the Arab work force on the Jewish economy which, in turn, has served to escalate the socioeconomic disadvantage faced by Arabs in the labor market.

In terms of our interest in ethnic relations and stratification, our findings have underscored two major phenomena. On the one hand the analysis reveals the constraints imposed on the Arab economic sector. On the other hand the analysis demonstrates that the integration of Arabs into the Israeli (Jewish) economy has entailed considerable social and economic disadvantages for the Arab minority. Our findings show that educational gains notwithstanding, adequate job opportunities for the better educated highly skilled Arabs are hard to come by. One consequence of this is a growing mismatch between educational attainment and occupational rewards, particularly among young Arabs. It appears to be much harder for the highly educated Arab individuals to convert their educational assets into occupational status and commensurate income levels.

In order to understand the sources of this mismatch we outlined the changing structure of the Arab economy, and the industrial composition of the Arab labor force. The most striking feature of the change was the shift of the Arab economy from agriculture to an economy based largely on public services. Although manufacturing in Arab communities has also expanded in recent decades, it still plays a relatively small role in the Arab sector of the labor market. In general, the change in the Arab economy entailed a substantial decline in self-employment and ownership of means of production, and large-scale commuting to work in Jewish communities.

Commuting of Arab workers into the larger labor markets dominated by the majority Jewish population leads to ethnic competition over a relatively fixed pool of jobs. As a consequence, the commuting of Arabs is accompanied by their economic subordination. Arabs employed in the bi-ethnic labor market in direct competition with Jews suffer the detrimental consequences of discrimination, especially as pertains to occupational positions. They are unable to obtain high status jobs and to convert their human resources into socioeconomic rewards. Nevertheless, they benefit somewhat from the higher earning levels available in the Jewish labor market. By way of contrast, employment in Arab communities provides Arab workers with a measure of protection. In the absence of competition, Arab workers are able to fill positions which are otherwise held by Jews. Furthermore, in comparison to Jews they are able to achieve high status positions with relatively lower levels of education.

The differences between the outcomes for Arabs employed in and outside Arab communities led us to explore more closely the institutionalization of job discrimination. We defined job discrimination as the segregation of Arab and Jewish workers in different occupational categories and the concentration of Arab employees in low status jobs. Key factors here, we argued, are employer hiring decisions and the legal framework which sets the ground rules. We pointed out that Israeli law prohibits discrimination on the basis of religion and nationality in very general terms. At the same time discriminatory behavior is made possible by the rules of "local preference" of employees, and by the application of security considerations in hiring practices. More importantly, there is clear indication that employer practices of job discrimination, whether legal or illegal, are widespread. Furthermore, they appear to be sanctioned by the normative system of the dominant Jewish group.

The competition perspective which we applied to the study of the labor market is also relevant for the understanding of employment patterns among Arab women. Labor force participation of Arab women in the market economy has only recently begun to rise. Most Arab women are confined to place of residence and are limited to only a few occupational positions. In the case of women, the impact of the ethnic labor market on individual attainment is even more pronounced than among men. Our findings reveal that, similarly to men, Arab women employed in Arab communities are advantaged relative to Arab women employed outside the Arab labor market. Moreover, Arab women, especially those employed in Arab communities, are occupationally advantaged relative to Arab men. The Arab market provides women with such protection by allocating them to the few occupation positions considered suitable for women. In these positions Arab women are relatively free from competition with men, on the one hand, and with Jewish women on the other.

From a competition perspective it is also significant to examine the effect of discrimination against Arabs on the economic well-being of Jewish employees. Our analysis shows that, on average, Jews benefit from discrimination against Arab workers. However, those at the top of the socioeconomic hierarchy benefit most from economic discrimination, and the advantages decrease as one descends the occupational ladder. In this regard the data demonstrate that an increased presence of Arab workers in an occupational labor market triggers a competitive process with unequal resources. In order to gain access to jobs Arab workers must render themselves more attractive to employers. To do so they offer their labor at a lower cost than Jewish workers who otherwise would be preferred. This competition process appears to be detrimental not only to the earnings of Arabs but also to the earnings of some members of the Jewish group. More specifically, competition with Arab employees is likely to depress the relative income of those Jewish workers who are employed in the same, typically low status, occupations.

In studying the relationship between Arabs and Jews in the Israeli labor market it is critical to note that we have described a system in which the rules of competition themselves are structured by the Jewish group. In this system rules and regulations serve to minimize the threat to the superordinate Jewish group and consequently handicap the subordinate Arab population. Thus, the state system, though exogenous to our analytical model, was considered germane to the issue as a factor which serves to structure and constrain labor market competition. Indeed, an additional and indirect indication of the intertwining of the political and economic spheres is the phenomenon of commuters "against the stream"—Jews who work in Arab communities. These commuters do not operate as a "middleman" minority, nor do they benefit from a protected market. In large part they represent ethnic group control carried out in the occupational sphere.

The data on Jewish-Arab inequality presented in this study lead us to revise and expand the concept of competition commonly used in the literature and to attempt to provide a more comprehensive and more powerful model for understanding ethnic group relations in the labor market. One central use of the concept of ethnic competition in the sociological literature was nurtured by the view of labor markets as "clearing houses" for the demand for, and the supply of, individual workers. According to this view, some workers are less desirable to employers due to their ethnic or racial origin and are consequently compelled to supply their labor at a lower cost. In this atomized view of labor market competition, there is little room for group action and the notion of ethnicity is limited to its handicapping impact on individuals' activities.

From the data and analysis presented throughout this book it is evident that ethnic competition should be perceived as asymmetric at two levels: the collective and the individual levels. Although analytically distinct, these two conceptual levels are interrelated. Indeed a comprehensive discussion of ethnic relations and labor market inequality must take into account the interdependence between the collective and the individual spheres. Specifically, we contend that group competition leading to the collective subordination of an ethnic group facilitates and reinforces economic discrimination at the individual level.

At the collective level competition takes place between well-defined, organized groups that populate (or aim to populate) a common space. The members of each group share a common heritage, and they collectively present claims for scarce resources (i.e., land, jobs, wealth). Over time the competition between groups may result in their unequal control of resources. This, in turn, leads to the institutionalization of superordinate-subordinate ethnic relations. Indeed, the institutionalization of asymmetric power relations is reflected in the legal system and in state agencies, as well as in economic enterprises and the labor market.

When the asymmetric relationship between superordinate and subordinate groups is anchored in the state apparatus it is difficult for the subordinate group to accumulate resources and mobilize. Since the state often dictates the rules under which competition may take place, the subordinate group typically faces unfavorable conditions. That is, the subordinate group has limited ability to develop an industrial base and provide economic opportunities for its members. Under these circumstances an adequate solution to economic needs of individuals cannot be found within the ethnic group. Hence, individual members are compelled to seek alternative solutions to their individual needs. Often they may seek employment in labor markets dominated by the superordinate population and in enterprises owned by them. In these markets the ethnicity of the subordinate workers handicaps them in the competition for jobs and becomes a liability. As the number of subordinate members seeking to satisfy their personal needs in markets dominated by the superordinate group increases, so does the potential pool of cheap labor as an immediate target for economic exploitation.

"Integration" of the two ethnic groups in the same labor market implies intensification of competition for the same jobs and rewards. According to neo-classical economics such competition should force the labor market into equilibrium regardless of employer prejudice. Assuming that employers seek to maximize profits, and that the market is competitive, it is sufficient that at least some employers will hire the (less expensive) subordinate workers instead of the (expensive) workers from the superordinate group for earnings discrimination to diminish. Accordingly, exclusionary discrimination does not necessarily lead to discrimination in earnings and the labor market may be divided vertically into firms that employ subordinate workers and those that exclude them. In both cases wages are determined according to worker productivity regardless of ethnicity and, consequently, this tends to reduce the wage gap between the two groups.

Although the logic embodied in this approach brings to the fore the dynamic nature of individual-level competition, it ignores the role of ethnic competition at the collective level. Ethnic competition at the collective level, we have argued, is central to understanding the conditions under which competition among individuals in the labor market takes place. More specifically, when ethnic subordination is reinforced by segregation and regulations coupled with prejudice, individual members find it extremely difficult to negotiate equal socioeconomic returns on their human resources.

The dependency of the subordinate population on resources controlled by the superordinate group serves to reproduce the system of ethnic inequality both at the individual and at the collective levels. On the one hand, employment in the same labor market creates a semblance of social and economic integration as large numbers of individuals from both ethnic groups are employed side by side. On the other hand, the presence of a subordinate ethnic minority in the labor market provides members of the superordinate group with the opportunity to exercise economic discrimination. Such "integration", then, may accentuate the reality of discrimination and deprivation and may fuel discontent and mutual hostility.

Under circumstances of discrimination and deprivation, subordinate group members are likely to resort to collective action in an attempt to redress socioeconomic inequality. In search for a solution they can adopt either economic or political recourse, or both. A common economic solution pursued by ethnic groups is the development of an independent economic system in an ethnic enclave. The ethnic enclave is separated to some extent from the economic system controlled by the superordinate group. It is characterized by enterprises and businesses owned by members of the subordinate group. Owners of these businesses tend to hire members of their own ethnic group. Consequently, in the enclave labor market minority employees enjoy job opportunities that are usually denied them outside the enclave. In the enclave they can attain a wide variety of jobs; not only low status, low pay, unskilled and semi-skilled jobs, but also professional, semi-professional, managerial, and other white-collar positions. Additionally, in the ethnic enclave, members of the subordinate group are more likely to receive higher returns on their human capital resources. It should be noted, however, that the ability of a group to develop an independent economic system in the ethnic enclave is itself dependent on the level and nature of control exercised by the superordinate group. The greater the control over the economy exercised by the superordinate group the greater the need of the subordinate population for an independent economic enclave. But at the same time, the greater the control exercised by the superordinate group, the greater is the difficulty to attain the resources needed to develop such an alternative mono-ethnic economic system.

The solution provided by the ethnic enclave is only one of several possible strategies which may be adopted by ethnic minorities. An additional course of action is political mobilization. It should be noted, however, that political and the economic actions are by no means mutually exclusive. Indeed, in most cases they nurture and reinforce one another. Under conditions of competition and group subordination, political mobilization aims to change the rules according to which competition takes place. Subordinate groups that resort to political mobilization may make use of legitimate political means, or even resort to open and violent conflict. In the extreme case such action will involve an open struggle in an attempt to break-off and establish an independent ethnic-national entity.

In light of the distinctive historical circumstances in which Jews and Arabs were brought together, the possibility of open conflict between the two groups is an ever present threat. Within this context it is possible to delineate what we consider to be a central Israeli dilemma. This dilemma derives from the premise that resource accumulation and conflict are strongly interrelated.

Some proponents of the competition approach argue that increasing intergroup competition and greater resource parity are likely to lead to ethnic mobilization and conflict. As stated by Olzak (1983:362) ". . . as groups come to compete in the same labor markets and increase their access to similar sets of political, economic, and social resources, ethnic mobilization will occur". In other words, as competing ethnic groups approach parity in accumulated resources, the greater the possibility of open conflict between the groups. Indeed, such a view seems to be at the heart of Israel's policies toward its Arab citizens. This is clearly revealed in government regulations as well as individuals' actions. In Jewish Israel's consciousness, the Arab population is viewed as a foe and an ever-present threat. According to this view, providing

Israeli Arabs with the opportunity for accumulation of resources would encourage further competition over limited resources. Not only would it deprive the Jewish collective, but it would also increase the potential for outright conflict. It should be emphasized, of course, that underlying these discriminatory practices is the premise that subordinate group mobilization cannot take place unless the resources accumulated by the group reach a critical mass. While in extreme cases subordinate groups may lack the resources to mobilize and challenge the superordinate group, such extreme resource deprivation can be maintained only under extremely oppressive conditions and for short periods of time.

An alternative view contends that increasing parity among competing ethnic groups does not necessarily lead to conflict. Competition is likely to result in strife when it is perceived as outrageously unfair. Indeed, this view shifts the emphasis from group competition *per se* to the rules by which competition is governed. Indeed, our study has demonstrated that competition between Jews and Arabs is structured in a way that favors the former over the latter group. To the extent that this structured inequality is perceived as unfair and unjust by members of the subordinate group, their disadvantage is likely to lead to unimpeded conflict. For example, Belanger and Pinard (1991:448) hypothesized that ". . . ethnic competition leads to ethnic conflict and ethnic movement if, and only if, the competition is perceived to be unfair".

The Israeli dilemma presented in our study reflects the uncertainty regarding the relationship between ethnic resource competition and accumulation, and the possibility of open conflict. One view contends that growing parity between competing groups increases the likelihood of ethnic conflict. Accordingly, the motivation of the Jewish majority group to deprive the minority Arab population from accumulation of resources constitutes a strategy to minimize the threat to the former group. This conviction eventually leads to oppressive and non-democratic policies that condone discriminatory actions at the institutional and the individual levels. A second view, however, suggests that discriminatory policies constitute unjust action which, in turn, increases the chances of resentment by the subordinate group and the threat of its mobilization. According to this second view it is not the accumulation of resources that leads to conflict, but rather the rules under which competition takes place.

The two opposing views are nurtured by the dual commitment to two basic principles on which the State of Israel was founded. On the one hand Israel was established as a democracy committed to equality of all citizens irrespective of race, religion, or ethnicity. This commitment is manifest in Israel's Declaration of Independence, in its democratic voting system and in the legal system. On the other hand, Israel was established as a state for the Jewish people committed to the goals of Zionism. As such it provides Jews with preferential treatment, while all other citizens are treated according to "what justice permits". The Israeli dilemma, then, stems from the view that the aforementioned principles are essentially incompatible. The contradictions concerning the nature of Israel as a nation state are deeply imbedded in the consciousness of the peoples of Israel and most likely will endure for years to come. Yet we contend that redressing economic discrimination against Arab citizens should not and cannot await their resolution. The patterns of labor market inequality revealed in our findings violate the "principle of equality" not only in the abstract sense, but even as construed within the existing framework of Israel's democracy. The Israeli dilemma cannot be resolved by the suppression of the Arab ethnic collective, but rather by the implementation of policies geared to the fair allocation of resources, at the collective level, and by ensuring equal access to opportunities, at the individual level.

Bibliography

Acker, J. 1980. "Women and Stratification: A Review of Recent Literature". *Contemporary Sociology 9:* 25–35.

Al-Haj, M. 1987a. *Social Change and Family Processes, Arab Communities in Shefar-Am*. Boulder: Westview Press.

————. 1987b. *The Employment Distress Among Arab University Graduates in Israel*. Haifa: University of Haifa, The Jewish-Arab Center, Occasional Papers on the Middle East (No. 8).

————. 1988. "The Changing Arab Kinship Structure: The Effect of Modernization in an Urban Community". *Economic Development and Cultural Change 36:* 237–258.

———— and H. Rosenfeld. 1990. *Arab Local Government in Israel*. Boulder, Colorado: Westview.

Allport, G.W. 1954. *The Nature of Prejudice*. Boston: Beacon.

Arnon, Y. and M. Raviv. 1980. *From Fellah to Farmer: A Study on Change in Arab Villages*. Settlement Study Center, Rehovot.

Arrow, K. 1973. "The Theory of Racism", pp. 3–33 in *Discrimination in Labor Markets*, edited by O. Ashenfeller and A. Rees. Princeton: Princeton University Press.

Atrash, A. 1991. "The Arab Industry in Israel—Developing Processes and Factories Set-up". Paper presented at the Conference on Aspects of Integration of the Arab Community in Israel, The David Institute for International Relations and Konrad Adenauer Foundation.

Averrit, R.T. 1968. *The Dual Economy*. New York: Norton.

Bar-Gal, T. and A. Sofer. 1976. "Changes in minority villages in Israel". *Ofakim Begeographia 1:* 1–77 (Hebrew).

Beck, E.M. 1980. "Discrimination and White Economic Loss: A Time Series Examination of the Radical Model". *Social Forces 59:* 148–68.

————, P.M. Horan and C.M. Tolbert II. 1980. "Industrial Segmentation and Labor Market Discrimination". *Social Problems 28:* 113–30.

Becker, G. 1957. *The Economics of Discrimination*. Chicago: The University of Chicago Press.

Belanger, S. and M. Pinard. 1991. "Ethnic Movements and the Competition Model: Some Missing Links". *American Sociological Review 56:* 446—57.

Bell, D. 1973. *The Coming of Post-Industrial Society*. New-York: Basic Books.

Ben-Israel, R. 1989. *Labor Laws and Legislation*. Tel-Aviv: Everymans University (Hebrew).

Ben-Porath, Y. 1984. "Israeli Dilemmas: Economic Relations Between Jews and Arabs". *Dissent* (Fall): 459–467.

Ben-Rafael, E. 1982. *The Emergence of Ethnicity: Cultural Groups and Social Conflict in Israel*. Westport, Conn.: Greenwood.

———— and S. Sharot. 1991.   *Ethnicity, Religion and Class in Israeli Society.* Cambridge: Cambridge University Press.

Ben-Sira, M. 1991.   *The Wage Gap Between Jewish Residents and Arab Residents of Israel in the Labor Market.* Tel-Aviv University, MA thesis.

Beneria, L. (ed.). 1982.   *Women and Development.* New York: Praeger.

Bergmann, B.R. 1971.   "The Effect on White Incomes of Discrimination in Employment". *Journal of Political Economy 79:* 294–313.

Bibb, R. and W. Form. 1977.   "The Effects of Industrial, Occupational, and Sex Stratification on Wages in Blue-Collar Markets". *Social Forces 55:* 474–96.

Blalock, H.M. 1967.   *Toward a Theory of Minority Group Relations.* New York: Wiley.

Blau, P.M. and O.D. Duncan. 1967.   *The American Occupational Structure.* New York: The Free Press.

Bloomquist, L.E. and G.F. Summers. 1982.   "Organization of Production and Community Income Distributions". *American Sociological Review 47:* 325–38.

Bohrnstedt, G.W. 1969.   "Observations on the Measurement of Change", pp. 113–33 in *Sociological Methodology,* edited by E.F. Borgatta. San Francisco: Jossey-Bass.

Bonacich, E. 1972.   "A Theory of Ethnic Antagonism: The Split Labor Market", *American Sociological Review 37:* 547–59.

————. 1973.   "A Theory of Middleman Minorities", *American Sociological Review 38:* 583–94.

————. 1976.   "Advanced Capitalism and Black-White Race Relations in the United States: A Split Labor Market Interpretation". *American Sociological Review 41:* 34–51.

Boserup, E. 1970.   *Women's Role in Economic Development.* London: Allen and Unwin.

Boswell, T.E. 1986.   "A Split Labor Market Analysis of Discrimination Against Chinese Immigrants, 1850–1882". *American Sociological Review 51:* 352–71.

Bowen, W.G. and T.A. Finegan. 1969.   *The Economics of Labor Force Participation.* Princeton: Princeton University Press.

Buraway, M. 1982.   "The Capitalist State in South Africa: Marxist and Sociological Perspectives". *Political Power and Social Theory 2:* 279–336.

Carmi, S. and H. Rosenfeld. 1974.   "The Origins of the Process of Proletarianization and Urbanization of Arab Peasants in Palestine". *Annals of the New York Academy of Science 220:* Article 6.

Cohen, A. 1964.   *Israel and the Arab World.* Tel-Aviv: Sifriat Ha'Poalim (Hebrew).

Cohen, A. 1965.   *Arab Border-Villages in Israel.* Manchester: Manchester University Press.

Cohen, A. 1978.   *The Economy of the Arab Sector in Israel During the British Mandate.* Givat Haviva: Center for Arab and Afro-Asian Studies, No. 14 (Hebrew).

Cohen, R. 1990.   *Complexity of Loyalties—Society and Politics in the Arab Sector in Israel.* Tel-Aviv: Am Oved (Hebrew).

Czamanski, D. et al. 1984.   *Employment Potential of University Graduates in the Arab Localities in Israel.* Haifa: Technion, Center for Research of City and Region (Hebrew).

Davis, J.F. 1978.   *Minority-Dominant Relations.* Illinois: AHM Publishing Corporation.

Doeringer, P.B. 1984.   "Internal Labor Markets and Paternalism in Rural Areas", pp. 271–89 in *Internal labor markets,* edited by P. Osterman. Cambridge: MIT.

Duncan, O.D. 1968.   "Inheritance of poverty or inheritance of race?" pp. 85–110 in *On Understanding Poverty: Perspectives from the Social Sciences,* edited by D.P. Moynihan. New York: Basic Books.

———— and A.J. Reiss Jr. 1956.   *Social Characteristics of Urban and Rural Communities, 1950.* New York: Wiley.

————, W.R. Scott, S. Lieberson, B. Duncan and H. Winsborough. 1960. *Metropolis and Region.* Baltimore: Johns Hopkins University Press.

Durand, J.D. 1975. *The Labor Force in Economic Development*. Princeton: Princeton University Press.

Eisenstadt, S.N. 1967. *Israeli Society*. London: Weidenfeld and Nicholson.

Esman, M.J. 1973. "The Management of Communal Conflict". *Public Policy 21*: 49–78.

Fiet-Stern, S. 1990. "'Commuting Against the Stream': Jewish Workers in Arab Labor Markets". Tel-Aviv: Unpublished M.A. Thesis.

Fischer, C. 1975. "Toward a Subcultural Theory of Urbanism". *American Journal of Sociology 80*: 1319–51.

Flapan, S. 1979. *Zionism and the Palestinians*. London: Croom Helm.

Fossett, M. 1984. "City Differences in Racial Occupational Differentiation: A Note on the Use of Odds Ratios". *Demography 21*: 655–66.

Frazier, E. 1951. "The Negroes' Vested Interest in Segregation", in *Race, Prejudice and Discrimination*, edited by A. Rose. New York: Knopf.

Freeman, R.B. 1973. "Decline of Labor Market Discrimination and Economic Analysis". *American Economic Review 63*: 280–286.

Friedlander, D. and C. Goldscheider. 1984. "Israel's Population: The Challenge of Pluralism". *Population Bulletin 39*: 1–39.

Frisbie, W.P. and L. Neidert. 1977. "Inequality and the Relative Size of Minority Population: A Comparative Analysis". *American Journal of Sociology 32*: 1007–30.

Ginor, F. 1979. *Socio-Economic Disparities in Israel*. Tel-Aviv: University Publishing Projects.

Glenn, N.D. 1964. "The Relative Size of the Negro Population and Negro Occupational Status". *Social Forces 43*: 42–49.

———. 1966. "White Gains from Negro Subordination". *Social Problems 14*: 159–78.

Gottheil, F. 1973. "On the Economic Development of the Arab Region in Israel" in *Israel: Social Structure and Change*, edited by M. Curtis and M. Chertoff. New Brunswick: Transaction Books.

Habash, A. 1973. *Society in Transition—A Social and Political Study of the Arab Community in Israel*. Michigan: Xerox University Microfilms.

Haidar, A. 1990. *The Arab Population in the Israeli Economy*. Tel-Aviv: International Center for Peace in the Middle-East.

Harari, Y. 1972. *The Arabs in Israel: Statistics and Facts*. Tel-Aviv: Center for Arab and Afro-Asian Studies.

———. 1974. *The Arabs in Israel 1973 (Facts and Figures)*. Tel-Aviv: Center for Arab and Afro-Asian Studies.

Hassdaya, M. and E. Kahana. 1982. "Bank Marketing in the Arab Sector in Israel", *Banking Review Quarterly 21*: 87–104 (Hebrew).

Hechter, M. 1975. *Internal Colonialism*. London: Routledge and Kegan Paul.

Heise, D.R. 1970. "Causal Inference from Panel Date", pp. 3–27 in *Sociological Methodology*, edited by E.F. Borgatta and G.W. Bohrnstedt. San Francisco: Jossey-Bass.

Hendeles, J. and A. Grippel. 1988. *Characteristics of Blue Collar Workers in Selected Industries*. Tel-Aviv: The Institute for Economic and Social Research (Hebrew).

Hodge, R.W. and P. Hodge. 1965. "Occupational Assimilation as a Competitive Process". *American Journal of Sociology 70*: 249–64.

———. 1966. "Comment". *American Journal of Sociology 72*: 286–89.

Iams, H.M. and A. Thornton. 1975. "Decomposition of Differences: A Cautionary Note". *Sociological Methods and Research 3*: 341–52.

Jones, F.L. and J. Kelly. 1984. "Decomposing Differences Between Groups: A Cautionary Note on Measuring Discrimination". *Sociological Methods Research 51*: 342–351.

Kasarda, J.D. 1978. "Urbanization, Community and the Metropolitan Problem". pp. 27–57 in *Handbook of Contemporary Urban Life*, edited by D. Street. San Francisco: Jossey-Bass.

Kaufman, R.L. 1984. "A Structural Decomposition of Black-White Earning Differentials". *American Journal of Sociology 89:* 585–611.

Kessler, R.C. and D.F. Greenberg. 1981. *Linear Panel Analysis.* New York: Academic Press.

Khalidi, R. 1988a. *The Arab Economy in Israel, The Dynamics of a Region's Development.* London: Croom Helm.

Khalidi, R. 1988b. "The Economy of Palestinian Arabs in Israel", pp. 37–70 in *The Palestinian Economy,* edited by George T. Abed. London: Routledge.

Kimmerling, B. 1983. *Zionism and the Economy.* Cambridge, Massachusetts: Schenkman.

Kislev, R. 1976. "Land Expropriations: History of Oppression". *New Outlook 19:* 23–32.

Klinov, R. 1989. *Arabs and Jews in the Israeli Labor Force.* Jerusalem: The Hebrew University of Jerusalem, Working Paper No. 24.

Kraus, E. 1986. "Edah and 'ethnic groups' in Israel". *Jewish Journal of Sociology 28:* 5–18.

Kraus, V. and R.W. Hodge. 1990. *Promises in the Promised Land: Mobility and Inequality in Israel.* New York: Greenwood.

Kretzmer, D. 1987. *The Legal Status of the Arabs in Israel.* Tel-Aviv: International Center for Peace in the Middle East.

Labovitz, S. and R.B. Hagedorn. 1975. "A Structural-Behavioral Theory of Inter-Group Antagonism". *Social Forces 53:* 444–48.

LaGory, M. and R. Magnani. 1979. "Structural Correlates of Black-White Occupational Differentiation: Will U.S. Regional Differences in Status Remain?" *Social Problems 27:* 157–69.

Landau, I. 1969. *The Arabs in Israel—A Political Study.* Oxford: Oxford University Press.

Lewin-Epstein, N. 1986. "Effects of Residential Segregation and Neighborhood Opportunity Structure on the Employment of Black and White Youth". *Sociological Quarterly 27:* 559–70.

———. 1989. "Labor Market Position and Antagonism Toward Arabs in Israel". *Research in Inequality and Social Conflict 1:* 165–91.

——— and M. Semyonov. 1985. "Noncitizen Arabs in the Israeli Labor Market: Entry and Permeation". *Social Problems 33:* 56–66.

———. 1986. "Ethnic Group Mobility in the Israeli Labor Market". *American Sociological Review 51:* 342–51.

Lieberson, S. 1970. "Stratification and Ethnic Groups". *Sociological Inquiry 40:* 172–81.

———. 1975. "Rank Sum Comparison Between Groups", pp. 276–91 in *Sociological Methodology,* edited by D. Heise. San Francisco: Jossey-Bass.

———. 1980. *A Piece of the Pie.* Berkeley: University of California Press.

Light, I.H. 1972. *Ethnic Enterprise in America: Business and Welfare among Chinese, Japanese and Blacks.* Berkeley: University of California Press.

Logan, J. 1976. "Industrialization and the Stratification of Cities in Suburban Regions". *American Sociological Review 82:* 333–48.

———. 1978. "Growth, Politics and the Stratification of Places". *American Sociological Review 84:* 404–16.

Lustick, Ian, 1980. *Arabs in the Jewish State.* Austin, Texas: University of Texas Press.

Marshall, S.E. 1985. "Development, Dependence and Gender Inequality in the Third World". *International Studies Quarterly 29:* 217–40.

Mason, W.M., G.Y. Wong and B. Entwisle. 1983. "Contextual Analysis Through the Multilevel Model", pp. 72–103, in *Sociological Methodology,* edited by Samuel Leinhardt. San Francisco: Jossey-Bass.

Martin, W.T. and D.L. Poston Jr. 1972. "The Occupational Composition of White Females: Sexism, Racism and Occupational Differentiation". *Social Forces 50:* 349–55.

McFarland, D. 1969. "Measuring the Permeability of Occupational Structures: An Information-Theoretic Approach". *American Journal of Sociology 75:* 41–61.

Metzer, J. and O. Kaplan. 1985. "Jointly but Severally: Arab-Jewish Dualism and Economic Growth in Mandatory Palestine". *Journal of Economic History 45:* 327–45.

Meyer-Brodnitz, M. and D. Czimansky. 1986a. "The Industrialization of the Arab Village in Israel". *Rivon Lekalkala (Economics Quarterly) 128:* 533–46 (Hebrew).

———. 1986b. *Economic Development in the Arab Sector of Israel.* Haifa Center for Urban and Regional Study (Hebrew).

Miari, S. 1986. *The Arabs in Israel: A National Minority and Cheap Labor Force, A Split Labor Market Analysis.* Loyola University of Chicago, Unpublished Ph.D. Dissertation.

Morris, B. 1987. *The Birth of the Palestinian Refugee Problem.* Cambridge: Cambridge University Press.

Nachmias, C. 1979. "Community and Individual Ethnicity: The Structural Context of Economic Performance". *American Journal of Sociology 85:* 640–52.

National Insurance Institute. 1989. *Annual Survey.* Jerusalem.

Noel, D.L. 1968. "A Theory of Ethnic Stratification". *Social Problems 16:* 157–72.

Oded, Y. 1964. "Land Losses Among Israel's Arab Villages". *New Outlook 7:* 10–25.

Ofer, G. 1976. "Characteristics of Israel's Industrial Structure in Comparative Perspective", pp. 19–35 in *Readings in Economics,* edited by N. Halevi and J. Coop. Jerusalem: The Falk Institute for Economic Research (Hebrew).

Olzak, S. and J. Nagel (eds.). 1986. *Competitive Ethnic Relations.* Orlando: Academic Press.

Olzak, S. 1987. "Causes of Ethnic Conflict and Protest in Urban America, 1877–1889". *Social Science Research 16:* 185–210.

Oppenheimer, V.K. 1970. *The Female Labor Force in the United States.* Population Monograph Series No. 5. Berkeley: University of California Press.

Owen, R. 1988. "Economic Development in Mandatory Palestine: 1918–1948", in *The Palestinian Economy,* edited by George T. Abed. London: Routledge.

Pampel, F.C. and K. Tanaka. 1986. "Economic Development and Female Labor Force Participation: A Reconsideration". *Social Forces 64:* 599–619.

Parcel, T.L. 1979. "Race, Regional Labor Markets and Earnings". *American Sociological Review 44:* 262–79.

———. and C.W. Meuller. 1983. *Ascription and Labor Markets: Race and Sex Differences in Earnings.* New York: Academic Press.

Parkin, F. 1979. *Marxism and Class Theory: A Bourgeois Critique.* New York: Columbia University Press.

Patai, R. 1953. *Israel Between East and West.* Philadelphia: The Jewish Publication Society of America.

Peled, Y. and G. Shafir. 1987. "Split Labor Market and the State: The Effect of Modernization on Jewish Industrial Workers in Tsarist Russia". *American Journal of Sociology 92:* 1435–60.

Peres, Y. 1971. "Ethnic Relations in Israel". *American Journal of Sociology 76:* 1021–47.

Portes, A. and L. Jensen. 1989. "The Enclave and the Entrants: Patterns of Ethnic Enterprise in Miami Before and After Mariel". *American Sociological Review 54:* 929–49.

Reich, M. 1971. "The Economics of Racism", pp. 107–13 in *Problems in Political Economy: An Urban Perspective,* edited by D.M. Gordon. Lexington, Mass.: D.C. Heath.

———. 1978. "Who Benefits From Racism?" *Journal of Human Resources 13:* 529–44.

Rekhess, E. 1977. *Arabs in Israel and the Land Expropriations in the Galilee: Background, Events, and Implications.* Tel-Aviv: Shiloah Institute for Middle Eastern and African Studies Series, No. 53 (Hebrew).

Rogers, D., L. Brian, F. Pendelton, W.J. Goudy and R. Richards. 1978. "Industrialization, Income Benefits and the Rural Community". *Rural Sociology 43:* 250–64.

Rosenfeld, H. 1964. "From Peasantry to Wage Labor and Residual Peasantry: The Transformation of the Arab village", in *Process and Pattern in Culture,* edited by R. Manners. Chicago: Aldine.

———. 1973. "Hamula". *Journal of Peasant Studies 1:* 243–44.

———. 1978. "The Class Situation of the Arab National Minority in Israel". *Comparative Studies in Society and History 20:* 374–407.

———. 1981. "Change and Contradictions in the Rural Family", in *The Arabs in Israel: Continuity and Change,* edited by A. Layish. Jerusalem: Magness.

Semyonov, M. 1981. "Effects of Community on Status Attainment". *The Sociological Quarterly 22:* 359–372.

———. 1988. "Bi-Ethnic Labor Markets, Mono-Ethnic Labor Markets, and Socioeconomic Inequality". *American Sociological Review 53:* 256–266.

———, D.R. Hoyt and R.I. Scott. 1984. "Place, Race and Differential Occupational Opportunities". *Demography 21:* 258–70.

——— and Y. Cohen. 1990. "Ethnic Discrimination and the Income of Majority-Group Workers". *American Sociological Review 55:* 107–114.

——— and A. Tyree. 1981. "Community Segregation and the Costs of Ethnic Subordination". *Social Forces 59:* 649–86.

——— and E. Yuchtman-Yaar. 1992. "Ethnicity, Education, and Occupational Inequality: Jews and Arabs in Israel". *International Perspectives on Education and Society 2:* 215–224.

Shafir, G. 1989. *Land, Labor and the Origins of the Israeli-Palestinian Conflict 1882-1914.* Cambridge: Cambridge University Press.

Shalev, M. 1989. "Jewish Organized Labor and the Palestinians: A Study of State/Society Relations in Israel". Pp. 93–133 in *The Israeli State and Society: Boundaries and Frontiers,* edited by B. Kimmerling. New York: State University of New York Press.

Shapira, A. 1977. *Futile Struggle: The Jewish Labor Controversy, 1929–1939.* Tel-Aviv: Hakibbutz Hameuchad (Hebrew).

Singleman, J. 1978. *From Agriculture to Services: The Transformation of Industrial Employment.* Beverly Hills: Sage.

Smooha, S. 1976. "Arabs and Jews in Israel: Minority-Majority Group Relations". *Megamot 22:* 397–423 (Hebrew).

———. 1978. *Israel: Pluralism and Conflict.* Berkeley: University of California Press.

———. 1980. "Existing and Alternative Policy Towards the Arabs in Israel". *Megamot 26:* 7–36 (Hebrew).

———. 1984. "Three Perspectives in the Sociology of Ethnic Relations in Israel". *Megamot 28:* 169–206 (Hebrew).

———. 1985. "A Critique of an Updated Establishmentarian Formulation of the Cultural Perspective in the Sociology of Ethnic Relations in Israel". *Megamot 29:* 75–92 (Hebrew).

Snyder, D. and P.M. Hudis. 1976. "Occupational Income and the Effects of Minority Competition and Segregation: A Reanalysis and Some New Evidence". *American Sociological Review 41:* 209–34.

Spilerman, S. and R.E. Miller. 1977. "City Nondifferences Revisited". *American Sociological Review 42:* 979–83.

Stendel, O. 1973. *The Minorities in Israel.* Jerusalem: The Israel Economist.

Stier, H. and N. Lewin-Epstein. 1988. "The Sectoral Structure of the Israeli Labor Market". *Megamot* (Hebrew).

Summers, G. and F. Clemente. 1976. "Industrial Development, Income Distribution and Public Policy". *Rural Sociology 41:* 248–68.

Sussman, Z. 1974. *Wage Differentials and Equality Within the Histadrut.* Ramat Gan: Massada (Hebrew).

————. 1973. "The Determinants of Wages for Unskilled Labor in the Advanced Sector of the Dual Economy of Mandatory Palestine". *Economic Development and Cultural Change 22:* 95–113.

Szymanski, A. 1976. "Racial Discrimination and White Gain". *American Sociological Review 41:* 403–14.

————. 1978. "White Workers Lose from Racial Discrimination: Reply to Villemez". *American Sociological Review 43:* 776–82.

Taeuber, A.F., K.E. Taeuber and G.C. Cain. 1966. "Occupational Assimilation and the Competition Process: A Reanalysis". *American Journal of Sociology 72:* 273–85.

Thurow, L.C. 1969. *Poverty and Discrimination.* Washington, D.C.: Brookings Institution.

Tienda, M. and D. Lii. 1987. "Minority Concentration and Earnings Inequality: Blacks, Hispanics and Asians Compared". *American Journal of Sociology 93:* 141–65.

Tyree, A. 1981. "Occupational Socioeconomic Status, Ethnicity and Sex in Israel: Considerations in Scale Construction". *Megamot 27:* 7–21 (Hebrew).

————. and M. Semyonov. 1992. "Revisiting Ethnic Discrimination and Majority Group Advantage". Paper presented at the American Sociological Association Meetings, Pittsburgh.

Villemez, W.J. 1978. "Black Subordination and White Economic Well-Being". *American Sociological Review 43:* 772–76.

———— and C.H. Wiswell. 1978. "The Impact of Diminishing Discrimination on the Internal Size Distribution of Black Income: 1954-1974". *Social Forces 56:* 1019–1034.

Wallace, M. and A.L. Kalleberg. 1981. "Economic Organization of Firms and Labor Market Consequences: Toward a Specification of Dual Economy Theory", pp. 77–117, in *Sociological Perspectives on Labor Markets,* edited by Ivar Berg. New York: Academic Press.

Ward, K.B. 1984. *Women in the World System: Its Impact on Status and Fertility.* New York: Praeger.

Waschitz, Y. 1975. "Commuters and Entrepreneurs". *New Outlook 18:* 45–53.

Wilcox, J. and W.C. Roof. 1978. "Percent Black and Black-White Status Inequality: Southern versus Non-Southern Patterns". *Social Science Quarterly 59:* 431–34.

Wilensky, H.L. 1968. "Women's Work: Economic Growth, Ideology and Social Structure". *Industrial Relations 7:* 235–58.

Williams, R.M. 1947. *The Reduction of Intergroup Tensions.* New York: Social Science Research Council.

Wilson, K.L. and A. Portes. 1980. "Immigrant Enclaves: An Analysis of the Labor Market Experience of Cubans in Miami". *American Journal of Sociology 86:* 305–19.

Wolkinson, B.W. 1989. "Equal Employment Opportunities for Israeli Arab Citizens". Golda Meir Institute for Social and Labor Research, Tel-Aviv University (Discussion Paper 48).

Young, K. 1982. "The Creation of a Relative Surplus Population: A Case Study from Mexico", in *Women and Development: The Sexual Division of Labor in Rural Societies,* edited by L. Beneria. New York: Praeger.

Youssef, N.H. 1972. "Differential Labor Force Participation of Women in Latin America and Middle Eastern Countries: The Influence of Family Characteristics". *Social Forces 51:* 135–53.

Zarhi, S. and A. Achiezra. 1966. "The Economic Conditions of the Arab Minority in Israel". Arab and Afro-Asian Monograph Series, No. 1. Givat Haviva: Center for Arab and Afro-Asian Studies (Hebrew).

Zureik, E. 1976. "Transformation of Class Structure Among the Arabs in Israel: From Peasantry to Proletariat". *Journal of Palestine Studies 6:* 39–66.

————. 1979. *The Palestinians in Israel.* London: Routledge.

About the Book
and Authors

The Arab Minority in Israel's Economy considers the Arab population as an integral, albeit disadvantaged, part of Israeli society. Using data from a thirty-year period, the book looks at Arab participation in the economy, especially in the labor market, showing how significant socioeconomic inequality persists despite a fundamental tenet of Israel's declaration of independence asserting equality of political and social rights of all its citizens.

Taking an ethnic competition perspective, the authors explore the extent of inequality, uncovering the institutional and social processes that influence it. They examine the role of local labor markets and individual human resources, giving special attention to the growing labor force participation of Arab women. They also consider the gains of the majority Jewish population that have resulted from competition and economic discrimination against Arabs.

Although the Arab community in Israel has been studied in the past, this book is unique in its detailed analysis of employment activity within and outside of the Arab sector and in examining both Arabs and Jews within the stratification system. The book fosters deeper understanding of Israeli society and of multi-ethnic societies more generally.

Noah Lewin-Epstein is professor of sociology and director of the Institute for Social Research at Tel Aviv University. **Moshe Semyonov** is the chair of the Sociology Department at Tel Aviv University and professor of sociology at the University of Illinois–Chicago. Together they have authored *Hewers of Wood and Drawers of Water*, a study of Arabs in the Occupied Territories.

Index

Acker, J., 88
Achiezra, A., 6, 47
Al Haj, M., 16, 20, 32–34, 57, 87–88, 145
Allport, G.W., 69
Arab populations, occupational structure
   of, 71
Arab women, female employment ratio
   (ERAF). See Employment patterns,
   Arab women
Arab women
   labor force participation, 87–88, 91, 93–
     94, 96–97, 99, 103, 107–109, 114–115,
     125, 150
   occupational status, 88, 94, 96–97, 99–
     100, 102–103, 107, 109
   unskilled jobs, 109
Arabs
   economic status, 5
   occupational status, 20, 35, 70, 96–97,
     99, 101–103, 148
   socioeconomic status, 82, 99, 114
Arnon, Y., 5
Arrow, K., 115
Atrash, A., 109
Averrit, R.T., 128

Bargal, T., 5
Beck, E.M., 116, 127–128
Becker, G., 109
Belanger, S., 154
Bell, D., 24
Ben Israel, R., 79
Ben Porath, Y., 43
Ben Rafael, E., 1–2, 12, 21
Ben Sira, M., 62
Beneria, L., 88
Bergmann, B.R., 116
Bibb, R., 128

Bi-ethnic labor markets. See Labor
   market, bi-ethnic
Blalock, H.M., 69, 137
Blau, P.M., 63
Bloomquist, L.E., 63
Bohrnstedt, G.W., 135
Bonacich, E., 9, 13, 69, 116–117, 131, 137
Boserup, E., 93–94, 96
Bosewell, T.E., 10
Bowen, W.G., 91
Buraway, M., 9

Cain, G.C., 116
Carmi, S., 51
Clemente, F., 63
Cohen, A., 46–47, 59
Cohen, R., 20
Cohen, Y., 132
Commuters against the stream, 136, 139–
   145, 151. See also Jewish commuters
Competition, 8, 70, 75, 78, 82, 93, 98, 102,
   105, 108, 114–117, 123, 125–128, 132,
   134, 148–154
   Arab, 44
   direct, 70–71, 136, 149
   economic, 1, 9–11, 66, 101, 105, 126,
     138–139, 148
   ethnic, 11, 78, 82, 148–149, 151–152, 154
   group, 151, 154
   individual level, 152
   job, 69
   labor market, 9, 12, 40–41, 44, 151
   resource, 138
Competition effect, 116, 125–126, 128, 132
Competition hypothesis (approach,
   model), 116, 126, 130–131, 153
Competition perspective (view), 117, 136,
   150

Czamanski, D., 48, 50–51, 59

Davis, J.F., 137
Decomposition, 67, 75, 84–86, 102–106,
    118–119, 121–122
Dependence, 3–4, 6, 87. See also Internal
    colonialism
Discrimination, 74, 76–79, 81, 94, 102,
    105, 115–116, 118, 120, 123–124, 127,
    131, 149–150, 152
    covert, 21, 46
    employer, 82
    ethnic, 62, 115–116
    gender, 116
    institutional, 21–22, 31
    job, 78–80, 117, 150
    labor market, 58, 66, 75–76, 78–80, 82,
        86, 105, 116–124, 132, 136
    occupational, 75
    overt, 21, 128
    racial, 115–116
    socioeconomic, 11, 12, 62, 68, 70–72, 78,
        105, 108, 114–115, 117, 120–124, 131–
        132, 136, 150–152, 155
    wage, 78, 117
Dispersion, measure of, 51, 59
Dissimilarity, index of, 29, 36, 51
Doeringer, P.B., 63
Dual economy theory (approach), 127
Duncan, O.D., 63, 84, 119, 144
Durnard, J.D., 88, 91, 93

Economic integration process, 68
Economic rewards. See Socioeconomic
    rewards
Economic well-being, 116–122, 150
Eisenstadt, S.N., 1, 12
Employment, 48, 56, 79, 83, 87–88, 91, 93–
    94, 98–99, 101–103, 105, 109, 112, 119,
    125, 138–139, 145, 147, 149, 152
    agricultural, 92–93, 98, 108–109
    Arab, 87, 136
    female, 87–88, 91, 94, 109
    Jewish-Arab ratio of, 48
    patterns, 98–99, 109–110
    place of, 99, 109
    public sector, 101–102, 112
    public service, 92, 109
    ratios, 89–90, 108, 110
    sector of, 107
    self, 51, 58, 149
    urban, 101–102

Employment opportunities, 63, 81–82, 91,
    99, 107, 131
    Arab sector, 33, 34, 70, 99
Employment patterns, Arab women, 87–
    88, 92–93, 97–99, 107–108, 150
Employment policies, 56
ERAF. See Employment patterns, Arab
    women
Esman, M.J., 3, 138
Ethnicity effect, 62
Expropriation of uncultivated land,
    emergency articles for, 46

Feit-Stern, S., 146
Finegan, T.A., 91
Fischer, C., 70
Flapan, S., 44, 59
Fossett, M., 69
Form, W., 128
Frazier, E., 69–70
Freeman, R.B., 124
Friedlander, D., 16
Frisbie, W.P., 69, 120

Ginor, F., 23
Glenn, N.D., 69, 116, 121
Goldscheider, C., 16
Gottheil, F., 5
Greenberg, D.F., 125, 134–135
Grippel, A., 79

Habash, A., 20
Hadashot, 82
Hagedorn, R.B., 117
Haidar, A., 32, 48, 94
Harari, Y., 50
Hassadya, M., 51
Hechter, M., 3
Heise, D.R., 134
Hendeles, J., 79
Hodge, R.W., 9, 62, 116–117
Hoyt, D.R., 69, 120
Hudis, P.M., 116, 127, 132, 134–135

Iams, H.M., 84
Income inequality, 67, 123
    measure of, 123
Indirect standardization, model of
    (technique), 119, 144, 147
Inequality, 30, 68, 78, 95, 132, 154
    ethnic, 3, 12, 68, 77, 152
    Jewish-Arab, 151

labor market, 151, 155
occupational, 95–98
social, 6
Internal colonialism, 4, 6
Israeli labor force, types of Arab
  populations
  commuters, 70–72, 74–77, 79–80
  residents, 70–72, 74–77, 79–80
  segregated, 70–72, 74–78

Jensen, L., 79
Jewish-Arab, employment ratio of. *See*
  Employment, Jewish-Arab ratio of
Jewish commuters, 12, 139–145, 151
Job segregation, 79, 96, 115, 125, 126–128,
  130
  effects, 116, 126, 131
  hypothesis (perspective), 117, 126
  processes, 128
Job categories, 63, 114
  diversity, 63, 66
  opportunities, 47–48, 58–59, 66, 69, 78,
    93, 108, 148, 153
Job ratio, 98
Jobs
  blue collar, low status. *See*
    Occupations, low status
  distribution of, 60
  high status, white collar. *See*
    Occupations, higher status
  low paying, 44, 69, 101, 108, 114, 117,
    127
Jones, F.L., 84, 109

Kahana, E., 51
Kallberg, A.L., 128
Kaplan, O., 8, 41, 43, 59
Kasarda, J.D., 63
Kaufman, R.L., 127–128
Kelley, J., 84, 109
Kessler, R.C., 125, 134–135
Khalidi, R., 5, 22, 46, 48, 59
Kimmerling, B., 8, 42–44, 59
Kislev, R., 45–47, 51
Klinov, R., 31
Kraus, E., 13
Kraus, V., 62
Kretzmer, D., 21, 31, 36, 46

Labor, skilled and unskilled, 24, 68, 79
Labor Force Survey of Persons, Aged 25–
  64, 19

Labor market
  bi-ethnic, 75–78, 149
  ethnic, 76, 99–103, 105, 108, 150
  local, 63–64, 72, 87, 92–93, 99, 101–102,
    107, 110, 115, 118–119, 131
  mono-ethnic, 78
  occupational structure of, 93
  protected, 99, 101, 104–105, 108–109,
    138, 145
  segregation effect, 188–191
Labowitz, S., 117
LaGory, M., 69
Landau, I., 20
Law
  emergency land requisition, 46
  employment land requisition, 46
  employment service, 79–80
  land acquisition, 46
  workers, male and female, 79
Lewin-Epstein, N., 22, 63, 69–70, 117, 129
Lieberson, S., 7–9, 70
Light, I.H., 70
Lii, D., 63, 69
Logan, J., 63
Lustick, I., 3, 22, 31, 45–46, 139

Magnani, R., 69
Market Discrimination Effect, 76, 105–
  107, 118
Martin, W.T., 69
Mason, W.M., 82
McFarland, D., 59–60
Metzer, J., 8, 41, 43, 59
Meyer-Brodnitz, M., 50
Miari, S., 10–11, 46
Middleman minority theory (approach),
  137, 139, 143, 145, 151
Miller, R.E., 69, 121
Mismatch
  educational, 56–57, 59
  labor market, 56
  occupational, 56, 59
  spatial, 54
Mono ethnic labor markets. *See* Labor
  market, mono-ethnic
Morris, B., 16
Mueller, C.W., 63

Nachmias, C., 63
Nagel, J., 11
National Insurance Institute, 28

Net differences, index of, 89–91, 95–96, 110
Neidert, L., 69, 120
Noel, D.L., 7–8

Occupational categories, 52, 59, 95–96, 125, 150
Occupational opportunities, 7, 30, 54, 56, 62–63, 70, 136, 144
  comparing Jewish women to Arab women, 144
  comparing men and women, 144
Occupational segregation, gender linked, 109
Occupational status, 13, 24, 27, 35, 56–58, 64, 71, 74, 83, 99, 101, 105–107, 112–113, 121, 139, 143–144, 147
  attainment, 72–74
  comparing Arab men and women, 97, 103–105, 144
  comparing Arab women and Jewish women, 89–91, 107, 144
  comparing Jews and Arabs, 72–74, 105–107
Occupational structure, 23–24, 51–52, 63, 125, 136
Occupations
  higher status, 24, 26, 52, 72, 94, 96–100, 108, 121
  low status, 33, 35, 54–55, 58–59, 69, 71, 79, 101, 108, 114, 117, 121, 136, 149–150
  low paying. See Jobs, low paying
  manual, 95
  semi-professional, 95–97, 108
  skilled and unskilled, 23, 26, 55, 78, 94–95, 109, 153
  socio-economic index of (SEI), 83
Oded, Y., 46
Ofer, G., 23–24
Olzak, S., 11, 153
Oppenheimer, V.K., 88
Overflow thesis, 121
Owen, R., 41, 43, 59

Pampel, F.C., 91
Parcel, T.L., 63
Parkin, F., 114
Patai, R., 137
Peled, Y., 9–10
Peres, Y., 14
Person to job ratio, 66

Pinard, M., 154
Portes, A., 70
Poston, D.L., 69
Protected labor market view (approach), 138, 143, 145

Raviv, M., 5
Rates, labor force participation, 89
Ratios
  Jewish to Arab, 33
  population to job, 92
  population to market, 54
Reich, M., 115–116
Reiss, A.J., 63
Rekhess, E., 46
Residential communities, Jewish to Arab ratios, 33
Reverse commuting. See Jewish commuters
Rogers, D., 63
Roof, W.C., 69
Rosenfeld, H., 5, 7, 24, 32–34, 51, 93–94

Scott, W.R., 69, 120
Segmentation, 114
  economic, 41
  labor market, 41
Segregated labor markets, 70, 75, 78
Segregation, 69–70, 79, 96, 114–117, 126, 128, 132, 134, 138, 152
  community, 62, 98
  ecological, 2, 21, 28, 59, 66
  ethnic, 115
  geographic, 44
  Jewish-Arab, 62
  job. See Job segregation
  labor market, 72, 77
  occupational, 98, 121, 132
  regional, 29
  residential, 14, 30, 62, 69, 77
  social, 2
  spatial, 30, 45, 48, 62, 68, 77
Segregation vs. competition hypothesis, 125, 134
SEI. See Occupations, socio-economic index of
Semyonov, M., 22, 30, 57–58, 62–63, 66, 69–70, 120–121, 124, 132
Shafir, G., 8–10, 40–41, 44
Shalev, M., 41, 44, 114
Shapira, A., 42
Sharot, S., 21

Singleman, J., 24
Smooha, S., 2–3, 34
Snyder, D., 116, 127, 132, 134–135
Socioeconomic inequality, 5–7, 11, 22, 35,
    62–63, 72, 75, 103, 132, 152
  Arab women, gender linked, 87, 94,
    96–98
  determinants of, 63
  sources of, 75
Socioeconomic (economic) rewards, 35,
    58, 62–63, 82, 101–102, 114, 131–132,
    138, 149
Sofer, A., 5
Spilerman, S., 69, 121
Split economy theory. *See* Dual economy
    theory
Split labor market thesis (perspective), 9–
    10, 114, 116–117, 131, 136
Stendel, O., 17
Stier, H., 129
Summers, G., 63
Sussman, Z., 44
Szymanski, A., 115–116

Tanaka, K., 91

Taueber, A.F., 116–117
Thornton, A., 84
Tienda, M., 63, 69
Tyree, A., 30, 62, 69–70, 83, 65, 106, 124,
    140, 145

Villemez, W.J., 116, 120, 124

Wallace, M., 128
Ward, K.B., 94
Waschitz, Y., 5
Wilcox, J., 69
Wilensky, H.L., 88
Williams, R.M., 69
Wilson, K.L., 70
Wiswell, C.H., 124
Wolkinson, B.W., 80–81
Workers, blue collar, 52, 55, 58, 79
  skilled and unskilled, 44, 132

Young, K., 94
Youssef, N.H., 87
Youchtman-Yaar, E., 57–58

Zarhi, S., 6, 47
Zuriek, E., 3–7, 22, 45–46, 51